CAN A BISHOP BE WRONG?

Can a Bishop Be Wrong?

edited by
Peter C. Moore

MOREHOUSE PUBLISHING

Copyright © 1998 by Peter C. Moore

Morehouse Publishing
P.O. Box 1321
Harrisburg, PA 17105

Morehouse Publishing is a division of the Morehouse Group.

Printed in the United States of America

Cover design by Corey Kent

Library of Congress Cataloging-in-Publication Data

Can a bishop be wrong? / edited by Peter C. Moore.
     p.   cm.
   Includes bibliographical references.
   ISBN 0-8192-1726-3 (pbk.)
   1. Spong. John Shelby. I. Moore, Peter C., 1936–
BX5995.S77C36   1998
230' .3'092—dc21   97-36015
                                                 CIP

FOR

John H. Rodgers

THEOLOGIAN

VISIONARY

STATESMAN

FRIEND

Contents

Books by John Shelby Spong
(And their abbreviations as used in this volume)

Honest Prayer (Seabury) 1972 (*HP*)

This Hebrew Lord (Seabury) 1974, 1988, 1993 (*THL*)

Christpower (Hale & Hale) 1975 (*CP*)

Dialogue: In Search of Jewish-Christian Understanding (Seabury) 1975 (*DS*)

The Living Commandments (Seabury) 1977 (*TLC*)

The Easter Moment (Seabury) 1980 (*EM*)

Into the Whirlwind: The Future of the Church (Seabury) 1983 (*ITW*)

Beyond Moralism: A Contemporary View of the Ten Commandments (Harper & Row) 1986 (*BM*)

Living in Sin? A Bishop Rethinks Human Sexuality (Harper & Row) 1988, 1990, 1995 (*LS*)

Rescuing the Bible from Fundamentalism: A Bishop Rethinks the Meaning of Scripture (Harper San Francisco) 1991, 1992, 1995 (*RBF*)

Born of a Woman: A Bishop Rethinks the Birth of Jesus and the Treatment of Women in a Male-Dominated Church (Harper San Francisco) 1992, 1995 (*BOW*)

Resurrection: Myth or Reality? A Bishop's Search for the Origins of Christianity (Harper San Francisco) 1994 (*RMR*)

Liberating the Gospels: Reading the Bible with Jewish Eyes (Harper San Francisco) 1996 (*LTG*)

Acknowledgments

I WOULD LIKE TO ACKNOWLEDGE a number of people who helped make this book possible. First, of course, are the authors of each chapter. They worked hard and, given their other academic and pastoral commitments, sometimes under severe time constraints. Next, I would like to recognize my sub-editor, and the editor of most of my other publications, the tireless and competent Denyse O'Leary of Toronto. Denyse O'Leary has many works to her credit. Her thorough editing, combined with frequent content suggestions, makes her an invaluable member of this team. She also shares the authors' Anglican orthodox faith, and so writes and edits from "the inside." I want to thank Robert Munday for his helpfulness in providing articles, bibliographies and other important data—all of which saved me a lot of time. I am also very grateful to my Administrative Assistant Beth Bogard VanderWel for helping me with many details, and for her willingness to be interrupted on countless occasions from other duties. David Mills, who was originally to submit a chapter of his own, graciously bowed out in the interests of brevity. However, his editorial helpfulness in several places has been deeply appreciated. I want to thank Todd Wetzel and Episcopalians United for their encouragement, and for the support they gave which helped make this book possible. Last, but not least, I want to thank Allen Kelley and all the people at Morehouse Publishing for their helpfulness in seeing this book into print.

Introduction

Peter C. Moore

"The Christian church doesn't really believe what it claims to believe" says the smiling Muslim evangelist to the bewildered Nigerian. "One of their bishops even admits so! Here's a book that proves it. It's called *The Resurrection: Myth or Reality?* by someone named Spong. He's a Christian bishop."

I AM TOLD THAT CONVERSATIONS like this are not infrequent in parts of the world where zealous Muslims seek advantage in evangelizing over their unsuspecting Christian competitors. A far greater number of uninstructed people in the West encounter Bishop Spong's writings. Some have heard that traditionalist believers consider him to be a bitter scourge of orthodoxy and the chief heresiarch of the age. Others, especially many ordinary people who are searching for spiritual meaning in their lives, hear that he is a bold and visionary architect of a Christianity suited to the modern age.

The book you hold in your hand is not an attempt to give a balanced assessment of the views of John Shelby Spong, if by "balance" you mean that equal time must be given to both sides. Rather this book is an attempt to correct an imbalance. John Spong has had virtually an open field. Despite the protests of a few scholars in other parts of the English-speaking world, notably England and Australia, few if any North American voices have been raised to critique his views. The works of the Episcopal bishop of Newark are thus a concern to anyone who cares for the life and mission of the church in the modern world. Now ten scholars, all of whom are Anglican, several of whom are young and represent a rising voice within the church, have risen to challenge him on his own preferred turf—the printed page.

Each chapter stands on its own, although together they amount to a remarkably unified and weighty challenge to the bishop's thought and an effective rebuttal of his conclusions. Written for the educated layman rather than scholars, these essays analyze Bishop Spong's writings from several different angles. However, the authors have a united confessional stance: basic creedal faith.

We have made every effort to avoid ad hominem arguments, but wish to question many of his cherished assumptions and most of his conclusions. We lay this challenge at his feet, and the feet of those who are inclined to agree with him, in the hope of persuading them at least to re-examine their assertions and give historic Christianity another look.

Seeing the Positive

Each writer sees something positive in the effort of John Spong to relate the Christian faith to the modern world. However, they are united in the opinion that he has essentially placed himself outside the Christian tradition and is using his privileged position as a bishop to attack it.

This is, of course, not a new thing. The Christian heritage is full of examples of leading churchmen and theologians who argued forcefully for positions which at the time were and, in the light of history, have been seen to be heterodox. Though some of these were far more popular than the bishop, eventually the church closed ranks behind individual champions of orthodoxy who brought back sanity and faithfulness and enabled the church to move on.

What is striking about the case of John Spong is that so few people have risen to challenge him. It may be that as the culture has become less able to provide answers to a searching generation, the church has focused more on mission and evangelism and has viewed his mounting denials of its major doctrines as the rants of an eccentric and, therefore, felt that debate with him would be a distraction from its mission. More likely, I think, the mainline denominations, facing shrinking memberships and budgets, have been consumed with issues of institutional survival, and have lost their taste (and courage) for theological debate—especially as serious, substantive debate may threaten their unity and survival. Further, in a world of shrinking borders, multiculturalism, and religious wars, theologians have elevated tolerance of other points of view to such a level that religious controversy is not to be tolerated no matter what the provocation.

For whatever reasons, we are faced with a spokesman of the church—and not just the Episcopal Church—who has captured the attention of the media with a deconstructed vision of Christianity in which old truths are demolished to make way for a radically new creed. With a corpus of thirteen books and many shorter works to date, some of which have sold quite well, it is time for an assessment of his thought by his intellectual peers. It is as an honest appraisal of "Spongism" that this volume is offered, in the hopes that others—perhaps even those more sympathetic to the bishop's conclusions than we—will be prompted to do the same.

Begin at the Beginning

To gain perspective on the developing thought of John Spong, I reached back to two articles of his which appeared in *The Christian Century* in 1979. Both indicated very clearly where the bishop was headed and revealed the fundamental assumptions and methods that have inevitably led him to his current opinions. They show that the bishop's controversial views are the logical expression of a theologically consistent attempt fundamentally to recast the Christian faith. With this attempt, and not just with selected conclusions, the authors are in profound disagreement.

In "The Emerging Church: a New Form for a New Era" (January 10, 1979) he argues that in order to remain relevant to its culture, the church must always respond to the dominant forces that influence that culture and reshape its expression of the gospel to meet that challenge: "When the force an institution is organized to deal with disappears, it is inevitable that the new force will call out a new response. Not to change is to become a museum." (p. 11)

This is a clear statement of the old maxim that "the world sets the agenda for the church." On this view the church is not the bearer of a divine revelation, but a human institution organized to deal with "forces." Throughout the article's brief overview of 2,000 years of history, there is no sense that the church exists to critique the world, nor that it brings a transcendent perspective that judges every age. For Bishop Spong, the church's task is to respond to the world not try to convert it There is barely a hint that the large cultural forces that have shaped modern Western civilization may have been anything but positive. He does, however, see one profoundly negative influence: religious folk who tenaciously remain committed to orthodox faith. These people deserve only his opprobrium, and in his mind are to be lumped together with all who in the name of God carry out inquisitions, pogroms, heresy trials, witch-hunts, holy wars and crusades. (See his second article from *The Christian Century* below, p. 920) The bishop sees the church's task in every age to reshape itself in such a way that it still has a place in the ever changing mosaic of society: "This cultural hunger is even at this moment calling the church to new frontiers, new shapes and forms, as we once again seek to respond structurally to the attitudes of our world." Note who is doing the calling. (p. 16)

How the church relates to the world is, of course, a matter of historic debate within all churches. To suggest, as Bishop Spong does, that the church exists primarily to respond to cultural forces gives the world altogether too much power. Commenting on the words of Eamon Duffy of the Cambridge University divinity faculty, who said that "the 'world' is the place where ordinary men and women live and must find their salvation," Cardinal Ratzinger wrote: "You know neither the church nor the world if you think that they could meet without conflict or that they could even coincide. [The task of the Christian] is to recover the capacity for nonconformism." (*New York Times* Magazine, November 24, 1985)

Or as Dietrich Bonhoeffer, a man who paid dearly for his conviction that the church is sometimes called to resist the forces which drive the world, put it: "The Church is always on the battlefield... struggling to prevent the world from becoming the Church and the Church from becoming the world. The world is the world and the Church the Church, and yet the Word of God must go forth from the Church into all the world, proclaiming that the earth is the Lord's and all that therein is." (*The Cost of Discipleship*, New York, Macmillan, 1960, p. 252) Bishop Spong's vision of a church which engages the world and shapes its expression of the gospel to meet its challenge loses its intrinsic appeal because it fails to draw its inspiration from first listening to the Word of God. Cultural critic Theodore Roszak pointed out that (God's ancient people) the Jews were the most alert listeners of history because (in contrast to the other gods who were silent) the invisible God spoke to them from beyond their world. (*Where the Waste Land Ends*, Garden City, Doubleday, 1973, p. 103) When it responds first to God and not, as Spong would have it, first to the world, the church rediscovers the balance so well stated by John Stott: "The Christian calling is at one and the same time to worldliness (in the sense of living in the world), to holiness (in the sense of being kept from the world's evil) and to mission (in the sense of going into the world as servants and witnesses). (Commenting on John, chapter 17 in *Christ the Liberator*, Downers Grove, IVP, 1971, p. 81)

A Major Omission

In Bishop Spong's *Christian Century* article there is as yet no obvious indication of the far-reaching changes in church doctrines he will soon demand. But even back in 1979 we are given a telling insight into his biblical hermeneutic that will allow and even require such changes. In order to promote his campaign for unfettered change in response to the world's commands and directions, he must overlook the biblical message of the Fall. Hence he argues that the key to understanding the Scriptures is the "forgotten" idea that all creation is good. (Scripture does not, of course, forget the idea creation is good. It amends it.) John Spong's premise is that all of life is good and that the church's task is to bless and sanctify life as it is. From this assumption (one, as some of the following chapters will show, he applies selectively) flow inevitably all his moral and doctrinal innovations.

There is no sense in what he writes of the central concept of redemption, which has governed the church's reading of Scripture; namely, that an originally good creation was later corrupted by sin and in need of redemption, and therefore that the church cannot bless and sanctify life as it is. A proper Christian response to Spong's optimistic assumption is Duke theologian William H. Willimon's: "Too often Christians have treated the modern world as if it were a fact, a reality to which we were obligated to adjust, rather than a point of view with which we might argue. The Bible doesn't want to speak to the modern world; the Bible wants to convert it." (*Leadership*, Winter, 1977, Vol. 18, No. 1., p. 30)

The second article, entitled "The Continuing Christian Need for Judaism" (September 26, 1979), illustrates another theme we have come to recognize in his writings, namely, his use of other religions to chastise those in the church who resist his revisionist program. In it we also recognize his consistent method, that of separating the Christian symbols (when he is not denying them outright) from their historical reality, and giving them a meaning better fitted (he thinks) to the modern mind.

First, he says that Hebrew faith is "the call to step boldly into tomorrow, to embrace the new, and to find no security in tradition, for God is always in front of his people calling them to step boldly into the future." (p. 919) This he uses to criticize a Christianity that he thinks remains mired in the past and closed to the future. But any Jew would, of course, recognize this description of Judaism as, at best, a half-truth, and as any logician will tell you, when a half-truth is turned into a whole truth it becomes a whole error.

Judaism, as it has emerged over the centuries, is quintessentially a religion of tradition. "Without our traditions, our lives would be as shaky as—as a fiddler on the roof," sings Tevye in *Fiddler*. Like its heir Christianity, Judaism looks both backwards to its defining moments of revelation and deliverance, and forward toward the kingdom that is to come, whose life in no way contradicts the revelation, but rather completes it. The great festivals of Judaism all celebrate historical events which have ongoing relevance. (See Eugene B. Borowitz's description of the development of rabbinic Judaism in *The Encyclopedia of Religion*, Vol.8, Mircea Eliade, ed., New York, Macmillan, 1987, pp. 129–148.) Biblical faith is a combination of "already" and "not yet." By erasing the already and sanctifying the not yet, John Spong has uprooted both Judaism and Christianity from their historical foundations and reshaped them into variations on the twentieth-century myth of progress. He seems to have confused tradition with traditionalism, a distinction that Yale theologian Jaroslav Pelikan clarified when he said that "tradition is the living faith of the dead; but traditionalism is the dead faith of the living." (*The Christian Tradition*, Vol. 1, Chicago & London: University of Chicago Press, 1971, p. 9)

Symbolism and Fact

Second, in his treatment of the Ascension, he argues that because Christianity has been removed from the "prophetic correction of Judaism," it literalized a symbolic event by portraying the Ascension of Christ as humankind's first voyage into space. He thinks that Luke intended the Ascension to be only a "symbolic event lifted out of the Old Testament and told to open the eyes of faith to behold Jesus as he really is." (p. 921) No thoughtful Christian would deny the symbolic dimension of the Ascension. Christian interpreters through the ages have seen rich Old Testament symbolism in the Ascension—for example, in Elijah's ascension into the glory of heaven, which happened at the time when he bestowed his spirit upon his follower Elisha.

But John Spong insists that a Jew like Luke would have seen no problem separating religious symbolism from history. I doubt this. A mainstay of Hebraic thought, as of Christian thought, is that God works through real historical events to disclose his purpose and plan. Therefore, by separating the abstract truth of the Ascension from the concrete historical event Luke records, John Spong reveals that his real debt is not to Hebraic but to Greek thought. He thereby guts the Christian story of any determinative meaning and any real transcendent objective authority. It becomes something into which one can place one's own meaning while continuing to claim some authority for it. But if doctrines are only symbols, why should anyone care what meaning John Spong or any other individual gives to them?

What is not clear from these examples and his later work is whether John Spong himself realizes these problems. The certainty with which he writes, the scorn with which he treats his detractors, and the crusading zeal with which he embraces all that is new raise questions about how self-reflective he is able to be. Or, to put it another way, how genuinely open, flexible, and liberal he really is.

It would be misleading if my preceding remarks left the impression that the purpose of this book is to score theological points. Theological differences of the magnitude that are described in the following chapters are matters of life and death—for the church as well as for individuals. "The church exists by mission as fire exists by burning," said Swiss theologian Emil Brunner; and what John Spong has repeatedly made clear is that his program leads to embracing religious relativity and thereby ending the Christian mission as it has been understood for 2,000 years: "Can we with integrity continue to support and engage in a missionary enterprise designed to convert?... I will not make any further attempt to convert the Buddhist, the Jew, the Hindu or the Moslem. I am content to learn from them and to walk with them side by side toward the God who lives, I believe, beyond the images that bind and blind us all." ("Evangelism when Certainty Is an Illusion," *Christian Century,* January 13, 1982; and THE VOICE, January 1989)

I want to reply to this blanket rejection of the church's historic missionary call with the words of Bishop Stephen Neill: "Tell that to the converts!" Millions of people, including a great many of Spong's fellow Anglicans, have found life in Jesus Christ that they did not find in other systems. To deny them the opportunity to hear and believe the gospel is to cut them off from that life and invite the church to write its own epitaph.

It is with the hope both of alerting people to the real problems and dangers of Bishop Spong's thought, and of challenging him to a deeper reflection and a new openness to the claims of historic Christianity, that this volume is dedicated. It is a hopeful exercise in which we engage. We too believe in change, but in a different way from John Spong. We do not believe in change for change's sake, but change for the gospel's sake. We do not seek to follow the world, but to serve the world by presenting to it a gospel from outside it. None of us is beyond the Spirit's reach. Our God is sovereign and has a reputation for surprises.

In offering this book, we write for all those who, bewildered by contemporary theological warfare, are willing to begin by uttering the simple prayer *Dominus illuminatio mea.*

The Essential Spong

James M. Stanton

ONE EVENING when I tuned in by chance to the Comedy Channel's *Politically Incorrect*, I noticed Bishop John Shelby Spong. "But who in the world," I asked myself, "could possibly be more politically correct than the bishop of Newark?"

And so it proved. Spong fed his audience just the kind of well-worn gag lines they craved—a thumb to the nose at traditional morality, religious orthodoxy, and the Christian church.

What struck me most at the time was the attitude of the Episcopal Church to all this. Does General Motors pay its executives to go on TV and make tasteless jokes about air bags? But when Spong ridicules traditional Christian morality and beliefs on TV, far from being fired by the body he supposedly serves, he is applauded—not only by the cable TV audience but by some Episcopalians. Isn't it all a little perverse, in the strictest (and nonerotic) sense?

To help us understand what is going on, let us consider this thesis: "If Bishop Spong did not exist, it would be necessary to invent him."

At face value, the thesis is preposterous, of course. One might immediately ask, "necessary to whom?" To TV talk shows like *Oprah* and *Politically Incorrect*? Not really. There are plenty of more interesting and bizarre cases of human interest out there.

Is he necessary to the clergy of his own denomination? I doubt they would miss spending an inordinate amount of time mopping up the debris after Bishop Spong's pronouncements or mollifying scandalized parishioners who are outraged by his provocative blasphemies—and ready to bolt for more traditional church homes? No.

Is he perhaps necessary to those serious biblical scholars and theologians who desperately need his unique gifts for presenting their assured scholarly results to the people? Is Spong, in other words, a sort of heterodox C. S. Lewis, that rare individual with both scholarly acumen to understand and the eloquence to popularize? No, among academics of my acquaintance (liberal, conservative, or so-so), the consensus seems to be that the bishop's scholarship is something of an embarrassment, often either outdated or out of left field, and usually over-simplified. As Tom Wright has written, "Spong sometimes sounds like a 1960s' man born (or at least writing) out of due time."[1]

His prose style is, at best, ordinary and he has bad habits in scholarship, such as

1. shamelessly quoting himself in his own footnotes. (For example, in *Living in Sin?* of the 63 footnotes, Spong cites himself 17 times. In *Rescuing the Bible from Fundamentalism*, there are 37 footnotes, 10 of which are self-referencing.)

2. dismissing his critics peremptorily, casting aspersions on their intelligence, intentions, and personalities. (For example, Pope John Paul II, former Presiding Bishop John Maury Allin, former Archbishop of Canterbury Robert Runcie, and former Bishop of London Graham Leonard are all lumped together as "sexist,"[2] well-known bishops of the Episcopal Church are accused of having "no knowledge whatsoever of [recent] biblical studies";[3] the view of one past dean of an Episcopal seminary is characterized as "strange and antiquated" and "grandly impotent."[4] Spong says of the Virginia Theological Seminary, his own alma mater, as a whole, it is "today more interested in propaganda than in education, more concerned about orthodoxy than truth, more afraid of the future than welcoming of it, and more defensive of its version of Christianity than it is open to the leading of the Holy Spirit."[5])

3. in general, painting himself as a heroic rescuer of the downtrodden or a sort of Galileo who suffers persecution bravely for the sake of truth.[6] Being a Galileo-like champion is a challenging pose to maintain, especially while enjoying the rank and privileges of a bishop. But it is evident that persecution has changed since Galileo's day.

In short, it is not scholars who need Bishop Spong. As Luke Timothy Johnson has observed, his "readers struggle on to the end through his repetitions, non sequiturs, and narcissistic self-referentiality" only to find that what he has done is to "embrace... the spirit of modernity with its inability to stomach the miraculous," and comes up with "what all enlightened people think anyhow."[7] And that is, perhaps, the real reason he is necessary. Certain kinds of critical thinking—or whole campaigns of scholarship, some of which span generations—deserve a bad name. Unintentionally, but very effectively, Spong is giving it to them.

The fundamentalist has no better friend than John Shelby Spong. No one demonstrates better the futility of liberal religion. Spong's writing career is a trajectory demonstrating, as a priest once remarked to me, that "liberal theology is the theology of people who are on their way out of the church." Hence the fundamentalist owes Spong a debt of gratitude for demonstrating the essential failure of the liberal, historical-critical tradition to engender a vital Christian faith of any description.

Starting from the mildest of critical views of Scripture, the most easygoing of skepticisms about the details of the Gospel resurrection accounts, Spong has gone on to champion *Eros Uber Alles,* castigate St. Paul as a self-hating closet homosexual, debunk the whole historical fabric of the Gospels, and finally liberate his flock from the need for theism as a basic tenet of the faith.

How, then, does he recite the Creed when celebrating services? He says he does so with a deep and profound respect for the Creed. He would not vote to change a bit of the wording, or even drop out phrases which he thinks have been responsible for gross injustices done to, for example, the Jews or women. "I do not think any of us can rewrite history," Spong says.[8] But it is the meaning *behind* the Creed, just as it is the meaning *behind* the Bible, that sustains Spong. Out of the experience of God in Jesus came the affirmations that found their final form in the Creed. "Jesus was of God. I assert that this is true *for me...*"[9] (emphasis added). The bishop writes, "The day has passed for me when, in the name of tolerance to the religious insecurities of others, I will allow my Christ to be defined *inside* a killing literalism."[10] He claims that he accepts the meaning of these theological statements, but he makes clear that this meaning could only be set free "when the literalism of the symbol had been destroyed."[11]

But was God really in Christ? Is that a true statement of the way things are? Is it objectively true? For Spong, all the theological statements come down to *personal* truths. He is entirely subjective. Furthermore, no theological statement or biblical narrative means what it appears to mean. The real meaning lies always "under," or "behind" the ostensible one. For those who have the time and the inclination to work through the Creed, or the sacraments, or indeed the Bible itself, and find a comfortable measure of "fit" between the words and what one believes, this may make sense. In reading Spong, one is reminded of the phrase from George Steiner, the "mandarin madness of secondary discourse."[12]

That is not what the church has meant when it has proclaimed that "God was in Christ." Right through Scripture and the church's history, the message is not that we finally depend on our own understanding, our own achievement (however mandarin!) in groping our way to God, but that God comes to us, calls us to turn around ("repent") and deny ourselves, and place our whole trust in his grace. The good news is not that there are some among us, like Bishop Spong, who can work their way to a "meaningful" restatement of what the Creed once represented. It is that Jesus of Nazareth is "the way, the truth, and the life" against which all "*my* christs" appear pale and ineffectual.

Who Are the Fundamentalists, and What's So Bad About Them?

Spong does not really define the term fundamentalist. But according to him, fundamentalists support segregation of the races[13] and outlaw the teaching of evolution.[14] They fear inquiry and will probably even turn violent when biblical ambiguities, contradictions, and problems are pointed out.[15] They believe the Bible, even though it turns out that they do not really know it or read it—unlike Bishop Spong, who says that he reads it daily.

But for the purpose of this essay, I will attempt to define what Bishop Spong thinks a fundamentalist is. The essential characteristic is revealed by the term he uses for them: literalists. The villainous person from whom Jack Spong intends to rescue the Bible is precisely that person who trusts the plain meaning of the Bible, who, in other words, regards it as truthful.

Put another way, for Jack Spong, a fundamentalist is anyone

who takes the Bible's statements more seriously than he does. This is actually a very large and diverse group: it includes almost everyone who is well known in religion from Athanasius to Augustine to Aquinas, from Martin Luther to Martin Luther King, Jr., from Billy Graham to Billy the Kid. It even includes Edgar Cayce and the *National Enquirer* (known among other things for its cover stories on "Healing Herbs from the Bible"). By Spong's implicit definition, Jewish scholar Pinchas Lapide, who credits the historical reality of Jesus' resurrection, is a fundamentalist. In Spong's terms, it is really difficult to find a nonfundamentalist, at least among those who give a hoot about the Bible one way or another. Indeed, it is hard to imagine why anyone who took the plain meaning of the Bible less seriously than Spong would bother to read it at all.

Historically, of course, the term *fundamentalism* meant something more specific. Historical American fundamentalism lay on one side of a basic cultural rift between the heartland attitudes and values of the Midwest and the cultured despisers of the same who tended to inhabit the Eastern Seaboard academies and imitate European trends. In reaction to liberal critics of traditional Protestant Christianity, a group arose to assert the "fundamentals" of the faith. Their fundamentals were not restricted to the classical credal tenets: dispensationalism and premillennial eschatology were mixed in with the theory of inerrancy of Scripture, which many of us now equate with "fundamentalism."

While reflecting on Bishop Spong's campaign to rescue the Bible from fundamentalism, it's worth remembering that historical fundamentalism itself was an effort to rescue the Scriptures and Christianity from liberalism. And, in turn, liberalism was an attempt to rescue Christianity from the hazard of being outdated in the face of Darwinism and other nineteenth-century scientific theories. The nineteenth-century liberals predicted that the capacity for supernatural faith would inevitably wither away in the twentieth century. The church was supposed to prepare itself to offer a nonsupernatural version of its faith.

But history played a trick on the liberals. Based on their predictions, we would expect the thriving churches of our own time to be those that are equipped with liberal modernist gospels. Those benighted churches that clung to the beliefs of the fundamentalists should have withered away in the face of history. But anyone with eyes to see or statisticians to count can observe that almost the opposite is true. Liberalism, which married the spirit of the age, is eking out a poor living on a widow's pension of sentiment and endowments. Literalists hold sway, even when their proclamations are not as doctrinally refined or theologically balanced as their own scholars might wish. Alister McGrath notes that a liberal like Spong can no longer believe that his message will be rewarded with popularity; on the contrary, there is almost a stoic death wish in it, an apprehension of dwindling resources and empty choirs. People like Spong can comfort themselves only with being part of the Faithful Remnant who hold out against the forces of darkness.

Spong as a Fundamentalist

I wonder whether Bishop Spong realizes that, in his own way, he is a fundamentalist. Certainly, his list of fundamentals would read differently than that of the people he opposes. The straw man fundamentalist that Spong depicts swallows Scripture's literal meaning like the camel in Jesus's figure of speech. In fact, the fundamentalist actually assumes that Jesus really said that!

Spong, on the other hand, would question Scripture's assertion that Jesus really delivered that one-liner and would denigrate the acumen of the fundamentalist who accepted such testimony on face value. But don't get the idea that the bishop's skepticism is consistently applied. It is not. If, as he reports it, the medical researchers at Cornell are "convinced that sexual orientation is inborn," Spong takes that opinion as... well, as gospel.[16] If Elaine Pagels[17] or Rosemary Radford Ruether[18] or Michael Goulder (the "nonaggressive atheist" biblical scholar whose work underlies Spong's book *Liberating the Gospels*)[19] publishes a minority opinion that commends itself to Spong's view of church history as one prolonged suppression of minorities and the distortion of primeval "religious experience," as Spong reconstructs it—well, then these opinions are revelations by which all other views must be judged. Never mind that the "assured opinions" of scholars rise and fall almost as frequently as hemlines.

The irony is that Spong in his own way is a fundamentalist.

The charge can be demonstrated from his own method of critiquing the Bible.

Spong articulates what may be called a hermeneutical principle: "Without awareness of the original source and motivations of a text... the Bible cannot be used with integrity, nor can it be quoted in debate to prove some point that in all probability the original authors would never have considered" (*LS*, 105). It is by means of this principle that he proceeds to debunk what most of the Bible has to say about sexuality. The biblical writers were so caught up in their own prejudices that they could not recognize the possibility of meaningful "mutual" forms of sexual relationships beyond marriage. Therefore, one could not use their laws to justify, for example, disallowing homosexual unions as understood today.

For instance, according to Spong, the Priestly writer in the Pentateuch, whom critical scholars refer to as "P," was the latest of the redactors in ancient Israel who worked over the biblical texts held to come down from Moses. He was, therefore, at the point *farthest removed* from the "original" form of Hebrew religion. Furthermore, as can be shown from a careful analysis of his work, P was a wholly disreputable guy (or guys). Spong can hardly find words equal to the task of describing this legalistic, patriarchal figure[20] bent on retaining and imposing priestly power on the poor unfortunates dependent on his reworking of the faith.[21]

After Spong has revealed to us the whole sick, distorted, myopic efforts of the Bible writers from P to Paul,[22] he asks, What enduring message does the Bible have to convey? What "Word" do we come to through the flawed and fallible words of the Bible?

The enduring Word, he says, "is heard in the biblical story of creation": "It is the Word proclaiming that life is good, that everything that is shares in the divine origin and must therefore be celebrated and affirmed" (*LS*, 156).

But where does this canon within the Canon come from? In the first chapter of Genesis, we find the formula, "And God saw that it was good." Yet the first chapter is also ascribed to P. Now, by Spong's own principle, we cannot interpret a biblical passage in a way that cannot be supported by the original writer's intention! If P was the legalistic and inhospitable author of the "laws" of Israel, condemning among other things the very sexual liberties that the bishop wishes to promote, then clearly he cannot be interpreted to support the notion that "everything... must therefore be celebrated and affirmed." P could never be interpreted to condone a new sexual ethic.

Yet Spong does precisely this. He uses a biblical author to justify a position which "in all probability the original authors would never have considered." Since this is what he accuses fundamentalists of doing, it is only fair to draw the conclusion that Spong himself is a fundamentalist!

The Don Quixote of Newark

When his views "lifted [him] as an author onto both a national and international stage," Spong says he found himself "hated and feared by some and at the same time a kind of religious hero for others." He assures readers of *Resurrection: Myth or Reality?* that he truly "coveted neither response." Coming from the man who shared condom jokes on TV with Doctor Ruth, this is significantly harder to believe than the sun's standing still for Joshua. So what kind of "religious hero" is he?

Perhaps he is a bit of a Don Quixote, self-appointed and misunderstood knight-errant defending his Beloved Lady, the Scriptures and the Christian faith, against the captivity and aspersions of the literalists. At first glance, this may be hard to believe. Isn't Spong actually saying that his Lady is somewhat dishonest? After all, he is the one who asserts that the Bible really is false, that it does lie—at least literally. Is he not the one who says that the giants really are just windmills He is intent on rescuing her from those literalists who say—falsely, Spong believes—that she tells the truth on a literal level.

How does the bishop of Newark seek to rescue the Scriptures? He starts by stating that they lie—at least literally.[23] If you or I knew someone who characteristically answered questions of literal fact with literal falsehoods, we would call that witness a liar. We would dismiss the shenanigans of any devious interlocutor who tried to twist his or her literal lies into testimonies of some Deeper Truths of Religious Experience.

The Gnostic Spong

Spong is not, of course, the first person who ever attempted to rescue the Bible from fundamentalism. Marcion classed Jews and benighted Christians as fundamentalists who were swallowing unsavory and, to the "modern" second-century mind, unbelievable Hebrew Scriptures. He junked the Old Testament, prepared his own bowdlerized Gospels and Epistles (not unlike the Jesus Seminar, only without the colored beads).

Those who are lumped together under the name of gnostic were generally rescuers along the lines of Bishop Spong. What characterized the gnostics? First, they claimed to decode the false literal meaning of Scripture by some arcane procedure known only to the Initiated. This allowed them to penetrate to a higher—and hidden—Truth.

What distinguishes the gnostic, then, is not symbolism per se. The orthodox have consistently marked the analogical depths and resonant symbolic meanings in sacred texts. The difference between the gnostic and the orthodox is that the orthodox reader assumes that the literal meaning is true as well. Of course, it often has another—and perhaps deeper—truth. For the orthodox, the scriptural revelation is a truth that reveals truth. But for the gnostic, the Scripture is a falsehood in which a truth is hidden, to be revealed only by applying his (or her) esoteric knowledge and methods.

What about today's gnostic? It could be argued that one thrust of the Reformation was to give the Scriptures to all members of the church. It could be further argued that the thrust of historical-critical methods has been to take them away again, to bind them to interpretations of the adept and unavailable to the plain reader. But that is an argument for another, more general discussion.

Having taken away the literal meaning of the Scriptures, Spong applies a specific technique to get at their meaning, a form of interpretation described by the afore-mentioned Michael Goulder as "midrashic." It is not at all clear from Spong's work that he has a systematic grasp of midrashic interpretation as practiced in ancient Jewish commentaries on the Bible. At any rate, he gives no definition of the method and merely asserts that midrashic commentary is at work in every instance in the Gospel records. But even if Goulder and Spong are correct, this midrashic form is one that has been unavailable to scholar and commoner alike for eighteen or nineteen centuries. Assuming that God had any serious interest in communicating with us, it seems terribly careless of him to misplace the necessary key to revelation, leaving us at the mercy of those nasty literal falsehoods for so long a time. A prudent individual might hesitate to entrust his or her destiny to so forgetful a God.

Genesis and Genitalia

As we have seen, orthodox Christians acknowledge the symbolic and inward dimensions of a biblical event, but they do not throw out the account of a literal event. As Aquinas insisted, God could speak in words like we do, but He could also speak in events. He could say "rock" as we can, in order to communicate, or he could say "rock" and there would be a rock. For the orthodox, God's vocabulary includes all created things. For the gnostic, physical events are unworthy of God and pretty much unrelated to Him. It was easier to separate God from the physical world than to deal with the relationship of a Holy God to a world afflicted with death and sin. But for the orthodox, separating God from the world was not an option. God was the Creator of the heavens and the earth, of all things visible and invisible. Sin and death plainly were at work in the world, but that did not cancel the connection of all creatures with their Creator. Hence, the God of the orthodox had a claim on what was done with all things, including us and, specifically, our physical members.

Bishop Spong writes that it was sex that drove him to the Bible. If so, he shows another characteristic similar to the gnostics. Ancient gnostics saw no conceivable connection between the sweet sentiments they attributed to Jesus and the intrusively simple, day-to-day regulations of money, sex, and power dictated by the God of the Scriptures. Gnostic sexual codes generally fell into one extreme or the other: either complete abstinence for the truly enlightened (because bodies were too "icky" for them); or complete license (because physical things were too trivial to merit regulating).

Ancient gnostics especially disliked the book of Genesis because it portrayed God as the approving Creator of all these things and the author of maleness, femaleness, and fecundity. The Gospels and Epistles confirmed the value and significance of this arrangement, asserting that the faithful relationship between male and female constituted a divinely sanctioned sign of God's own love. Ancient gnostics rejected the whole literal meaning, burying it in symbolism. Modern gnostics follow suit. Gender is rejected as meaningless. The ethereal quality of "caring," "mutuality," or some other quality is the sine qua non. Bishop Spong is compelled to say that he has seen marriages between a male and a female that lacked these qualities (no surprise there—though many of us would be slower to judge a whole relationship based on our impressions), and furthermore that he has seen same-sex relationships that were deeply caring. So the plain, incontrovertible sign of a union between a man and woman with vows of fidelity and the desire for God's blessing in fulfilling God's purpose is kicked out the window. "Inner" and ineffable qualities, always hard to discern and never as apparent on one occasion as another over the course of a lifetime, become the keys and tokens to fulfillment or salvation.

And who will judge the durability of these feelings of caring and commitment? The participants? Maybe, but how many young people since the Sixties have said "but we Love each other" and lived to regret it? How many children are growing up without fathers because we live in a society where intimate decisions are made on the basis of feelings rather than "coarse" plain promises and covenants?

It is worth noting that Bishop Spong promotes what appears to be permissiveness,[24] especially in *Living in Sin?* at precisely the historic moment when that attitude is poised to wreak havoc on the lives of countless people, many of them innocent children who either were left to grow up without an intact family or who never grew up at all because they were not objects of desire—and thus were killed in the womb before they ever saw the light of day.

The Worship of Desire

We must not lay at one bishop's door the weight of our national worship of death. But Spong is particularly tragic at a historic moment when cultural wars are centered, as James Davison Hunter says, on the most private of areas, our bodily lives. The hot issues of our time are body issues: AIDS, abortion, sexual orientation, the family as an institution that balances the overweening demands of the state. The church is certainly not the only institution that has a word to say about what we do in and with our bodies. The family, schools, every level of licensed meddler from the NEA to the AMA to the FDA to the First Lady's Global Village engaged in raising every child, to the Joint Chiefs of Staff: every institution has staked a claim. If there is anything that is distinctive about the church in this struggle—in the secular dimension—it is this: the church is perhaps the only institution that promotes its agenda solely through persuasion. It has no recourse to compulsion.

It is an irony that at this moment a bishop pledged to protect the coherence and integrity of this institution's message is the one to tell it to mind its own business and obediently applaud the carnival and carnage of our civilization's struggles. If the church cannot speak a clear word, if persuasive voices are unable to pursue any real reconciliation between our lives and the Creator's will for us, then what options are left for settling our differences? In the absence of discourse, there is only maneuvering, manipulation, and compulsion. Without persuasion, there is only Power.

Concealed and Revealed

There are indeed falsehoods abroad, but they do not originate from Scripture nor are they any part of the Christian faith. Falsehood is at the core of the modern world. What is concealed are the flaws in that worldview, which are revealed in the conflicts of our time. Lay it on the doorstep of the Enlightenment if you wish, with its faith in a severely denatured version of human reason. But however we trace the footsteps to where we stand, we should not leave out the prophet of this age, Nietzsche, who grasped that reason would give way to something stronger once God was dead to us. When God died, blood would rule. Our century has borne him out. Force prevailed where the common ground essential to discourse crumbled. Everyone sees this when we speak of Mengele and the death camps. Why is it so hard to see when discussing abortion mills and Doctor Kevorkian? Because to see it poses a threat to the worship of desire—our own desires rather than other people's.

The failure of Modernism is obvious to us in totalitarian states that have gone down in flames. In the United States, it is disguised in the social struggles and in the degraded moral level of our political and personal life. But the disguise is wearing thin.

Is it unrealistic to expect the church to buck this trend? After all, each of us who are members of the church were also weaned on this world. We have imbibed its conflicts, been seduced by its corruptions. At best, we are in remission from its fatal illness. Unclean members of an unclean people, who are we to speak?

And how are we to speak when our designated spokesmen do nothing more than echo the disordered desires and ravings of our time and place? How are we to speak to our time when we are unable to hear from our God? How are we to hear from God when our own lusts and vanities are roaring in our ears?

The Ego vs. the Ego Eimi

Starting with his first treatment of the Resurrection, his explorations of sex and sin and his attempt to rescue the Bible from literalism, and proceeding through his second and less literal account of the Resurrection and his eventual highjacking of Jesus from the Gospels, Bishop Spong follows the trajectory of liberal theology. With what must surely seem to him the best of intentions, he has become a bishop fighting a holy war to make the church safe for atheism. The Church of Spong is unsafe only for orthodoxy. Everything else would find a home.

It is worth considering that all of the new theologies that differ from each other in so many respects have united in opposing one thing—what we variously call the catholic or orthodox or credal or Trinitarian faith. Docetics, Arians, Gnostics, or challenging modern-critical scholars, all agree on targeting this orthodox faith. Could there be something that desires above all to silence this faith? And if so, could it be that the motive behind it is neither truth nor our welfare nor the glory of our God?

There remain only two things to be added. First, Spong styles himself a judge of the church, but that is not his actual role. Rather, his continued presence as a bishop in this church constitutes a judgment upon us. While Spong's published positions are well outside any meaningful definition of the Christian faith, this has not taken him outside the church. By retaining his office while making a travesty of the faith he was ordained to guard, he has dragged much of the church into darkness with him.

Our confidence is not that we understand perfectly those mysteries in which we are afloat. Rather, it is that we stand upon the Rock. A bishop in particular bears an enormous responsibility. He would be foolish to say to himself, "I can trust my way because of who and what I am as a unique individual, what I think and what I see, or even what makes plain sense to me." That brand of confidence is the modern vision. Modern history shows it is misplaced.

The Christian's confidence is not idolatrously placed in his own little "I am this" or "I am that." Our confidence is that we are in Christ, the One who could rightly say "I AM." As a

Christian, my confidence is not in my ego, but in his "ego eimi."
There lies our authority and our priesthood. St. Paul described
this confidence as our armor and called it "putting on Christ."
The great Anglican priest and poet George Herbert depicted it in
his poem "Aaron" as an act of vesting:

> Christ is my only head
> My alone only heart and breast,
> My only music, striking me ev'n dead:
> That to the old man I may rest,
> And be in him new drest...
> So holy in my head,
> Perfect and light in my dear breast,
> My doctrine tun'd by Christ, (who is not dead,
> But lives in me while I do rest)
> Come people; Aaron's drest.

This vesting in Christ is what qualifies the fallible, sinful
human to stand as priest, to call the people together and to
teach them. It is the very opposite of playacting, of wrapping
one's self in a falsehood. It is wrapping one's self in the Truth,
and it reveals the truth that might otherwise be disguised behind
our egotistical pretensions. The tragedy is that false and bad doctrine had to actually be taught in the church in order that the
deceptive nature of the modern world can be revealed for what
it is. But, as we have been warned, the world is particularly adept
at deception. There are powers abroad that appeal to our vanity,
powers that would, if possible, deceive even the elect. Bishop
Spong, for instance, has cast himself as the Rescuer of Scripture,
the one anointed to tilt at the windmills of literalism, racism,
sexism, and other assorted -isms. But this is a deception. He is
not a knight—not even Don Quixote. The story in which he
appears is a different tale.

In the sad case of John Shelby Spong, he has exchanged the
vestments of Christ for others that are more stylish, more flatter-
ing to our vanity, but that in the end are utterly insubstantial. In
this case, therefore, Aaron is not dressed. In the end it requires
only a little child's transparent honesty to speak the word... that
he is naked.

Endnotes

1 *Who Was Jesus?* (Grand Rapids, 1992), p. 67.

2 *Rescuing the Bible*, p. 5.

3 *Born of a Woman*, p. 11.

4 *Living In Sin?*, p. 47 and *Rescuing the Bible*, p. 228.

5 *Rescuing the Bible*, p. 232.

6 The Galileo theme is a favorite: See *Living In Sin?*, Epilogue; *Rescuing the Bible*, pp. 9-11; *Resurrection: Myth or Reality*, Preface and chapter 1; *Born of a Woman*, chapters 1 and 12; *Liberating the Gospels*, chapter 1.

7 *The Real Jesus* (New York, 1996), p. 33ff.

8 *Born of a Woman*, p. 179.

9 Ibid., p. 180.

10 Ibid., p. 12.

11 Ibid., p. 181

12 Cited in Robert Wilken, *Remembering the Christian Past* (Grand Rapids: Wm. B. Eerdmans, 1995), p. 12.

13 *Rescuing the Bible*, p. 2ff.

14 The heroic figure of Charles Darwin is cited in virtually every one of Spong's books. At the same time, Spong recalls in derisive terms the whole Scopes Trial in showing how fundamentalists opposed evolution. Yet, this is basically a "guilt by association" tactic. Edward J. Larson, *Summer for the Gods* (New York, 1997), shows how the fundamentalists in general did not originally attack Darwin's theories of biological evolution, but the social implications of evolutionary theory. "Some articles in The Fundamentals dating from 1905 to 1915 criticized the theory of evolution, but others in that series accepted it" (p. 32). What fundamentalists most stridently resisted was modernism. Bryan came to fight evolution because of the way in which the theory was used to justify World War I!

There is an interesting gaff when Spong writes, "Bishop William Wilberforce made a public career out of attacking Darwin" (*LS*, 1988, p. 227). William Wilberforce died before Darwin published his *Origin of Species*, and made his career by fighting the institution of slavery and slave-trading in England-on the basis of Scripture, no less-in the early years of the nineteenth century. Samuel Wilberforce was the bishop who came eventually to attack Darwin. Spong's text has been corrected in more recent editions.

15 Violence of the fundamentalist or literalist Christian is often a thinly veiled theme: "A major function of fundamentalist religion is to bolster deeply insecure and fearful people. This is done by justifying a way of life with all of its defining prejudices. It thereby provides an appropriate and legitimate outlet for one's anger. The authority of an inerrant Bible that can be readily quoted to buttress this point of view becomes an essential ingredient to such a life. When that Bible is challenged, or relativized, the resulting anger proves the point categorically" (RB, p. 5). The "religious agenda" of fundamentalists inspires hostility, violence, even child abuse (LG, p. 329ff.). My experience in the church is that this "community of the Holy Spirit" more often responds to nontraditional suggestions not by interacting rationally but by killing or attempting to discredit the messenger" (LS, p. 227).

16 Spong speaks repeatedly of the "explosion" of new knowledge that helps us understand sexuality in new ways. He does not document this "new knowledge," however. In a remarkable passage, he *does* say "I have verified that my conclusions [with respect to homosexuality] possess high levels of probability with the help of Dr. Robert Lahita, associate professor of medicine at Cornell Medical Center in New York City" (LS, p. 78). He never, however, indicates that the scientific community is itself in a quandary about the causes of sexual orientation—as it has been for more than a century. John Money (regarded by many as the dean of sexuality researchers) has written, "special interest groups adopt their own dogmas, doctrines, hypotheses, theories, and ideologies, and set themselves up as religious, legal, moral, political, or professional authorities." But, he concludes, "on the basis of today's store of scientific knowledge, the best answer that can be given to the question of causation is that [sexual orientation] develop[s] in stages, and [has] more than one contributing cause...In sexology, application of the scientific maxim or law of parsimony decrees that a sexual effect has a sexual cause. Therefore, in childhood, the postnatal developmental cause of homosexuality has its most likely source in the development of juvenile sexual (sexuoerotic) rehearsal play." *Gay Straight and In-between* (New York, 1988), pp. 122-124.

17 "If Professor Elaine Pagels is accurate... male dominance and theological orthodoxy were merged in the struggles to rout the heretical thinking of the democratizing Gnostics, who were

open to women, and to consolidate ecclesiastical power in the hands of men only" (*LS*, p. 220). Spong never thinks to criticize Pagels, however. Her theory quickly becomes established truth.

18 "Personal unity comes," Dr. Reuther attests, "when one connects 'the many parts of the self through multiple relationships with other people'" (*LS*, p. 71). This attestation is sufficient to warrant it as truth. Spong does not see fit to critique the idea or contrast it with what, for example, Jesus taught about finding the whole self (e.g., Matt. 16:24-25). Rather, he goes on to declare, "There is nothing unnatural about *any* shared love" (emphasis added). This would seem to be a very naïve notion.

19 "There is a sense in which this whole book is my attempt to make accessible to the general public the insights of Michael Goulder" (*LG*, p. xiii). The identification of Goulder as a "nonaggressive atheist" is made by Spong, quoting Goulder himself (p. xii).

20 The writer of the creation myth was "anti-female" (*LS*, p. 129): Spong asserts that the P writer was "less misogynist" than the earlier writers of the tribal myth, but against women nevertheless (see p. 127); the "Levitical condemnation of homosexuality is a pre-modern illustration of ignorance,"(p. 147); the laws of priestly writer(s) were "rigidly enforced" (p. 103); the priestly writers were "racial purists" and were motivated by the notion that "foreigners" were to blame (Spong calls them "scapegoats") for events that resulted in the Exile—"No protest was heard against this xenophobia" (p. 31).

21 "The enforcement of the law [in the post-exilic period] moved Judah into one of the uglier phases of her national history" (*LS*, p. 31). Spong, incidentally, writes: "The book of Deuteronomy suggests that the search [for racially pure bloodlines] went back ten generations." But even on his own showing, Deuteronomy was pre-exilic! How, then, could it be used as evidence for a later period?

22 "Both the religious and ethical directives of the Bible were formulated out of a patriarchal understanding of life, with the interests of men being primary" (*LS*, p. 133).

23 "Can modern men and women continue to pretend that timeless, eternal, and unchanging truth has been captured in the words of a book that achieved its final written form midway into the second century of this common era?... Have we embraced the

meaning of the subjective quality of a particular language, the truth *lost at worst and distorted at best* in the translations?" (*RB*, p. 15, emphasis added). Spong makes the point in *LS* that "Human beings always form their understanding of God out of their own values, needs and self-understanding. We do make God in our own image" (p. 122). This dictum applies as well to the writers of the biblical books as to our own time. So it is easy to posit that all formulations, no matter how ancient, are limited and distorted. There are two sides to this coin: First, no written word can really be called a "Word of the Lord." ("It is certainly possible, indeed probable... that what was articulated in Paul's writing was not God's unchanging word but Paul's ill-formed, culturally biased prejudices. Responsible Christians cannot close their minds to the knowledge explosion in the field of human sexuality by hiding behind a Pauline quotation and claiming that this is 'the word of the Lord'" (p. 153). Second, the authority of Scripture is not found in what it says or in what its authors intend, "but in the community that assigns authority" to its words. Therefore, "If the authority is in the community, then the right to change, revise, and render inoperative various parts of Scripture must also be vested in the community" (p. 107). Clearly, these positions do not regard the Bible as "true" in any substantive sense.

24 Spong would, of course, reject the notion that he stands for "permissiveness." Yet, consider the following statement: "The enhancement of life... comes through a loving human relationship that does not violate any commitments the involved persons have previously made *that are still operative*" (*LS*, p. 226, emphasis added). This formulation vests the whole judgment of what a "commitment" is, and whether or not previous commitments are "operative" in individual discretion alone. This is the very definition of "permissive."

Works Considered or Consulted

Bonhoeffer, Dietrich. *Worldly Preaching*. Nashville: Thomas Nelson Inc., 1975.

Braaten, Carl E., and Robert W. Jenson, eds. *Reclaiming the Bible for the Church*. Grand Rapids: Wm. B. Eerdmans, 1995.

Johnson, Luke T. *The Real Jesus.* New York: HarperCollins Publishers, 1996.

Lapide, Pinchas. *The Resurrection of Jesus.* Minneapolis: Augsburg Publishing House, 1983.

Pannenberg, Wolfhart. *Faith and Reality.* Philadelphia: Westminster Press, 1977.

Ramsey, Michael, and Dale Coleman, eds. *The Anglican Spirit.* Cambridge, Mass.: Cowley Publications, 1991.

Wright, N.T. *Who Was Jesus?* Grand Rapids: Wm. B. Eerdmans, 1992.

Flight from Transcendence
William G. Witt

IT IS NOT IMMEDIATELY OBVIOUS that Bishop Spong has a
doctrine of God. After all, the controversial bishop has made his
reputation by publishing books that focus on questions of biblical studies, not systematic theology. Nonetheless, I would suggest
that not only does Bishop Spong have a doctrine of God, but that
his doctrine of God largely determines a priori the conclusions
he reaches in his discussion of the Bible. This may not be evident
immediately because of the particular hermeneutic Spong
employs when discussing the Bible. Accordingly, to understand
Spong's doctrine of God we must begin first with a discussion of
his hermeneutical agenda, that is, his view of how the Bible is to
be interpreted.

Mythology
Let us start with Spong's notion of mythology. His hermeneutic
approach owes much to the demythologization program initiated fifty years ago by the New Testament scholar Rudolf
Bultmann. Like Bultmann and other liberal Protestant theologians, Spong uses the concept of myth in the following ways.

1. Myth is a way of speaking of the other world in terms of this
world. It uses this-worldly metaphors or symbols to refer to the
divine. We might call this a *history of religions* definition of myth.

2. Myth explains unusual this-worldly phenomena in terms of
divine intervention. Myth is a story of the gods coming to earth.

Events on earth are explained in terms of otherworldly causality. This is myth understood as *divine intervention*.

3. Myth entails a prescientific view of natural law. The cosmology of the world is three-storied, with heaven above, earth in the center, and hell beneath. Hence Bultmann's famous statement that no one could use a light bulb or the wireless and continue to believe in the miracles of the Bible. Spong echoes Bultmann's fascination with the three-decker universe but has moved beyond concerns about light bulbs and radios to a passion for space flight and rocket ships. This is a *prescientific worldview* definition of myth.

4. Myth is simply a fable or an untrue story. Ancient people used to make up stories to explain how the universe worked. Today we know that these stories are not literally true and that science (or reason) can explain all these things. Myth belongs to a precritical worldview. This could be called the *Enlightenment* or *popular* definition of myth.

Spong incorporates all four definitions in his discussion of myth, without clearly distinguishing between them. His purpose in identifying the mythological elements in Scripture is to move beyond mythology to a "deeper" appreciation of Scripture. Spong's approach involves a two-step progression. It is only after he has decided in the first step that myth cannot be taken literally that it is then demythologized to provide a deeper (existentialist or experiential) meaning in the second step. Spong's discussion of the virginal conception provides an illustration of the approach.

First, the Matthew and Luke accounts of the virginal conception are full of contradictions that cannot be reconciled. He writes: "...It is impossible to ignore the fact that mutually contradictory details are present. At the very least, mutual contradiction means that someone is wrong, and it opens the possibility that none of the Gospel writers is correct in the literalness of their assertions" (*RBF*, 210). We are thus free to lay aside the literal meaning of the passages.

Second, the biblical writers had a prescientific view of the universe. "The common belief at that time was that God dwelt just beyond the sky, which was not far above the earth... this deity seems to have been limited by a Ptolemaic world-view" (*RBF*, 211).

Third, we know better than that now, because science has enlightened us: "We... have flown in airplanes many thousands of feet above the earth. Human beings have journeyed to the moon, and human technology has devised the means by which we have viewed with dramatic closeness every planet that rotates around our sun... The inescapable conclusion is that God was bound at the time of Jesus' birth to a view of the universe that is today abandoned by every literate human being" (RBF, 211–212).

Fourth, it is impossible, therefore, that Jesus could have been born of a virgin: "Of course these narratives are not literally true. Stars do not wander, angels do not sing, virgins do not give birth, magi do not travel to a distant land to present gifts to a baby... The virgin birth tradition of the New Testament is not literally true" (RBF, 215). It is important to note the logical jump that Spong makes here: (a) The New Testament writers believed in a three-decker universe (myth definition 3); (b) We live in a world of airplanes and rocket ships (myth definition 3, 4); (c) Therefore, Jesus was not born of a virgin (myth definition 2). Spong also carelessly lumps together several things that might operate on different levels historically, scientifically, or theologically—wandering magi, celestial phenomena, virginal conceptions. In Spong's discussion of the virginal conception, anything suggesting that God might have acted in a miraculous or out-of-the-ordinary manner seems to be suspect.

Having finished step one, we move to step two.

Because we know that the stories of Jesus' virginal conception are not literally true, they must convey some other kind of truth. The virgin birth is a story that hides a deeper spiritual truth (myth definition 1). "Underneath the level of the fanciful, literal details the message of the birth narratives was and is simple. This was the early church's way of saying, 'What we have met and experienced in Jesus the Christ we do not believe human life alone is capable of creating. He must be of God' " (RBF, 216). Lest we misread Spong here, it should be noted that other passages in his writings clearly show that he does not believe in the incarnation of God in Christ, or the resurrection of Jesus in any literal sense. As with Bultmann, the ultimate point of the Jesus-event has to do with my understanding, not with an objective act of

God in history. It would seem, then, that Spong's approach parallels Bultmann's fairly closely.

It should also be noted that nowhere in his writings does Spong make a theological or philosophical case against miracle or divine intervention. Rather, Spong leads his reader to assume that he has actually developed such a case against a literal reading of the accounts of divine intervention in the virginal conception or bodily resurrection of Jesus by subtly blurring different definitions of mythology. Thus, by asserting the questionable premise that the biblical writers believed in a three-decker universe (which does not fit well with our modern scientific cosmology) and by pointing to the rather obvious fact that the biblical writers never flew in spaceships or airplanes, Spong draws the totally unwarranted conclusion that Jesus could not have been born of a virgin and could not have risen bodily from the grave. The reader is not meant to notice the obvious illogicality of the argument, because Spong has not alerted him or her to the sleight-of-hand move from an imperialistic Enlightenment equation of a prescientific worldview as mythology, to a total rejection of divine intervention in history.

Such a blatant example of an illogical leap leads the reader to suspect that Spong's case against mythology may be hiding a more subtle agenda. If his argument against divine intervention is fallacious, might it not disguise his real reasons for rejecting the biblical accounts of the virginal conception or the bodily resurrection of Jesus? I would suggest that Spong's real reasons for rejecting the notion of divine intervention are that he has an a priori commitment to an epistemology, a notion of religious experience, and a doctrine of God in which divine intervention is impossible.

Spong's Epistemology

Spong approaches religious knowledge in terms that Lutheran theologian George Lindbeck has dubbed "experiential-expressivism" (*The Nature of Doctrine: Religion and Theology in a Postliberal Age*, 20 ff., 30–45). Experiential-expressivism originated in nineteenth- century liberal Protestant theology, beginning with the German theologian Friedrich Schleiermacher, who combined a Pietist tendency to interpret the subject matter of Christianity in terms of our experience of faith with a neo-Kantian theory of knowledge. From Pietism, Schleiermacher borrowed the notion that Christianity is about my religious experience. From the philosopher Immanuel Kant, Schleiermacher accepted the fundamental distinction between *noumena* (things in themselves) and *phenomena* (things as they appear to be). There can be no knowledge of things in themselves, but only of things as they appear to consciousness. Knowledge, for Kant, had a strictly regulative function.

Schleiermacher's epistemology led him to the conclusion that the object of Christianity was not knowledge of God in himself but only of God as experienced in our human consciousness. The object of Christian religious experience was the feeling of absolute dependence on God. In its numerous variations, Schleiermacher's hermeneutic appeared again and again in the nineteenth and twentieth centuries as the leitmotif of liberal Protestant theology. Spong's hermeneutical program is one more variation.

At the heart of Spong's hermeneutic lies a notion of pure experience that is not and cannot be articulated. For example, he summarizes this view in his book *The Resurrection*: "What is real... is that behind our religious systems, our holy words, our power claims, and even behind our fears lies an experience that transforms, deepens, and calls us into what Paul Tillich has called 'the new being.' " Spong speaks of this experience over and over again in the most glowing terms. It is an experience that leads into "eternal truth," it has dramatic power to change lives, it is "mind-altering, consciousness-raising" (*RMR*, 37, 44, 100, 244).

Although Spong speaks so rapturously of religious experience, it is very difficult to discern precisely what he means, because his notion of experience is ultimately a totally subjective one, incapable of being articulated in any meaningful way. Spong understands this experience to be noncognitive and prelinguistic, culturally and historically timeless (*RBF,* 75, 230–231; *RMR,* 9, 99).

Of course, human experiences are always conveyed and communicated in terms of particular languages, cultures, and historical contexts. Spong is quite aware of this even as he repeatedly rejects any notion that experience can be permanently articulated in propositions. For example, when discussing the relationship between experience and language, he says: "The experience is always primary, the reflective understanding of the experience is always secondary, and the tales that illumine or explain the understanding are always tertiary.... An intense experience ultimately has no form. As soon as it achieves form it is distorted. The only means we have to do this is by and through the use of words and symbols" (*BOW*, 33). Indeed, the problem of the relation between experience and linguistic interpretation creates a genuine tension in Spong's theology. On the one hand, he knows that there can be no preservation of experience without language; on the other, he seems to believe that there is something inherently evil in the tendency to express timeless experience in propositional terms, and labels all such attempts with his favorite term of opprobrium, "literalism."

Nonetheless, since experience cannot be articulated except through language and propositions, Spong shows himself a true child of postmodernity by repeatedly emphasizing the historically and culturally contingent nature of all attempts to communicate human experience. He insists that the writers of the New Testament were very much people of their own times and thought in the frame of reference peculiar to the first century. "They were bound by the limits and subjectivity of their own language, their own history, and their own way of life" (*RBF*, 228). At the same time, Spong at least concedes that the modern period itself cannot escape from its own entanglement in history and culture: "The formulations of today or tomorrow will be no more eternal than the formulations of first-century people." "To freeze the interpretation of the experience in the words of any era, including our own, would be to guarantee the eventual loss of the truth of the experience" (*RBF,* 169, 231).

How, then, does he reconcile these two claims? On the one hand, Spong speaks of a timeless, prelinguistic, pure experience. He castigates those who strive to capture this experience in permanent propositions. Yet he insists, nonetheless, that it is impossible to convey experience except with language and symbols and emphasizes repeatedly that we are all subject to limitations of culture, language, and history. The answer to this question is the key to interpreting Spong's religious epistemology and, thus, his entire way of reading Scripture. From the moment that religious experience occurs, there will be an attempt to communicate it to others, although the very attempt to do so freezes the experience in a moment of time. This now substitutes words for the reality of the experience. These words become the interpretation that is handed down to us in mythology, Scripture, and ritual. The interpretation, in words that point to but cannot capture the religious experience, is inevitably expressed in terms of that limited worldview that provides the context in which the original experience occurred. Thus, the articulated linguistic expression of the original experience, like a snowball careening down a slope, picks up cultural and linguistic baggage as it rolls along (*RMR*, 33, 41; *RBF*, 25, 228).

The modern interpreter's job, then, is essentially to scrape away the dross to get beyond, but also go through, the language that not only stands in the way of but also provides the only access to the original experience in order that one might recover something of that experience for oneself. (*RMR*, 31; *RBF*, 31–32, 222). Ironically, while Spong criticizes those who wish to freeze biblical interpretation in the language of literalism, his goal is similar to those he criticizes. Despite his endorsement of the language of historicity and cultural perspectivism, Spong is interested neither in history nor in culture in themselves. On the contrary, his hermeneutic is itself a flight from both. The goal of Spong's hermeneutic is to escape from the vagaries of history to seek a pure, timeless experience that is immune from those vagaries. The mistake of literalists is not that they search for unchanging truth, but that they confuse the interpretive dross of history and culture with the unchanging reality of subjective experience itself.

In the light of Spong's account of religious experience, it becomes evident why he rejects the notions of miracle and divine intervention as mythological. Ultimately, his problem with the narratives of Scripture is their very narrativity, the fact that they speak in the language of history and cultural conditionedness. They have served their purpose to the extent that the biblical stories that witness to God's action in the life, death, and resurrection of Jesus of Nazareth point beyond themselves to a timeless moment of pure experience in which Spong and modern people can themselves participate. They can be of no use to us if those narratives are understood as referring to actual historical events in which God has revealed himself in a concrete and unrepeatable history. Literalists might appeal to Scripture in an attempt to speak of a historical revelation, but history is lost in the limited culture of a first-century worldview. Literalists pretend to find a definitive Word from God in Scripture, but ultimately language is incapable of communicating divine revelation. To speak of a revelation of God in word or deed is to objectivize the eternal, subjective experience, in which alone (Spong believes) God can be known.

The Trivialization of the Holy

There seems to have been a decided shift in Bishop Spong's doctrine of God. In Spong's early work, *This Hebrew Lord*, he praises Hebrew thought and criticizes Greek thought. Hebrew thought is wholistic, Greek thought dualist. The Hebrews could not possibly have believed in the dualist notion of the immortality of the soul. Rather, they believed in the "continuing life of the whole person," that is, resurrection. In this book, Spong discusses biblical concepts in the manner of the mid-twentieth-century biblical theologians. He notes that the Hebrews believed that God was revealed in history (*THL*, 19, 21–22, 33-36, 64, 69, etc.).

All of this contrasts with Spong's later writings. In his book *The Resurrection*, Spong rejects the notion of bodily resurrection as "crudely physical" (84). In *Living in Sin?* and *Born of a Woman*, he laments that the God who is portrayed in the Old and New Testaments is an immoral, sadistic, and patriarchal deity. Far from believing that God is revealed in history, Spong now insists that the essence of the biblical message has to do with "timelessness." Rather than indicating the existence of separate writers (as a Spong-like historical-critical scholar might conclude), the noticeable shifts from *THL* to the later works reveal more about Bishop Spong's tendency to embrace the latest trends in fashionable biblical scholarship than anything else. In *THL*, Spong was still under the spell of the liberal wing of the biblical theology movement. Now his authorities tend to be more postmodern or radical feminist.

In his earlier work, Spong may still have endorsed something like an orthodox notion of the transcendence of God—although there are indications that monist tendencies were already evident in his writings (*THL*, 144). Here he says, "To the Hebrew, God and the world were not antithetical, nor were they identical. God was the creator; the world was the creature. God was bigger than the creation, but the creation revealed the creator's glory" (*THL*, 33). Spong notes with apparent approval that the Hebrews believed that the world was created ex nihilo, from nothing. All this seems to have been abandoned in Spong's current doctrine of God. Far from believing in a transcendent deity, Spong has now clearly embraced a position in which God is in some sense identical with the world. The transcendence of God has been lost in a kind of radical immanentism (or monism): "...I no longer look for God or for ultimate meaning in some distant place beyond this world," says Spong, "I rather seek these realities in every moment and in every relationship. For me the transcendence of God is no longer something different from the immanence of God. Transcendence is always a dimension of the immanent. The immanent is the point of entry; the transcendent is the infinite depth of being discerned behind any moment, beyond any point of entry" (RMR, 289).

Spong now identifies God with Paul Tillich's "Ground of Being." There are also echoes of Hegel's notion of an evolving deity in Spong's notion of God: "God is not a heavenly man, an external force, or a judging parent. God is the creating spirit that calls order out of chaos. God is the life force that emerges first into consciousness, then into self-consciousness, and now into self-transcendence, and ultimately into we know not what. God is the love that creates wholeness, the Being at the depths of our being, the Source from which all life comes" (RMR, 290). Spong takes the logic of his pan (en)theist deity to its logical conclusion— that evil itself must find a home in the nature of deity: "Perhaps the presence of evil pushes us to see the shadows present in both God and life that Carl Jung talked about and to seek that interrelatedness that makes even suffering a pathway to God" (RBF, 69).

What has led Spong to endorse a monist doctrine of God? One can only speculate here because, as so often, Spong asserts rather than argues his point. I would suggest that a crucial factor in this move is Spong's hermeneutic of religious experience. Repeatedly Spong suggests that the only pathway to knowledge of God lies in a moment of timeless, prelinguistic religious experience that cannot be located in either the external world or in propositional statements. This inevitably moves us away from transcendence, toward interiority. Such an experience is, in effect, an experience of one's own subjectivity. It is a small step from arguing that God is known only through the experience of one's own subjectivity, to identifying that subjectivity in some way with that which it experiences. If God is known in a timeless experience of the self, might God not be identified in some manner *with* the self?

Although Spong insists repeatedly that experience cannot be captured in language or images, he continually associates the content of religious experience with language of "love," "life," and "self." It is in his explorations of these three motifs that Spong most frequently is led to immanentist interpretations of the divine nature. "We have come to the dawning realization that God might not be separate from us but rather deep within us" (*RBF,* 33).

An Unnecessary Incarnation

A monist, or immanentist, doctrine of God has clear implications for Spong's understanding of Christ. If the entire creation is already in some sense identified with God, then it makes little sense to speak of an incarnation of God in Christ in any literal sense. How can God become a human being, if in some sense all human beings are already identified with God? Any distinction between Jesus of Nazareth and other human beings, then, must be qualitative at best. We see in Jesus the potential that is inevitably in store for all of us. Spong's Christology is therefore adoptionist. Jesus Christ is not God become human, but rather a human being in whom God was especially present. Spong emphatically denies that St. Paul (or any other New Testament writer) understood Jesus to be the God-man of later Christology. Paul would not have said that "Jesus is God," nor was he a Trinitarian (*RBF,* 123–124, *BOW,* 25). Such notions belong to a later generation of Christians who had forgotten their Hebrew roots. For early Christians, like Paul, "Jesus the Christ was a special human life through whom God had uniquely acted and in whom God was uniquely present." (*RBF,* 124). Hence when Spong uses incarnational language, he is not speaking of the incarnation of God in a particular human being. Rather, he is identifying God with all humanity (*BOW,* 40).

Salvation as Self-Acceptance

Given his monist doctrine of God and his adoptionist Christology, Spong's understanding of salvation follows rather predictably. Since the religious experience of "love," "life," and the "self" is to be identified with the very nature of God, so the meaning of the love and life reflected in the mission of Jesus is to be found in Jesus' own self-acceptance. As Jesus affirmed his own self to be identical with the Ground of Being, so we are invited to affirm the being that is identical with our own selves: "The biblical portrait reveals a Jesus who had the courage to be himself.... . He both lived out the meaning of the Ground of Being in his own life and through his love gave to others the capacity to enter their own being at deeper and deeper levels" (RBF, 242).

Spong insists that Jesus loved life so much that not even the boundaries of death could stop that love. Lest, however, we be led by such enthusiastic language to presume that Spong has finally forgotten that the God he believes in does not act outside the realm of purely subjective experience, Spong makes it clear that he is not talking about the resurrection of the dead Jesus in any literal sense. Resurrection is but one more example of mythological language that is really referring to a timeless and unspeakable experience. Resurrection is not primarily something that happened to Jesus, but something that happens to us (RBF, 240–241).

The nature of salvation is fairly clear then. As Jesus affirmed himself and recognized his own identity with God's presence, so also we are to affirm ourselves and embrace our own divinity. As Spong interprets the message of the Gospel of John: "How can one worship the source of being, the great 'I Am,' except by having the courage to be the self God created each of us to be? The Christian is the one called so deeply into life, into love, and into being that he or she can say with Christlike integrity, I AM!" (RBF, 207). Spong assures us that such self-acceptance leads inevitably to affirming the selves of others as well. "I worship Jesus when I claim my own being and live it out courageously and in the process call others to have the courage to be themselves" (RBF, 242).

Of course, one might well ask whether self-acceptance leads inevitably to the love and acceptance of other selves. The earlier Spong seems to have been aware of this problem. Apparently influenced by the doctrine of sin that some in the biblical theology movement discovered in the New Testament, the early Spong endorsed what he called a doctrine of "original sin" found in Paul. He praised the Hebrew idea of creation and the fall that expressed a deep insight into the meaning of life. He saw sin as a basically self-centered attempt at ego building that results in more separation rather than community (*THL*, 69, 73).

The Spong of the later writings seems to reject any notion of a doctrine of original sin or the fall. He seems unaware that love can be self-centered or that self-affirmation might not be the road to salvation. He asks for the evidence that the creation began good and then fell into sin: "Are not the human qualities we now call selfishness or self-centeredness the result of the drive to survive far more than of the fall into sin?" (*RBF*, 34–35). Spong now blames the doctrine of a fall into sin on St. Augustine rather than the "Hebrews' deepest insight." In fact, Paul's understanding of sin is perceived to be pathological (*BOW*, 215–217, *RBF*, 108 ff.).

Of course, this does not mean that Spong has dispensed with sin entirely. Clearly, his vicious attacks on the idolatry of those he calls literalists—in language that reflects the passion of the Hebrew prophets—implies that some, at least, are outside the pale of salvation (*RBF*, 170, 232; *RMR*, 99). And then this poses the question of whether in a pan(en)theist universe there can be idols. If idolatry is the worship of the creature rather than the Creator, can any behavior be idolatrous in a world in which creatures share in God's very being? But leaving that unanswered question aside—in the end, Spong seems to recognize only two primary sins: lack of self acceptance and lack of inclusiveness. Because it would imply that people are not acceptable just as they are, it would presumably be exclusive to insist that Jesus' call to discipleship might demand change, perhaps even repentance from sin.

It should now be obvious that Spong's doctrine of God is unitarian. He has no interest in preserving the doctrine of the Trinity, though he wants to embrace the experience out of which that doctrine was forged (*RBF*, 232). The origins of Trinitarian doctrine can be traced to the repressive values of a patriarchal world: "God was a male called Father. Jesus the Christ was a male Son. These two male deities made up two prongs of the Christian Trinity." Just to be fair, the Spirit ought to have been female, but patriarchy prevented it (*BOW*, 205).

Of course, because Spong is a bishop, on occasion he finds himself in situations where he is required to recite the Trinitarian creeds. He can do this with a clear conscience because he applies the same hermeneutic to the creeds that he applies to Scripture. The creeds speak not about something God has done to create and redeem the world, but instead about human experience. When Spong says he believes in God the Father, maker of heaven and earth, he understands this to mean that all human beings are created in God's image and so should not be oppressed. When he says he believes in Jesus Christ, God's only Son, our Lord, he understands this to mean that God loves every one, even those who "seem intent on killing the love of God when that love is incarnate in human history." When Spong says he believes in the Holy Spirit, the Lord and giver of life, he understands this to mean that "each of us is created, loved, and invited by the Source of life into the fullness of life, into a heightened consciousness, into having the courage to be ourselves." The more human we are, the more we reveal the divinity within us (*RBF*, 249). So the Creed becomes one more opportunity to recognize God's monist incarnation in all of humanity, and to affirm our own self-worth.

Language and Experience

As we have tried to show, there is a reciprocal relationship between John Spong's epistemology of religious experience, his biblical hermeneutic, and his doctrine of God. To provide an adequate critique of his doctrine of God, we must first assess his account of religious experience.

The Roman Catholic philosopher and theologian Bernard Lonergan has pointed out that a common mistake of philosophers is to forget the difference between the way that infants and adults interact with the world. Infants do not use language; therefore their relation to the world is one of immediacy. Adults speak, and consequently their relation to the world is mediated by meaning and language. Radical empiricist philosophers like the logical positivists tend to forget this and develop philosophies that equate reality with immediate sense perception. In reaction, idealist philosophers, following Kant, recognize the cognitive mediation of knowledge but mistakenly conclude that the object of knowledge is merely *phenomenal*. Knowledge is about concepts rather than objects external to the self. In Spong's account of religious experience, we find a combination of the errors of both empiricism and idealism. With the empiricists Spong insists that the object of knowledge is direct and immediate. Religious experience is timeless, prelinguistic and not mediated by meaning. But with the idealists, Spong equates knowledge with the contents of consciousness rather than with perception of external objects. Hence religious experience seems to be an experience of the self.

In his radical distinction between experience and interpretation, Spong believes that in the order of knowledge, experience is primary (and formless), interpretation is secondary, and narratives follow last of all. In actuality, this is almost precisely the opposite of the way in which adult human beings really come to know. The relationship between language, narratives, and experience is mutually interdependent. Because knowledge is mediated by meaning, there simply are no experiences that are not first made possible by language, narratives, and tradition. Rather than language and enculturation representing an unfortunate secondary interpretive step following a universal and formless religious experience, it actually works the other way around. Concrete religious traditions with their attendant narratives, conceptual interpretations, and understandings are what make religious experience possible. Religious tradition is, in the words of George Lindbeck, an "external word" that molds and shapes the self. It is not merely the expression of a preconceptual religious experience. As people learn to interpret the self within the overarching narrative of a particular religion and become skilled in the symbols and practices of that particular religion, they become religious in a particular way and have concrete religious experiences. Accordingly, while there may be Christian, Jewish, Hindu, and other ways of being religious, there is simply no such thing as the kind of preconceptual, timeless, and prelinguistic religious experience that lies at the heart of Spong's hermeneutic.

We must conclude that Spong's demythologizing project of separating the mythological narratives of Christianity from a timeless religious experience undermines the Christian enterprise. Because he is so intent on interpreting Christianity in terms of an a priori hermeneutic of religious experience, it seems Spong is incapable of hearing the Christian message itself. He reduces the saving acts of God in Jesus Christ to their significance *for me* and divorces them from any objective status outside the self. But if we pay attention to the biblical narratives themselves, we discover that God's saving acts in Christ outside myself are, in fact, the central message of the New Testament.

As Edward P. Sanders, one of the foremost contemporary experts on Paul's theology, argues, Paul's doctrine of justification by faith is not about my self-understanding, but is simply one aspect of Paul's general theory of salvation through the crucified and risen Christ. Paul's understanding of salvation is that of incorporation of the self into the Christ-event, that is, my being united by faith to the crucified and risen Christ. It is not the reinterpretation of the Christ-event in terms of my own self-understanding. The risen Christ has logical and ontological priority to my own appropriation of salvation.

Similarly, at the heart of the biblical understanding of reality is the awesome awareness of a God who is radically distinguished from the human self and from creation. The New Testament scholar N.T. Wright has designated this notion of God as a creational, providential, covenantal monotheism. This biblical God has freely created and preserved the world, has entered into a covenant with the nation of Israel, and has fulfilled that covenant and redeemed the world in the life, death, and resurrection of Jesus Christ (*The New Testament and the People of God*, 248 ff.).

This notion of biblical monotheism, with its corresponding implication of a radical distinction between God and the world, has numerous implications that distinguish Christian monotheism from the understanding of the relation between the world and the divine found in ancient pagan religions, pan(en)theism, and the kind of "natural religious experience" embraced by Bishop Spong.

First, God's creation of the world is a free act. Accordingly, God is not dependent on the world for his own fulfillment. God does not need to have created a world and, indeed, might not have created a world at all. While God's existence is absolutely necessary, the existence of the world is utterly and radically contingent. It is not merely that the world might have existed differently, it might not have existed at all. Creation is, then, an act of sheer and overwhelming generosity—a gift, an absolutely gratuitous, free, and uncoerced sharing of divine goodness.

Second, if God is the Creator of the world, then God cannot be one of the items in the world that he has created. Nor can God be construed to be part of the world, as a monist or pan(en)theist substrate underlying the world's reality. God is present to the world not as one thing is present over against others, nor by sharing in the very existence of the world (as in monism), but in that most intimate and free act in which God gives to the world its very existence. While being utterly distinct from the created realm as its Creator, God is as present to each creature as is its very existence.

Third, such a God can be known only through covenant, not through general religious experience. The biblical God, in contrast to the gods of paganism, who are identified with the powers of nature, must freely give himself to be known in words and deeds that, while mediated through created realities, utterly transcend them. If the transcendent Deity must communicate in word and deed in order to be known at all, the notion of divine intervention (and thus miracle) is essential to Christianity. Of course, given the Christian understanding of creation, the concept that God intervenes is a bit of an oxymoron. God only needs to "step in" if the world is simply running along independently of the divine causality. We should rather say that when God acts or speaks in the created realm, he is doing so directly rather than through intermediate created causalities. Nevertheless, the immediate effects of such action are created effects.

Fourth, because God is not part of the created realm, the realm in which human beings come to knowledge, it follows that language about God is a special case. Since human language normally applies to created realities, language about the divine must be either symbolic, metaphorical, or analogical. This recognition provides a corrective to the false dilemma Spong poses in demanding a choice between literalism and nonreferential relativism. Rather, language use is rooted in the doctrine of creation itself. Human language and knowledge about God and the world are determined by the nature of God as Creator and the world as created. Because the created world exists prior to our knowledge of it, language is determined by the existence of realities that are prior to the knower, rather than vice versa. While language will never be able to encompass created reality in its complete intelligibility, language truly refers beyond itself. It is capable of pointing to its transcendent Creator because the creation reflects the perfections present in a higher and eminent manner in the God who has brought it into existence out of nothing.

We use symbolic, metaphorical, and analogical language to speak of God because it is the only language we have. Human beings can speak of spiritual (and uncreated) realities only through the use of language whose primary referent is physical, observable created realities. Attempts to discard metaphorical language as anthropomorphic or prescientific inevitably substitute equally metaphorical language for that rejected. A woman who had been brought up by very forward-thinking parents to think of God as "pure substance" once confessed to C.S. Lewis that she had always pictured God as a kind of vast tapioca pudding!

John Spong himself is no exception to this rule. Spong, rejecting the notion of a god who lives in the heaven of a three-decker universe and embracing the Ground of Being instead, merely substitutes imagery of immanence for that of transcendence. But did the biblical writers take the three-decker language literally? While the biblical narratives present God as dwelling in heaven, God at the same time is specially present at various sanctuaries (Bethel, Shiloh), on Mt. Sinai, in the desert tabernacle, in the cloud and pillar of fire that follow the Israelites in the desert, and later in the Temple in Jerusalem. Although the special place for worship of Yahweh is Jerusalem, he can be addressed by his worshipers wherever they are. It is impossible to escape from God's presence; he is in heaven but also in deepest Sheol (Ps. 139). "Do I not fill heaven and earth?" (Jer. 23:24); he lays the foundation of the earth and spreads out the heavens (Isa. 40:12; 48:13). In a classic study, Edwyn Bevan suggests that the reason the notion of God dwelling in heaven specifically came to be associated with Hebrew religion is that height is associated with transcendence. The great divide between religions is essentially that between monist religions and philosophies (like Hinduism and Neoplatonism) and the transcendence of Hebrew religion and Christianity. It would seem then that Spong understands correctly that the biblical view of a God in heaven is a threat to his monist enterprise (*THL* 144; *RBF* 145).

It is this doctrine of a transcendent Deity that provides the context for the doctrine of the incarnation of God in Christ. Because the pagan gods are part of the greater whole, they cannot truly partake of created reality without ceasing to be part of that greater whole and thus ceasing to be gods. In contrast, the biblical God is so radically transcendent (neither part of the greater whole of created reality nor a competing nature within that created reality) that he can become fully human in Christ in such a manner that neither the completeness of his incarnate humanity nor the completeness of his transcendent deity is compromised.

Because Jesus Christ is truly God become human, the incarnate Word of God is not merely the prime example of God's love for human beings, but is himself the self-communication of the divine love to human beings. It is because the personal identity of Jesus Christ is that of God incarnate that he is able to save sinful humanity. The word of grace that Jesus communicates to us is the very life of God, not merely the word of a God-like or God-filled creature.

Transcendence and Grace

The New Testament understanding of salvation and grace involves not simply a new self-understanding, but the actual transformation and re-creation of redeemed humanity as, through faith and the sacraments, it comes to share in the divine life mediated through the glorified humanity of the risen Christ. If, as in Spong's immanentism, created reality is insufficiently distinct from divine reality, then salvation in the biblical sense is unnecessary, because human nature is already (in some sense) identical with the divine nature. It is also impossible, because the monist god is incapable of acting in the created realm. On the other hand, Spong's caricature of the orthodox deity as merely being one competing reality set over against other realities in the created realm, leads to the destruction of humanity, since no two finite natures can meaningfully occupy the same metaphysical space. It is really only the Christian understanding of creation, in which God gives existence to the created world but neither competes with nor is a part of it, that enables the graced transformation of redeemed humanity, so that, in the words of the scholastic dictum, "grace perfects but does not destroy nature."

The three different ways in which God is present to humanity in creation, incarnation, and grace point to the triune identity of the biblical God. The doctrine of the Trinity, while not spelled out in Scripture, nonetheless is the inescapable implication of what the New Testament does tell us about the God who is revealed as Father, Son, and Holy Spirit. We know him in the history of Israel, the life, death, and resurrection of Jesus Christ, and the transforming presence of the Spirit of grace in Christ's body, the church. The New Testament writers do not (generally) refer to

Jesus as God, because they know that God is the one Jesus called Father; nonetheless, they do not hesitate to speak of Jesus in ways that in the Old Testament refer only to Yahweh. They apply to Jesus the divine name of *kurios;* they identify him as the Creator.

The doctrine of the Trinity follows inevitably from the principle that God must be who he has revealed himself to be. The God who truly has given himself to us as Father, Son, and Holy Spirit in the economy of salvation must be triune in himself if that revelation in history is a true revelation of his identity. The love that God has lavished upon us in creation, redemption, and transforming grace reveals an internal love shared between Father, Son, and Holy Spirit from all eternity, even apart from our own existence and even the existence of the universe. Our own salvation is the gift that enables us to become participants in this eternal love.

Far from separating God to an infinite and unknowable distance, it is precisely the distinction between the transcendent God and the world implicit in the doctrine of Creation that enables our own participation (by grace) in the triune life of God. If the Son and Holy Spirit were perceived to be lesser divinities, somewhere in the vast distance between God and creation, then at most they could provide pointers to an unknown God beyond themselves. But if the revelation of God in creation, redemption, and grace points to the triune identity of God as Father, Son, and Holy Spirit, then that revelation reflects a genuine giving of God himself to humanity. It is the orthodox doctrine of the transcendence of God that enables God truly to communicate to us his life and love.

Works Considered or Consulted

Barth, Karl. "The Triune God," *Church Dogmatics 1/1 The Doctrine of the Word of God,* Edinburgh: T & T Clark, 1975, 295-489. G.W Bromiley and T.F. Torrance, eds.

Bevan, Edwyn. "Height," *Symbolism and Belief,* Allen & Unwin, 1938.

Burrell, David. *Knowing the Unknowable God: Ibn-Sina, Maimonides, Aquinas.* Notre Dame: University of Notre Dame Press, 1986.

Eichrodt, Walther. *Theology of the Old Testament.* Philadelphia: Westminster Press, 1961, 1975, 2 vols., J. A. Baker, trans.

Frymer-Kensky, Tikva. *In the Wake of the Goddesses: Women, Culture and the Biblical Transformation of Pagan Myth.* New York: Macmillan, 1992.

Lindbeck, George. *The Nature of Doctrine: Religion and Theology in a Postliberal Age.* Philadelphia: Westminster, 1984.

Lonergan, Bernard. "The Origins of Christian Realism," *A Second Collection.* Philadelphia: Westminster, 1974, 239–261. W. F. Ryan, S.J., and Bernard J. Tyrrell, S.J., eds.

Lonergan, Bernard. *The Way to Nicea: The Dialectical Development of Trinitarian Theology.* Con O'Donovan, trans. Philadelphia: Westminster, 1976.

Sokolowski, Robert. *Eucharistic Presence: A Study in the Theology of Disclosure.* Washington, D.C.: Catholic University of America Press, 1994.

Sokolowski, Robert. *The God of Faith and Reason: Foundations of Christian Theology.* Notre Dame: University of Notre Dame Press, 1982.

Thiselton, Anthony C. *New Horizons in Hermeneutics: The Theory and Practice of Transforming Biblical Reading.* Grand Rapids: Zondervan, 1992.

Thiselton, Anthony C. *The Two Horizons: New Testament Hermeneutics and Philosophical Description.* Grand Rapids: Wm. B. Eerdmans, 1980.

Torrance, Thomas F. *The Trinitarian Faith: The Evangelical Theology of the Ancient Catholic Church.* Edinburgh: T & T Clark, 1993.

Wright, N.T. *The New Testament and the People of God.* Minneapolis: Fortress Press, 1992.

Modernity or Christianity?
John Spong's Culture of Disbelief
C. FitzSimons Allison

IN 2 CORINTHIANS 5:19, St. Paul tells us that "…God was in Christ, reconciling the world unto himself…." Bishop Spong seeks to reverse this proposition by reconciling himself to the world.

"I seek to stand with one foot inside my religious roots and the other firmly planted in my secular world," he tells us. "I am not willing to sacrifice either perspective"(*The Bishop's Voice,* April 1997).

It is clear, however, that religious perspective is precisely what he does sacrifice.

To begin with, he defiantly affirms that one can be a Christian while jettisoning belief in theism. Theism is caricatured as "an external Deity who *invades* human affairs periodically to *impose* the divine will upon this world… [theism] though still given lip service in worship settings has nonetheless died culturally"[italics mine] (*The Bishop's Voice,* October 1996).

Because the secular world no longer believes in such a Being who "is inevitably portrayed in human terms as a person who has a will, who loves, who rewards and who punishes"(ibid.). we must all relinquish our own belief in these enlightened times. Aside from the straw-man that he erects to represent biblical faith, complete with such unbiblical descriptions as "impose" and "invade," Spong seems unaware of the crucial and simple point that C.S. Lewis makes: personal and anthropomorphic descriptions of God are inadequate—but all the alternatives are worse. To be made in the image of a God who is less than personal is to turn our humanity toward a destructive, impersonal goal.

Orthodox Christianity has always warned against the danger inherent in using anthropomorphic language about God. God is affirmed to be more than, and only symbolized by, personal terms. Nonetheless, such terms remain the least misleading imagery available for conversation about God.

Decoding Modernity

A generation ago, Paul Van Buren attempted to accommodate the Christian faith to current secular assumptions in a very scholarly and disciplined work, *The Secular Meaning of the Gospel* (New York, 1963). Insisting that there was nothing of integrity in Christianity that could not be comprehended by the "mind of modern man," he tried to use modernity as a filter through which to pour traditional faith. Of course, the stress was on Jesus' humanity, not divinity.

Yet, ironically, the only reason that we have available to us an understanding of the humanity of Jesus at all is that the early church withstood the "mind of modern man" that existed in that day. The early church struggled hard to assert the full humanity of Christ against the "modern" and secular ethos that wanted to see him as a wholly divine figure, untouched by the world. The great heretics of the time, Arius, Apollinarius, Nestorius, and Eutyches, all proclaimed a divine Christ. One must go to an exotic and virtually unknown heresy, Psilanthropism, to find anybody who denied the divinity of Christ in the church's early history. If the church had practiced Van Buren's recommended epistemology, and not prevailed against the assumptions of those times, we would not now possess the revealed treasure (the full humanity of Christ) that Van Buren, this age, and Spong find so congenial.

The temptation today is to accommodate the Christian faith to the assumptions of an age that resists the affirmation of the divinity of Christ. But Scripture warns us against this temptation, especially in John 14:17, 22–27, where our Lord's emphasis is on "keeping his words" in the midst of a world which neither sees nor truly knows him.

Spong is a bishop attempting to reconcile Christianity to modernity. In doing so, he attacks those who differ with him, including his fellow bishops, as "immoral," "prejudiced," "superstitious," "illiterate fundamentalists," "ignorant," "religiously insecure," "incredible," "ill-informed," and "not living in the twentieth century." Religion for such people is "a precious narcotic, producing happiness and security, to which they cling with passion" (*The Bishop's Voice* and letters to Bishop Maurice Benitz). By contrast, Paul Van Buren, an honorable and respected scholar, never resorted to personal attacks on his critics. His commitment to modernity caused him to leave the church rather than subvert it.

But Spong's whole project is misconceived. As William Willimon wrote recently, the church has no business adopting an uncritical attitude toward modernity:

> Modernity has arrogance built into itself. Beginning as a search for certain irrefutable knowledge, a quest for the "facts," it likes to think of itself not as a point of view but simply as the facts. Therefore, all other ways of construing the world must converse with modernity on modernity's terms—or be labeled "primitive," "narrow," or "tribal." ...In leaning over to speak to the modern world, I fear we may have fallen in.... The point is not to speak to the culture. The point is to change it" (*Christianity Today*, May 19, 1997).

Scholarship, Please
Quite apart from the fact that Spong turns the Christian mission upside down in attempting to conform the gospel to the world (cf. Rom. 12:2,) he attempts to do so by a one-sided selection of authorities. For example, he quotes recognized scientific authorities who do not believe in Christianity but fails to cite those who do, for example, Polkinghorne, Peacocke, and T. Torrance. Much more seriously in the context of the Christian faith, he handles academic scholarship in the same way. He cites the Jesus Seminar group, Crossan, Borg, and Funk, who dismiss the creeds and claim that almost nothing in the Bible reflects what Jesus actually said or did. But he does not refer to scholars of international reputation who have devastated the Jesus Seminar, writers upon whom he rests his case. There is no evidence from his writings that he has ever studied the work of N.T. Wright, Luke Timothy Johnson, Brevard Childs, Gerald Bray, James Dunn, Anthony Thiselton, or Earle Ellis. Especially glaring is his omission of any reference to the work of Michael Wilkins and

J.P. Moreland, *Jesus Under Fire: Modern Scholarship Reinvents the Historical Jesus* (Zondervan, 1995). He dismisses this impressive body of literature as "defenders of traditional biblical ignorance." He implies that the only contemporary alternatives to the Jesus Seminar scholars are Pat Robertson, Jerry Falwell, and orthodox Catholic traditionalists (*Human Quest* 208 (3) 14–15, March–April, 1994).

Ordinarily, it would not be fair to blame an active bishop for being unfamiliar with the wide range of biblical scholarship that exists today. But Spong goes out of his way to present himself as a scholar, informed by the latest research. Yet he repeatedly (and wrongly) identifies the scholarly academy exclusively with those who have departed from the Christian faith. Worse, when he does cite such responsible scholars as Reginald Fuller and Raymond Brown, he falsely implies that they support his contentions. In fact, both have been at pains to distance themselves from Spong. Raymond Brown writes: "Spong is complimentary in what he writes about me as a New Testament scholar; I hope I am not ungracious if in return I remark that I do not think a single New Testament author would recognize Spong's Jesus as the figure being proclaimed or written about" (*Birth of the Messiah*, 1992, 704).

Spong has also attempted to undercut the work of evangelism. What are we to make of his visit to, and worship in, a Buddhist temple, which evoked the promise that he would never again try to convert people of other religions? If St. Patrick and St. Augustine of Canterbury had shared these views, Jack would possibly be a Druid today. And, while it may at first seem charitable to ignore real differences in belief, it soon becomes apparent to people of other faiths that the sincere beliefs they hold that differ from Christianity are regarded by Spong as being of no more importance than the Christian beliefs he rejects. Tolerance is certainly better than oppression, but it is inadequate in the long run. It requires no love and will ultimately be seen as condescension.

Again, Spong's caricature of missionary endeavor exposes his ignorance of the work and writings of Stephen Neill, Max Warren, Hendrick Kraemer, and others who have shown that Christianity is never its true self until it is being given away. Christians are not born but converted.

Neophilia

Spong also reveals a radical skepticism when he denies that it is appropriate to ask God for mercy in the *Kyrie* in the eucharist. Bishop Arthur Vogel points out that such a denial amounts to denying the validity of all prayer. He also adds that there is nothing "modern" about this skepticism about prayer. "It is as old as any denial of the Christian awareness of God."

Vogel goes on to show that questioning the legitimacy of the *Kyrie's* prayer for mercy should logically exclude a prayer for the blessing of same-sex unions. "It is difficult to see the consistency in so vigorously advocating a prayer for blessing while denying the legitimacy of prayer for mercy" (*The Living Church,* March 19, 1996). The consistency, however, lies in Spong's rejection of biblical theism in favor of the church's role in furthering political agendas, in this case that of the gay lobby. One of the blessings lost in this endeavor is reflected in Oswald Chambers' description of one of the functions of prayer in his devotional work, *Still Higher for Highest.*

> In his prayer Hezekiah tells God what he knows God knows already. That is the meaning of prayer—I tell God what I know He knows in order that I may get to know it as He does. (London: Marshall, Morgan and Scott, Blundell House, p. 118)

A neophiliac is someone who so loves the new that he cannot appreciate the old. Jack is such a neophiliac that in one of his earliest books, *Honest Prayer,* he claims that there was no such thing as honest prayer until modern times. The rich heritage of the prayers of St. John Chrysostom, St. Augustine, St. Bernard, St. Francis, Thomas Cranmer, Lancelot Andrewes, and George Herbert seems to have gotten lost somewhere in this assessment.

Scripture Under Fire

Bishop Spong's ambition to denude traditional faith of all aspects that are uncongenial to modernism necessitates an attack on Scripture, whose pervasive witness is a judgment on all ages and all "modern" times. Hence, we discover from Spong that Scripture is "patriarchal," "exploitative," "tribal," and a "primitive myth." John's Gospel is antisemitic, St. Paul is a self-loathing homosexual,

Scripture endorses slavery, and the Ten Commandments are immoral because they treat women as property. "Our primary understanding of God's grace came from a self-hating gay man." We are also told that Isaiah, Jeremiah, and the Psalmist did not anticipate Jesus because "people can't predict future events. It's a magical view of the Bible" (*The Living Church*, January 7,1996).

In *Rescuing the Bible from Fundamentalism*, Spong sees taking the Bible literally as the great heresy. Yet, left to himself, no one is as much of a literalist as Spong. He calls the Ten Commandments "immoral" because the last commandment declares that "man shall not covet his neighbor's wife." For thousands of years faithful people have read "man" as generic—otherwise, presumably, women would be free to sin in this particular way although men would still be bound by the commandment. Now, however, Spong informs us that the commandments must be discarded because "man" does not include women and the meaning of "wife" cannot embrace "spouse."

Similarly, according to Spong's view of the Bible, only men "are created in the image of this God" (*LS*, 125). In this instance, Spong does not seem to be a very careful reader, because the generic meaning of "man" is explicit in Gen. 1:27. "So God created man in his own image, in the image of God he created him; male and female he created them."

Concerning Christ's ascension, Spong quotes with approval his daughter's remark that "...if Jesus went up into the sky he would not get to heaven, he would go into orbit" (*The Times*, London, August 4, 1989).

In general, Spong fails to grasp the profound nature of symbols. They are never "only symbols." Because he fails to see that the symbol points to something beyond itself, he jettisons what the symbol points to and participates in. In spite of quoting Paul Tillich voluminously, he seems to have missed something crucial in Tillich's thought:

> He who says "only a symbol" has completely misunderstood the meaning of symbol; he confuses symbol with sign and ignores that a genuine symbol participates in the reality of that which it symbolizes. (Cegley, C.W. and Bretall, R.W. *The Theology of Paul Tillich*, New York: Macmillan, 1952, pp. 334–335)

This failure to appreciate the nature of symbols precludes for Spong any appreciation of the Ascension. In this feast we celebrate that reintegration of our nature with God, the Father who created it, in the person of God the Son who took it for himself and redeemed it. This meaning is inaccessible to one whose literalism about symbols causes him to consign them to ridicule.

Spong's treatment of St. Paul deserves special attention. His claim that the apostle was a self-hating, repressed homosexual is explained as follows:

> Nothing else, in my opinion, could account for Paul's self-judging rhetoric, his negative feeling toward his own body and his sense of being controlled by something he had no power to change (*New York Times*, February 2, 1991).

The alleged "negative feeling toward his own body" is an egregious mistake even for someone who is ignorant of Greek. In the famous passage in Rom. 7, Paul is not writing about his "body" but his "flesh." The Greek word for "body," meaning our physical person, is *soma*. But the word for "flesh" is *sarx*, and it refers to our fallen or lower nature. In Galatians 5, Paul includes in the long list of works of the flesh such nonbodily sins as idolatry, hatred, wrath, strife, and envy. To suggest that Paul hated his physical body is to completely misunderstand one of the rudimentary themes of the New Testament, that our self-centered selves are in a tragic bondage from which we need to be set free. A Manichaean heresy later equated sin with the body (*soma*) in the way that Spong reads incorrectly into Paul.

The other "evidence" for the claim that Paul's "thorn in the flesh" was homosexuality is his "sense of being controlled by something he had no power to change." Yet Christians from Paul onward, dealing with all varieties of problems, have described themselves in this way. The admission that we are unable to control our behavior apart from grace is the theme of Thomas Cranmer's confession in Morning Prayer. It is also Step One of every AA program of the twentieth century, and that experience has now expanded to a range far wider than alcoholism. This experience of bondage as a human condition is so universal that it seems particularly apparent in those who deny its reality.

As for the issue of what the thorn in Paul's flesh was, it was apparently something so evident to the Galatians that they might have turned away from him in disgust because of it, though they did not (Gal. 4:14). It could hardly have been homosexuality unless it were acted out or confessed, for which there is no evidence at all. A much more plausible conjecture has been that Paul suffered from something like epilepsy. But to speculate about the thorn is to miss the point in 2 Corinthians 12:7, which is that we are to depend on God's strength and not on our own. He can use our very weaknesses to show his power. The picture Spong gives of St. Paul as a self-hating neurotic is light years away from the confident, enduring, encouraging, indefatigable, and effective teacher, missionary, and apostle whom we see in Scripture.

Another charge that Spong makes against Scripture is that it accepts slavery, which gives him an opportunity to contrast modernity's superiority. His distorted claim that the church endorsed slavery ignores the historical context and deeper relationships of grace that eventually caused the evangelicals to help eradicate slavery from the British Empire through the efforts of William Wilberforce (whom Spong confuses with his son, Samuel). One of the best comments on this calumny is by Steven J. Keillor (brother of Garrison):

> Critics correctly note that the New Testament did not explicitly condemn Roman slavery; indeed, Paul commanded slaves to obey their masters. We can quickly see why that was so. First century Christians were a small persecuted minority sometimes tossed to the Coliseum's lions or lit up as human torches in Rome. The apostles did not waste quills or parchment writing to their scared flock about ideas to reform Roman society. No matter how noble the ideas or well-intentioned the believers, they could never carry them out. (*This Rebellious House: American History and the Truth of Christianity.* Downers Grove: IVP, 1996, p.41)

Blaming the church for living with slavery is like blaming Russian Seventh Day Adventists for living under Stalin or Jack Spong for living with the Berlin Wall. In his attempt to discredit the religion expressed in "Amazing Grace," he claims erroneously that John Newton wrote it on the deck of a slave ship with its "writhing human cargo below struggling to survive their kidnapping from Africa." In fact, Newton wrote the hymn many years later, after his conversion, in his study at Olney, Buckinghamshire.

The Critical Method

One of the difficulties faced by the generation that Jack Spong and I represent is the way Scripture has been taught to us. The Jesus Seminar is not a surprising offspring of the approaches we learned. Every method of studying the Bible for over 150 years comes with a hyphenated partner: higher-, lower-, form-, textual-, redaction-, historical-, and literary-criticism. The very word *criticism* has the inescapable connotation that we are the judge of Scripture and not vice versa.

This is not to say that endeavors to find the earliest sources of texts and the dates and authorship of the writings are unworthy exercises. The overwhelming focus on the Bible as an object of criticism, however, carries with it the inevitable loss of the verifying experience that the reader is an object of Scripture's revelation.

No wonder that many have found David Steinmetz's article, "The Superiority of PreCritical Exegesis" (*Theology Today*, Vol. 37, 1980, pp. 27–38) a refreshing liberation from the dogmatic claims of the historical-critical method that is now admitted on all sides to be impotent in establishing authority for Scripture.

> Until the historical-critical method becomes critical of its own theoretical foundations and develops a hermeneutical theory adequate to the nature of the text which it is interpreting, it will remain restricted—as it deserves to be—to the guild and the academy, where the question of truth can endlessly be deferred.

One can test Steinmetz's assertions by comparing Luther's commentary on Galatians with any number of contemporary ones. Luther will not help us decide whether Galatians 2 is describing the same trip to Jerusalem as that related in Acts 15. But we are unlikely to find a modern commentary that can open up the meaning of justification as Luther's commentary did for Charles Wesley. John's younger brother was so powerfully transformed that after the experience of hearing the gospel through this precritical commentary, his heart opened up and some 8,989 hymns poured forth in the following fifty years. One might truly say that there is a great difference between the eighteenth and twentieth centuries but three things have not changed: the nature of humanity, the nature of God, and the gospel that puts them together.

Jack Spong and I graduated from the same seminary only three years apart. The mottoes engraved in Greek on its shield are "The Word became flesh" and "The faith once delivered to the saints." Over the library, however, is carved "Seek the truth, come whence it may, cost what it will." The latter is mistakenly thought to be the motto of the seminary. There is a world of difference. The true mottoes are claims of objective fact to which we are witnesses. The library motto is a good corrective to the human tendency to freeze even correct teachings into ultimates, but it is empty of any connotation that Truth has sought and claimed us. "Seek the truth..." can imply that our ministries are essentially seeking ministries where nothing certain is given and everything is "up for grabs."

If I could influence Jack to read one book, it would be C.S. Lewis's *Pilgrim's Regress*. In that allegory, the protagonist, John, seeks from a Mr. Broad some specific directions as to whether he is to cross a canyon or not as he continues his journey.

> "That is a beautiful idea," says Mr. Broad, "the seeking is the finding."

> "Do you mean that I must cross the canyon or that I must not?" John repeats. But the only response he can wring from Mr. Broad is, "These great truths need re-interpretation in every age."

The oracle that provides such frustrating sophistication is not "wrong," it is simply inadequate. Questioning and searching are always appropriate, but they are no substitute for a basic decision for or against the gospel, and certainly no substitute for the crossing of the canyon itself. C.S. Lewis has no peer as a teacher for those of us misled by substituting a search of some kind for the claim of God upon our lives.

The Trivialization of God

The most obvious liability that results from putting too much faith in the clever ideas that are abroad in the world is that we will have little protection from the climate of the times. Our current religious climate can be accurately diagnosed as the *Trivialization of God*, which is the title of an excellent work by Donald McCullough, with its subtitle: *The Dangerous Illusion of a Manageable Deity* (Navpress, 1995). Karen Armstrong's book, *A History of God* (Ballantine, 1994) and Jack Miles' *God: A Biography* (Vintage, 1996) are, by contrast, examples of the world's condescending criticisms of God. Both authors are ex-Roman Catholics who write as though God were an object for us to study, whose actions and "growth" are evaluated by our standards. William C. Placher's *The Domestication of Transcendent Thinking About God* (John Knox, 1996) traces the roots of this reductionist tide to the seventeenth and eighteenth centuries.

Never in the history of the church has an age been more guilty of adherence to Reinhold Niebuhr's dictum: In the beginning God created us in his own image and ever since we have endeavored to return the compliment. Paul Vitz's *Psychology as Religion: The Cult of Self-Worship* (Eerdmans, 1977) shows how the psychological influence within the churches has reduced the hope of human transformation by grace, to psychological affirmations to enhance self-esteem. E. Brooks Holifield's book *A History of Pastoral Care in America: From Salvation to Self-Realization* (Abingdon, 1983) indicates in the subtitle what is happening in the training of our clergy. Rabbi Kushner's best-selling *When Bad Things Happen to Good People* has some wise things to say about the fact that bad things can happen to undeserving people (one could have discovered this more easily by reading Jesus' description of two disasters in Jerusalem in Luke 13:1–5). Kushner's solution to the mystery of innocent suffering is, however, to forgive God. Our God then is one we must forgive, another example of a "trivialization" of God.

The outstanding example of the arrogance of this present age toward God is the recent publication by Norman Mailer of *The Gospel According to the Son* (Random House, 1997), in which Mailer presumes to tell us what the gospel is according to Jesus. His own celebrity, he claims, has given him "a slight understanding of what it's like to be half a man and half something else, something bigger." His remark is a serious symptom of the trivializing of God. In no previous age have the "modern times" produced such presumptions about almighty God.

It is from breathing in the world's atmosphere of trivialization that one exhales contemptuous words about Scripture, outrageous statements about St. Paul, and exotic and baseless conjectures about our Lord. The idea that God could be evil stems from the fashionable pantheism among some extreme feminists that equates all nature with God instead of seeing nature as a now-imperfect creation of God. This leads to the inevitable recognition that there are dark and terrible things in nature (God), so we have to decide what is good and what is bad in nature (God). Or, as I have written elsewhere, "Monism dulls the ethical imperative [in a way] that makes it impossible for a just society to distinguish between good and evil. It leaves the individual, who does so distinguish, in the position of being the judge of God" (*The Cruelty of Heresy,* Harrisburg: Morehouse, 1994). This is the driving force that makes Spong the judge of Scripture. C.S. Lewis's description of the differences between theism and pantheism in *Miracles* is unsurpassed (Macmillan, 1947, Chapter 11, "Christianity and Religion").

One of the first things to be left out of the Christian faith, as a result of the trivialization of God, is God's wrath. But there is a sentimental cruelty inherent in the idea of a "manageable deity," because it cuts out any hope of final justice. God's anger is the inevitable flip side of his love. There can be no authentic love without implacable antagonism against the denials and betrayals of love. Abraham Heschel teaches us that "God is not indifferent to evil!... This is one of the primary meanings of the anger of God: the end of indifference." The trivialization of God will end by enhancing indifference toward what is wrong and destroying the human hope for justice.

It's a small step within modernity from being the judge of God to dismissing the creeds. The report to the Diocese of Newark in 1992 "Our Common Life" claims that when we say "...we believe in the teaching of scripture and the authority of the historic creeds... this tells us nothing." Hence the commitment to modernity in Newark is giving up that which Christians across denominational lines have affirmed each Sunday: the doctrine of the Trinity. Yet Roland Frye of Princeton says that "the formulation of the Christian doctrine of the

Trinity is one of the most impressive intellectual achievements in human history."

> It involved analyses of at least equal sophistication of those of present-day astrophysics and physical theory, and it achieved coherence of theological meaning while preserving the divine mystery. Five or six centuries were required for the full development of this careful, nuanced, and balanced formulation to preserve and present theologically the three persons whom Christians encounter as divine, without falling into polytheism, but maintaining a single and undivided godhead. (*Speaking the Christian God*, ed. A. Kimel, Grand Rapids: Eerdmans, 1992, p. 22)

Modernist contempt for historic Christianity leads to shocking ignorance of the basic outlines of the church's teaching on the Trinity. Spong writes:

> The idea that somehow the very nature of the heavenly God required the death of Jesus as a ransom to be paid for our sins is ludicrous. A human parent who required the death of his or her child as a satisfaction for a relationship that had been broken would be either arrested or confined to a mental institution" (*The Bishop's Voice*, October 1996).

It is very difficult to understand how anyone in the bishop's position could possibly be unaware that the separation of the Father from the Son in the preceding quotation was the teaching of the heretic Arius and that if the Councils of Nicea and Constantinople (and the Creed) were wrong in insisting that Christ was of "one substance" (essence) with the Father, then Arius was right and Good Friday was indeed "child abuse."

When Scripture and the historical creeds "tell us nothing," it then follows that we can make the same old mistakes again and again, mistakes as serious as confusing Christian faith with Arian heresy. Jack Spong and I had a teacher, Albert Mollegen, who quite dramatically demonstrated Athanasius's faithful rendering of the gospel against that of Arius by illustrating with a long, boney hand how "God redeemed mankind with his right hand but brought it back bloody!" The essential identity of Jesus Christ with the Father, so casually rejected when rejecting the Creed, results in the kind of horrid portrayals of God Spong describes.

A clergyman in his diocese once asked Bishop Spong how he could function with integrity as a bishop when, in examining candidates for the ministry, he does not personally hold the beliefs he expects of those whom he ordains. "Is this not a sign of his own hypocrisy? Thus far, I have not been satisfied with his answer that the questions in the ordination service (*BCP*, p. 526) are simply a matter of (individual) interpretation"(James P. Jones, *Central Florida Episcopalian*, May/June, 1997). One wonders whether verbal agreements or signed business contracts carry greater authority than public vows before an altar. If not, would one do business with the bishop? If so, what does it say about holy vows?

Honest to God
One of the surprising things in John Spong's writings is his discovery of and affection for a remarkable scholar, Michael Goulder. Although most of Goulder's work is now out of print, he has done careful research, resulting in such works as *Midrash and Lection in Matthew* (London: SPCK, 1974), which seems to undergird Jack's skepticism about the Gospels. Goulder's own academic journey has led him out of Christianity into atheism. Spong's fondest hope is to "preside over the liturgy that would restore Michael Goulder to the Anglican priesthood"(*LTG*, xv). Yet Goulder's departure from Christianity was not imposed upon him but was the action of an honorable man who no longer believed in Jesus Christ. Spong does not wish to convert him but to change the Christian faith to accommodate him.

More than fifty years ago, A.D. Nock made the claim that Paul was perhaps a homosexual, and Robert Graves long ago suggested that Jesus was the illegitimate son of a Roman soldier. But neither of these were Christian and neither could use the office of bishop to sell their views. It is typical of Spong's weight on the foot in modernity that he wants not to convert Goulder to the belief and trust of Christianity but to accommodate Christianity to Goulder's atheism.

One must be cautious about using statistics to verify truth. But Bishop Spong's claim that the church's failure to accommodate the present age is holding back its growth and impeding his own mission to the "alumni" who have left must be challenged. One would expect that where such a ministry has flourished for twenty years, its fruits should be showing. Instead, the Diocese of Newark had 44,423 communicants when he came in 1978 (*Episcopal Church Annual*, 1980) and only 24,648 in 1995—a loss of almost half.

The Rev. William Ralston of St. John's Church, Savannah, deserves the last word on this matter.

> I truly think that the troubles and disorders of the existential Church are an index in code of its derelictions in the matter of the doctrine of God. The Holy Trinity is a mystery, but it is neither irrational in meaning, inexplicable as sound religion, or incomprehensible as a form for the human experience of divine realities. And it is most certainly the historic (and philosophical) basis for the spiritual life of the Church. If you don't believe it, or choose to ignore it, then go your way. But don't try or claim to drag the Church your way. That is dishonest, and worse than dishonest. It is more grievous than heresy. It is treachery (*The Parish Paper*, June 2, 1996).

Works Considered or Consulted

Bray, Gerald. *Biblical Interpretation Past and Present*. Leicester: Apollos, 1996.

Hays, Richard B. *The Moral Vision of the New Testament: Community, Cross, New Creation: A Contemporary Introduction to New Testament Ethics*. San Francisco: Harpers, 1996.

Kegley, C.W., and R.W. Bretall. *The Theology of Paul Tillich*. New York: Macmillan, 1952.

Keillor, Stephen J. *The Rebellious House: American History and the Truth of Christianity*. Downers Grove: Inter-Varsity, 1996.

Kimel, A. editor. *Speaking the Christian God*. Grand Rapids: Eerdmans, 1992.

Thiselton, Anthony C. *Interpreting God and the Post-Modern World*. Grand Rapids: Eerdmans, 1995.

Rescuing the Bible from Bishop Spong
Ephraim Radner

> "The voice of my beloved! Behold he comes... "
> (Song of Songs 2:8)

The Basic Question: Does God Speak?

I ONCE KNEW A YOUNG UNIVERSITY WOMAN struggling with a severe depression. Following the violent death of one of her parents, she had grown increasingly despairing and had eventually come under the care of a psychiatrist. She was a member of my church, and one day we came to talk about how things were going. Along with some drug therapy, her treatment consisted of frequent discussions with her psychiatrist about a number of issues: her relation to her parents, her habits of self-regard and personal interactions, her sense of worth, and so on. All of this was helpful, she said.

But at a certain point she had come to a barrier in these discussions with her doctor. She had realized that, ultimately, the issues at stake appeared quite different to her doctor from how they appeared to her. Her doctor was attempting to get her to grasp the fact that the world was actually manageable for her if she could see that it was, at root, a place where despair was unnecessary. With proper "self-awareness," she would be able to "deal with" reality. She, on the other hand, had been confronting a very different set of questions: What is the sense of life and of death? What of her parent's life and death? Where did these lead and what did they mean? How do we choose our actions? What is good and evil about the choices we face, make, and confront in others? What is the significance of fear and of sorrow? How do we come to love, to give and to receive affection?

"My doctor's world is mute concerning all these things. He has no language to talk about them," she said. "Instead, I've been driven back to the Scriptures. God's language seems to grasp what I am asking." When God speaks, when God articulates his life in the specifics of directive and localized action, she said, the result is not a limiting God, but a world where "the true depth and mystery of my life is taken seriously and opened up to view."

I am reminded of this episode when I approach John Spong's view of Scripture. Not that Spong is particularly tainted with today's habitually parodied "therapeutic" mindset. He seems, in fact, little interested in helping smooth out the troubled psyches of his readers. But he does seem deliberately intent on affirming a vision of the world in which divine aphasia, a God who cannot speak, determines the basic shape of religious existence. And in this regard he stands in fundamental accord with the whole range of secular attitudes that have consigned the gripping and troubling aspects of human life to the unutterable, because what is mysterious is deemed unspeaking. Spong's rejection of Scripture's capacity to enunciate God's "words," because God after all cannot "speak," has as its outcome (and perhaps also its motive) the insistence that human life be lived in the shallow grave of its own Creator's inaccessibility. In the end, such an insistence offers only the most flabby and uninteresting of evasions of the compelling grasp of God's love for us in this world, to which Scripture not only testifies, but which it actually embodies— articulately, coherently, and profoundly.

This question of divine communication regarding the mystery of our existence is the lens through which I wish to reflect on Spong's understanding of Scripture. In doing so, I will admittedly sidestep some of the more titillating aspects of Spong's reading of the Bible. His scriptural analysis, as we all know, is notorious mainly for its outrageous speculative and reductionist judgments about Scripture's content: miracles didn't objectively happen, most of the Old Testament is filled with not-so-pious myths of violent ethnic self-justification and bigoted oppression. Most of his tired assertions can be countered analytically on the basis of objective historical and literary arguments, which have achieved a formidable scholarly mass since skeptics first began articulating challenges to Scripture's veracity in the first century. The "modern scientific consciousness" that Spong claims is crucial to asking new questions of Scripture has really made little difference in this regard. And handbooks of Christian apologetics, from Origen onward, address these perennial scoffings.

Far more pertinent to our own clear grasp of Scripture's positive character, however, is an exposition of Spong's underlying attempt in all of this to expel from the world's apprehension God's fundamental self-giving to the realities of our own existence. The reduction of Scripture that Spong promotes simply expresses this deeper denial of, or refusal to pursue, God's creative self-communication to the world of our experience.

Spong's Embrace of Divine Incoherence

Spong's denial of God's speech, so prevalent among the disaffected of our time, demands some response. For much of the argument strikes me as sheer lack of intellectual fortitude, which may also be a cultural symptom of the epoch in which we live: it seems to require too much *effort*, to be too *painful* to confront our lives as if God himself could touch them concretely. To see why Spong has so little use for Scripture, one need only note how rare it is for him to discuss who God is with any consistent and sustained focus.

It astonishes me that he can put forward as the sum of his theology and spirituality, not even the abbreviated substance of the books and sermons that someone like the mid-century writer Paul Tillich produced, but merely their titles: *Ground of Being, Source, Life, Love*. Spong obviously holds Tillich in high regard (cf. *RB*, pp. 240 ff). And abstract terms like these for Tillich have, to be sure, some intelligibility when moored to an explanatory apparatus, not to mention consistent historical demonstration. But when they are allowed to do all the work of referring to God, they inevitably end up by meaning nothing much at all because they indicate everything. Since other essays in this volume deal more fully with these broader theological terms, let us here simply observe the poverty of significance that Spong's unfocused language for God entails. In the process, we can also note how a lack of focus in signification about God forces the religious role of Scripture to be not so much contradicted as rendered meaningless.

Take the following paragraph at the end of one of his recent
books:

> Jesus was alive, totally alive, and in that vibrant vital life
> God was experienced. This God was perceived in Scripture
> and creed as a human form who lived just beyond the sky,
> who manipulated life by entering it and by withdrawing
> from it. That limited view has faded. This God is now per-
> ceived as the presence of life that animates the universe,
> that reaches self-consciousness in Homo sapiens and that
> breaks open to the essence of transcendence in Jesus of
> Nazareth. In the fullness of this life we enter the same
> experience of God that marked the life of Jesus. We wor-
> ship this God and acknowledge the saving power of this
> Jesus when we dare to live openly, fully, completely—
> affirming the life of God that is within us (RBF, 241).

This paragraph is typical Spong-speak. It plays with a number
of key abstractions that are never analyzed elsewhere, are lifted
up as if they themselves somehow clarify an otherwise miscon-
strued object, and are, when pressed, proved to be self-referring
and hence literal nonsense. For example, the dominant concept
here used to explain who God is—and who, by derivation,
Jesus is— is the concept of "life." What does Spong mean by
"life"? He does not, clearly, have in mind a strictly biological
definition; otherwise the biological death of Jesus would bring
to an end Jesus' vital relation to God. But does he mean to
imply that God's "life" animates the inanimate aspects of the
universe? Such an idea would fit awkwardly with another affirmation he makes: by linking the "presence of life" to its capacity to come to "self-consciousness" in human beings, Spong
might be asserting that the "life" that is God is not "self-conscious" apart from the existence of human beings—that is, God
is present in a bird, possibly in a stone, possibly in a microbe
or a quark, but God is not "self-conscious" except in a (biologically existent?) example of the species Homo sapiens. What
exactly animates the vast reach of the universe that exists in a
state of insentient being? Perhaps Spong means that God is the
principle of "evolving consciousness" within the universe,
something a few pop science writers have suggested. But what

does it mean to call God a "principle," when we are also calling God "life"?

In addition, if God is the principle or motive force of evolving self-consciousness, to what exactly does such self-consciousness tend in its "transcendence," a word used with reference to Jesus? If "life," which itself "animates" the universe—something that sounds rather embracing—is conscious of itself *somewhere* (a peculiarly limiting claim for a man of Spong's "universal perspective"), what transcendent object can it *also* be tending toward beyond itself? Is the "life *within*" us the same as the "essence of transcendence"? Finally, "living openly, fully, and completely" seems to be the same as being self-conscious of the Life that "animates the rocks." Doesn't this seem to indicate an identity of being between rock and human being? What, then, is there to "dare"? For even if a human being were to grasp hold of his or her "being" in the manner of a stone—whatever that might mean—such a "rock-headed" person could not be "inauthentic" to the "being" of "life."

An intellectually charitable assessment of this outlook might describe it as "monist," in the sense that it views reality as made up of just one substance (e.g., " life"). But, really, there is little of such rigorous monist viewpoints as held by Spinoza or Hinduism or even Hegel in any of this jumble. So, exactly *what* is there in it? The frustration that follows any attempt at analyzing Spong's terminology is not merely a matter of scholarly pedantry. The attempt—and consequently the frustration—is absolutely demanded on Spong's own terms, not least by his claim that this "reality" of God, as he gropingly puts it, logically excludes the character of scriptural language as referring to a truth. If God is the kind of thing Spong claims God is, then Scripture cannot be the kind of thing classical Christianity (let alone classical Judaism) has claimed.

The point to be emphasized here is that the kind of God Spong affirms is a semantically *nonsensical* abstraction. Therefore, anything Spong has to say about Scripture is, religiously speaking, bound up with nonsense.

Spong's Attack on Divine "Literalism"
Perhaps Spong's relegation of Scripture to the realm of the inherently nonsensical is not so apparent to all readers. Many of them

sympathetically seize upon Spong's critical tirades against the
"literal" significance of the Bible's many narratives and moral
imperatives: evolution contradicts Genesis (read in "literal"
terms), physical miracles are impossible, Scripture commands
many heinous actions of vengeance, violence, and oppression,
and so on.

Since the bulk of any book by Spong is devoted to this kind of
negative, as opposed to constructive, discourse, it is easy for those
in sympathy with such age-old concerns (voiced initially by
ancient Greek and Roman opponents of Judaism and
Christianity) to gloss over the fact that the basis of Spong's dismissal of Scripture's "literal" significance is not critical at all.

His dismissal is not based on a consideration of either evolutionary theory or Genesis' literary and linguistic substance; it is
not based on a consideration of the character of what has been
called "miracle" and its relation to what is commonly called a
"law of nature"; it is not based on a consideration of the moral
(let alone religious) dimension of holiness, evil, violence, and
historical existence. No, Spong's dismissal of Scripture's classical
Christian significance seems to be based not on the application
of critical analysis but on Scripture's sheer incapacity to be appropriated to the anti-conceptual mindset that lies behind Spong's
argumentative rejection of any divine metaphysics. Simply put,
Spong's God is incoherent, and Scripture is not: obviously they
cannot come together in his mind.

There is much more at root here, however, than an incongruity
of sense. Spong actually seems to suggest that Scripture's coherence
is *itself* anti-God. Indeed, the very principle of coherence, where
concepts and referents are actually susceptible of an analytic fit,
is for Spong a contradiction of a "God" who is deliberately consigned to abstracted incoherence. Spong's whipping boy, the
"literalizing" of Scripture's meaning—which he associates with
fundamentalists, Roman Catholics, bigots, and precritical hominids
(cf. *RB*, pp. 227–237 and passim)—acts as but the projected
object of his antipathy for the coherence of human experience
and reason, and the particularity of its communicated expression.
Could it be that the reason Spong attacks the practice of taking
the meaning of Scripture literally is that he hates the idea that
there might be some fundamental connection between human
reason, human experience and human speech?

An example of Spong's insistence that God lies beyond speech can be seen in the following quote:

> True discipleship is seen when we imitate this God pres-
> ence by living fully, loving totally, and having the courage
> to be all that God has created each of us to be. This is the
> power of Jesus and the presence of Jesus that for me lies
> behind the literal words of holy Scripture. This is the mys-
> tical presence that beckons to us when we follow the
> pointers in the biblical symbols, in the myths, in the leg-
> ends, and in the *midrashic* traditions toward their destina-
> tion. These were the creative but inevitably human ways
> that people used to capture in timebound words the God
> presence they met in Jesus. This is the ineffable wonder
> that Jesus offered that can only be seen when our eyes are
> opened and our consciousness is raised to the realm of
> the holy... The God experience lies beyond the literal
> words of the Gospels... Religious experience, the presence
> of God, is mystical at its core, and because it is mystical,
> then creeds, doctrines, scripture, and sacred stories will
> never be ultimate. For ultimacy belongs to God, not to
> the words that only point to God (*LTG*, 333–34).

Here Spong presents a number of familiar contrasts: timebound and timeless, literal and mystical, limited and ineffable, human and divine. On this score, Spong sounds less like a philosophical monist than a gnostic dualist! "Literalizing" God is something he links to a passed era and debased form of consciousness, some-thing old people from his childhood or contemporary people gripped by "insecurity" and "fear" still do. Literalizing God hap-pens when the articulate descriptions of God that human beings have fabricated become mistakenly identified with the "experi-ence of the God presence" itself within them. Scriptures, creeds, doctrines, sacred stories—all the articulate vehicles of conceptual expression by which human beings communicate with one another about God (not to mention *with* God and God *with* them)—are tied to this literalizing threat. They are themselves limited, narrow, and incomplete. And unless one is able to crack them open, get beyond them, pull aside their veiling illusions, in the end, they become socially dangerous. *Dangerous,* because they create experiential and religious divisions that tear apart rather than unite the social fabric.

Pulling Social Justice Out of a Hat

Any reader of Spong knows that he is nothing if not passionate about social justice (however broadly and vaguely defined). His earlier ministry was marked by a strong and positive witness for racial integration. But just where this passion for social justice comes from, religiously speaking, is not at all clear. It cannot quite come from instruction in a particular religious tradition, with articulated values concerning human life, since much of that tradition, as it is articulated, is according to him limited and narrow. At the end of his book (*RTB*, chapter 14), Spong describes his encounter with the "Word of God" as itself somehow being the disclosure of the principle of this justice; but he is explicit that the Word of God must be distinguished from the words of Scripture. Might one, perhaps, encounter the Word *in* Scripture, if not *as* Scripture? It's hard to see how on Spong's own terms. He himself dismisses much of the Old Testament as being incapable of such a role. And in the New Testament he dismisses much of the material that describes aspects of Christian experience, even of Jesus' teachings, that he finds contradictory to "the Word" (e.g., passages about divine judgment and punishment, regulative codes of behavior, historical descriptions of healings, and so on).

Spong's version of the "Word of God" seems to come to him almost *despite* the literal words of Scripture. It is discerned through a process of correlating the possible religious *experiences* of the Bible's purported authors with the *reality* of the ineffable, unlimited, mysterious God. Real human beings have the "experience" of the wordless God; and the words of Scripture are explicable only as the inevitably disposable indicators of that experience of ineffability. However obscure all this is—are experiences of God's presence ineffable, or just the presence itself? How do words about experiences actually indicate something that is beyond words? The implications for Spong's ethical motive is clear: social justice and its principles are, like God's presence, as inarticulately tethered as the divine.

That is why Spong can see no irony in claiming, as in the preceding quote, that Christian discipleship comes down to the same thing as fulfilling the promise of the U.S. Army: "Be all that you can be." If training in the exercise of killing can be as easily assimilated in its *verbal* form into the divine imperative for human life as "loving totally," it is only because, in Spong's overriding vision of the cosmos, language is meaningless and conceptual articulation impossible. *It really doesn't matter what one says or if one has anything to say—for the shapes of the world are not ultimately real.* God is found in the embrace of incoherence, of formlessness, of the unstructured, of indistinctness and of departicularization that rise above the world we experience.

Spong may call his social ethics and politics "inclusive," in the sense that he gives permissive latitude to a wide range of contemporary moral postures. But this "inclusivity" is logically linked to the way Spong insists that discrete things can have no ultimate divine significance. Specific persons, moments, beginnings and endings, time, and human life itself, with its histories, its dissatisfactions, its pointed angularities of unintegrated experience, its anguish and its terminations—all of these particularities of existence appear in Spong's argument as but transient phenomena, upon which God could not possibly lodge absolute care. Neither can they act, therefore, as regulative objects or touchstones of divine judgment How curious to find such an opponent of traditional Christian theism sound so much like an anti-humanist in this regard. And how odd that this man, so intent on revivifying Christianity for the modern world, ends by commending a personal version of the faith that is deliberately wedded to the indistinct, the ineffable, and the ineffective. This is the very thing that has rendered mainstream Christianity uninteresting to so many people. Spong seems to have donned the faded mantle of the decrepit religion he insists that he has come to restore.

When Spong actually says what he thinks Scripture is and is useful for, he merely repeats—over and over again—the justification that any high school student today is given for reading the works of different cultures and distant times: by seeing what was deeply important to other people, we can gain some insight into what can also be important to us. And so, for Spong, Scripture is a collection of stories and literary images expressive of the historical experience of its various authors' "God consciousness." In and of itself, this collection has little historical or moral or dogmatic value: it conflicts with the clear findings of science, critical historiography, and evolved social reasoning.

His latest attempt at biblical criticism, *Liberating the Gospels*, reiterates this thesis in a grinding monotone. The book is a laboriously extended effort to insist that a "God-experience" that the Jewish apostolic church thought was "exciting" can be imaginatively stimulating to those who today care to pick through its secretive remains. But severed as it is from any historically impinging God, the kind of document that Spong makes the Bible out to be holds far less promise in speaking meaningfully to the depth of our lives than does a serious television drama like *NYPD Blue*.

Divine Creation and Communication:
The Christian Claim

All this should show, by contrast, the proper and compelling manner in which the traditionally defined character of Christian Scripture may be described. Scripture, at the least, must be the *articulate* expositor of the relationship between the historical world and its creator, God.

If Scripture speaks, like Spong, of life, of love, of presence, and of mystery, it does so in a manner that lodges these realities in the world of time and breath, hope and disappointment. It denotes a "life" that has a shape as well as limits; it displays a "love" that has objects and subjects, that takes form within the spaces of assaulted as well as striving and expansive experience. Scripture details a presence that does not contradict or dismiss the color of the day, the mood of the soul, the boundaries of the body. It unveils a mystery whose filiation with eternity stretches back into the threshold of death, the walls of unrighteousness, the queries of the disappointed and the denied, and the intensely focused hopes of the unvindicated. Scripture will speak, in its concrete imperatives, historical descriptions, predictive indicators, and the human ear will hear the very voice of God.

It is not my purpose to mount an argument as to why this is *in fact* what Scripture does. I wish only to point out that the fact that Scripture speaks in such a way that the human ear (or mind or heart) can hear God speaking makes a good deal of sense. After all, if it were taken seriously in the realm of human relations, Spong's consistently applied principle of incoherence—upholding the aphasic God—would simulate a kind of insanity: people would speak or act in specific ways in reaction to certain things, and other people would be unable to react according to their words or gestures. There would be, in fact, no way to relate at all, only to circle about one another with suspicion, driven by fear, or enveloped in a mist of individual fantasy. How else would a group of disparate people get beyond the words of each individual and grasp a reality that lay unbounded by such literalizations? But why on earth would anyone think that the social habits of a psychiatric ward could engagingly apply to a world in which God and human beings shared a space of purpose and responsibility?

To assert a God, to assert the world as it is, and to assert that human life is defined, in a distinctive and essential way, by the exercise of coherent discourse, is, in effect, to make compelling the assertion that Scripture is the "words of God." It is also, conversely, to assert that the scriptural "words of God" are themselves susceptible to bearing the fulsome burden of God's mystery and love in such a way as to embrace the ostensible limitations of the world, even to the point of issuing commands and describing historical reality. If they could not, then the message of the world's redemption—the *real* world's redemption, and not just the projection of a wordless, worldless neural stimulus associated with "life"—would be meaningless. In our day, philosophers as different as Henry Dumery and Nicholas Wolterstorff have demonstrated the rational grounds for this kind of claim about verbal revelation.

And in every respect Scripture itself indicates the coherence of this assertion that God's love informs the real world in which we live. Scripture does this both through *what* it says about God and the world, and through the very fact *that* it says this, with words capable of human reception (if not always of full comprehension). On one side is a mute and incoherent "Being" hovering mindlessly through reality—Spong's vague attempt at explaining the divine "mystical presence," whose character is so divorced from the actual experience of time and space as to be meaningless. On the other side, the Christian Scriptures describe and refer their own existence to a God whose reality itself informs all that we confront in the world's disparate press. The world, as Genesis puts it, is the way it is in its concrete variety and hard edges because it is a product of God's character to communicate: "…and God *said*, Let there be…" The world in which we speak to one another is the way it is because it is a world brought into being by One who speaks to the world. This, in fact, is the central Judaic claim orienting the Scriptures and the tradition of Israel that passed them to the Christian church.

When Spong denies this claim, he mounts an odd anti-Jewish platform of his own. Everything that Spong rebels against as being somehow undivine—difference, historical particularities, cultural specificities, languages, diverse experiences—Scripture ascribes to the fact that the Creator is a communicating God. Creation, in all its variety, is a form of divine communication, a "word," a set of "words." But think of what this means! The very stuff of which our lives are made and which either so buoys us or so depletes and threatens us—our mortality, our friendships and enmities, our caresses and violences—this stuff of life is ours only because God stands to us as one who speaks to us. To the degree that life is coherent at all, it is because God is the speaker of all life.

The Psalmist, for instance, writes that,

> [God] scatters his hail like bread crumbs; who can stand against his cold? He sends forth his word and melts them; he blows with his wind and the waters flow. He declares his word to Jacob, his statutes and his judgments to Israel. He has not done so to any other nation; to them he has not revealed his judgments. Hallelujah! (Ps. 147:18–21, BCP).

There is a short distance here between God's creative ordering of the world of nature, its snows, winds, and frosts on the one hand, and God's work of establishing a particular people, Israel, and revealing to them the divine law. This distance, between the natural world and the world of human history, is held together by the common reality each shares as proceeding from the "word" of God. There is a world, because God speaks it into being so that it may stand in a relation to him as an object of his concern. There is a history for a particular people, Israel, because God speaks to its life with commands and directives, that it might be the beneficent object of his ordering in the sight of all other people. The distinctions that mark the existence of a world, with its temporal processes of birth and death and its differences between individuals and peoples, have come into being because God is a being who communicates.

Divine Love and the Scriptural Word of Christ

And we call God "love" itself because of his communicative character. For at root, the possibility of divine communication is established by the fact of divine love. There is no time without love; there is no space without love; there is no difference and distinction without love; there is no speech without love. The very fact that a universe exists at all derives from the fact that God is one who causes beings and persons to exist whom he might love and who might love in return. The nineteenth-century philosopher Hegel is well known for speaking of love as something that separates God from himself. Yet long before Hegel, Christians grasped that love is something that brings into being distinct objects and subjects, and that to enter into the mystery of God's love is to enter deeply into the reality that the universe is filled with meanings that pass from one subject to another, which are founded on the very act of communicating. If the world of the early and medieval church, with its interlocking of natural, historical, and religious symbols, seems so strange to us today, it is less because our scientific vision precludes such cosmic meaningfulness than because we have lost faith in the very love of its Creator.

The fact that God might communicate differently and in limited ways in different times and in different places and to different people actually confirms this sensitiveness to the reality of divine love. "In many and various ways God spoke of old to our fathers… "opens the Letter to the Hebrews. And that God should demonstrate the very peak and focus of such subsuming love in delimiting his speech to a single time and place and person was but a logical extension of this confirmation: "But in these last days he has spoken to us by a Son, whom he appointed the heir of all things, through whom also he created the world" (Heb. 1:2). The very word by which the world was made the object of God's love is also given in its own coming into the world, to be seen and grasped and heard. "In the beginning was the Word, and the Word was with God, and the Word was God… and the Word became flesh and dwelt among us, full of grace and truth; we have beheld his glory, glory as of the only Son from the Father" (John 1:1, 14). Thus the Christian gospel is, at root, an affirmation about the "literalness" of divine love.

There is a striking continuity between these three basic

Christian affirmations: God creates limited worlds out of love; God speaks in various limited ways to portions of these worlds; God gives himself to the world in a painfully limited way in the absolute fullness of that love. One can move backward and forward through these affirmations as through one single tissue of truth: if God loves the world in Jesus, the Christ, it is because God speaks to the world in words that can be understood; if God speaks to the world, it is because God is its creator; if God creates the world, it is because God has taken the flesh of Jesus in love.

It is clear why Spong's notion of an incoherent nondifferentiated God/consciousness/life-force has no room in it for the *particular* words of Scripture as being God's words. But we must now emphasize how this exclusion of words is also the exclusion of divine love, the love that enters the world as it is and dies for it. Spong's descriptions of the Gospels and of Paul are almost devoid of any grappling with the crucifixion of Jesus or of the cross of Christ as the Christian form of life.

One searches in vain for any sustained discussion of Paul's claim that Jesus "became" our "sin," or that he himself had been "crucified with" Jesus, or of Jesus' call to "take up one's cross," let alone of the full range of Jesus' various teachings concerning the need to "die" to the world and to possessions and to family. Many of the latter are couched in terms of divine "judgment," which, of course, Spong simply dismisses out of hand. But in this kind of dismissal and imperviousness to central topics of scriptural speech, is it not patent that Spong has recoiled from the very means by which our own historical existence is established as the object of God's love? Who can speak of the mystery of suffering and of disappointment, or of the disorienting turmoil of malice and violence in real lives, if they refuse to grant the coming-into-time—the concrete communication—of God's own life face to face with our own? The passage from the power of the Creator to the power of the Redeemer of creation is marked by the speech of God, the incarnation of God, and the suffering of God. Spong's vision of God, by contrast, is one of historically undifferentiated silence and lovelessness. Let those who have lost the capacity to console, to hope, and to act embrace such a pallid vision.

Humility, Scriptural Literalness, and Modern Consciousness

In light of Spong's refusal to admit that God speaks, we must seriously reassess the implications of the purported historical rupture between premodern sensibilities and the modern worldview informed by science. Spong is not alone in making this division crucial for his dismissal of Scripture's "fantastic symbols." In his eyes, the particular descriptive forms of Scripture are at best vestiges of an ignorant past whose "literalistic acceptance" can only be derided by informed persons of the "twentieth- and twenty-first-century world of science and technology" (*RTB*, 133). But here Spong betrays his flaccid grasp of God's creative embrace of history. For in a created world where the mystery of God's love is given in God's own embodied death, *every* aspect of historical experience, including developed knowledge about the physical world, can be measured only *within* the limits of a universe where God speaks. However we may wish to evaluate the theories and experimentally confirmed assertions of modern science, such scientific claims cannot logically be seen as capable of contradicting the God who speaks to us unless we also accept their contradiction of a God whose love is historically intelligible and real.

The history of Scripture's composition can be described in a variety of ways, with respect to its authors, its editors, its manuscript and translation traditions, and its context of reading. Spong seems to think that, having delineated some debunking theory about all this, he has destroyed any reasonable assertion that Scripture's words are God's literal words. But Spong has never really grappled with this secondary issue of *how* God's will and being and acts could take the form of literal words, visibly written on paper or memorized in the head or spoken with the mouth on given dates and in given places. The issue, for Spong, is more basic: *whether God has* a will and a being and is capable of acting in a world of visibilities and times and places.

How, then, shall we respond? If we say that God loves in this world, then we must say that God is indeed "capable." And if God has loved, we may rightly affirm the fulfillment of that capacity in the words joined to that love. It is really a matter of holy amusement, from that point on, as to the way in which we explicate the *how.*

The difference between the premodern and the modern outlook, then, has nothing to do with the issue of whether or not the words of Scripture are reasonably understood as being God's words. Any difference that exists is simply part of the unremarkable fact that there are various ways people in different periods must intellectually order things that are penultimate explications—with respect to the ultimate reality that God speaks in Scripture because God loves in Jesus Christ.

From the earliest years of the Christian church, readers of Scripture sought different ways to make coherent things that Scripture said. But none of these efforts, even in their variety, contradicted the basic and shared conviction that the words of Scripture were God's words, each of which demanded an effort to hear, to bend one's mind and spirit to understand, and finally to give way with a grateful heart. The very variety of interpretive strategies, in their consistent and constant deployment, was a testimony to (not a contradiction of!) the fact that scriptural words were divine words requiring unremitting attention, delighted engagement, and wondering reception. They were testimonies to the fact that, as St. Augustine observed, God has so ordered his particular words and his particular creation that at every point of time and place, as the Scriptures are read, he speaks to us and we can hear him.

For the mystery of our life derives from its origin in the deeper mystery of God's creative and subsuming love. When the Christian church has claimed that the Holy Spirit "inspires" Scripture, and that the Holy Spirit opens us to Scripture's divine truth, she has claimed no more, and certainly no less, than that the power of God's love is deep enough to order the breadth of our historical lives in their detail, so as to encounter his.

Why should it seem odd that interpretations of Scripture change, or come in different shapes from the perspective of historical persons like us? For what is the outcome if we each stand open to the astounding reality that God's love has established the very possibility of our being a particular person at all, of having a life and a death, and moving in a world of persons and of experience? Is it not that we shall each be *drawn* always and continually to give ourselves over, in every form and time and place in which we find ourselves, to the voice of the One who loves us? We shall handle God's words as we handle and touch the face of the one we love, from every angle, with every emotion, with every degree and curve of energy, out of sheer and inextinguishable awe and affection.

This is why the question of how exactly we take the scriptural accounts of this or that event or teaching is properly debatable only *within* the realm in which we give ourselves over to the historical ultimacy of God's words. It is a fruitless endeavor to argue about the meaning of Scripture's particular forms with those who reject altogether God's coming to us in time and space. Believers can tolerate such debate, in large measure because interpretive disagreement is governed by a common humility before the defining power of God's speech. Within this common humility, questions can indeed be asked about historical reference, about the meaning of this or that phrase, about the doctrinal implications of this or that scriptural perspective. But disagreement is never final, because the questions Christians have about Scripture are ones whose answers will always give way to the irreducibility of God's words, in their specificity, to command our whole attentive beings. And because God's words are ultimate with respect to the varieties of our hearing, and are themselves tied to the ultimacy of God's self-giving in the historical person of Jesus, humility about the findings of science and historical study and individual conscience and interpretive practice is not a veil for relativism. The humility of love that gives way to the words of God is a simple affirmation that "God was in Christ reconciling the world to himself" (2 Cor. 5:19).

The modern mind is as amenable to this affirmation as the premodern. It knows as well now as at any time that the realities of our existence are not exhausted by the inert descriptions given them through the conceptual frameworks of this or of any age. The self-described modern person knows that life and death, the fate of human persons and of natural objects, is mute and dumb before time and space's sightless face, except that time be the time of God, and except God be the God of space. We moderns know that there is no mystery to this or anything else unless it be granted by God and given over to us by God.

It is the most reasonable thing in this kind of world, a world perhaps of neutrinos and cloning, to recognize this as an inescapable fact: "The grass withers, the flower fades; but the word of our God will stand for ever" (Isa. 40:8). What we do with this recognition is bound to the invitation extended by the

Speaker behind the world's capacity to speak back, an invitation
that is life giving and loving because it is inescapably literal.

The clash between John Spong and the Christian tradition is a
confrontation between faiths: a mute faith in a mute world, and
a voiced faith fixed in the midst of the glorious sounds of a God
who touches us in love.

The poet Samuel Taylor Coleridge, a man well attuned to issues
of historical criticism and science, wrote a century earlier of
another world, literally held and approached by a God of love:

> But "a God that made the eye, and therefore shall *He* not
> see? who made the ear, and shall He not hear?" (Ps. 94:9)
> who made the heart of man to love Him, and shall He
> not love the creature whose ultimate end is to love
> Him?—a God *who seeketh* that which was lost, who cal-
> leth back that which had gone astray; who calleth
> through Its own Name; Word, Son, from everlasting the
> Way and the *Truth;* and who became man that for poor
> fallen mankind he might *be* (not merely announced but
> *be*) *the Resurrection and the Life...* Oh, prize above all
> earthy things the faith! (Letter of March 22, 1832)

Works Considered or Consulted

Dietrich Bonhoeffer. *Meditating on the Word.* Cambridge:
Cowley, 1986.

John Breck. *The Power of the Word in the Worshiping Community.*
Crestwood, NY: St. Valdimir's Seminary Press, 1986.

Brevard S. Childs. *Biblical Theology of the Old and New
Testaments: Theological Reflection on the Christian Bible.* Minneapolis:
Fortress, 1992.

A.G. Hebert. *The Throne of David: A Study of the Fulfillment of
the Old Testament in Jesus Christ and His Church.* London: Faber &
Faber, 1941.

A.G. Hebert. *The Authority of the Old Testament.* London: Faber
& Faber, 1947.

George Hunsinger, "What Can Evangelicals and Post-Liberals Learn from Each Other? The Carl Henry-Hans Frei Exchange Reconsidered." *The Nature of Confession.* T. Phillip and D. Okholm, eds. Downers Grove: Inter-Varsity Press, 1996.

Richard Swinburn. *Revelation. Oxford: Clarendon Press,* 1992.

Lionel Thornton. *Revelation and the Modern World.* London: Dacre Press, 1950.

Nicholas Wolterstorff. *Divine Discourse: Philosophical Reflections on the Claim That Speaks.* Cambridge: Cambridge University Press, 1995.

The Sin of Faith

Russell R. Reno

IN THE MINDS OF THOSE who have heard of him but not read him carefully, Bishop Spong is associated with two areas of controversy: sex and the Bible. In the first instance, Bishop Spong has positioned himself as a self-described courageous spokesman for a supposedly realistic, humane, and just revision of traditional sexual morality. He rings the bell for blessing premarital and postmarital sex, for affirming divorce, and—most ardently and with greatest vigor—for full acceptance of homosexuality in the life of the church.

In controversies involving the Bible, Bishop Spong has relentlessly pursued the slightest hint of a faith based on biblical authority. Bishop Spong sprays his opponents with the condemnations of "literalism" and "fundamentalism." True to his perception that the church is captive to biblical authority, he has written a number of books devoted to "critical exegesis." As a student of theology and an adept polemicist, he does not merely stumble upon these two areas of controversy. Sex and the Bible emerge as crucial foci in his vision of the Christian faith. If we have any hope of understanding Bishop Spong in his passionate convictions and deep certainties, as well as his intense and bitter renunciations, then we need to enter into this vision.

First and foremost, this vision is one of unveiling and uncovering. In his view, the biological and sociological "facts" of human sexuality break through the patina of prejudice. A disciplined and fearless engagement with modern historical criticism forces a reassessment of the authority of the biblical text. Deep feelings and intense experiences overwhelm reservations and hesitations based on an empty traditionalism. These patterns recur again and again in Bishop Spong's books.

In each instance, the approach might be best described as evangelical. "I have been a sinner," one imagines Bishop Spong saying. "I have wallowed in the mud of patriarchalism. I have enjoyed the comforts of a pharisaical traditionalism. I have surrounded myself with the finery of biblical literalism. Yes, friends, I too have been where you are. I too have looked backward rather than forward, feared change rather than embraced the future, fled from life rather than affirmed reality. But despair not. I have been to the mountaintop. I have seen the freeing truth. I have tasted the sweet honey of the Lord's mercy. Yes, friends, there is redemption. Let me show you the way."

We should listen to Bishop Spong. The violence and bitterness of his polemics, the certainty and intensity of his convictions, the spectral tissue of his reconstruction of the Christian faith all clarify the deep difference between the modern view of sin and redemption and the classical view.

As a controversialist, Bishop Spong has a very definite sense of what he is against. We need to discern the proper shape of his enemy. We need to understand his view of the sin that is abroad in society, in the church, and in our souls. Bound up with his view of sin is his understanding of grace. If we are to hear him speak fully and forcefully, then we must follow him on the path to redemption. We need to see how our repentance grows out of the word of grace and new life. We must hear his "Yes" in order to plumb the depth and scope of his "No." We must allow him to preach to us. Only then can we feel the fire he feels and fear the brimstone he fears. Only then can we know the horror of sin that he knows. And if we feel as he feels and fear as he fears, we might well come to know something of ourselves and our peculiar time. For Bishop Spong is nothing if not extreme, and the sheer passion of his convictions brings into sharp relief the theological choices we face, both as individuals and as a church.

Biblical Fleshpots

Sin beset Bishop Spong from his youth. His mother gave him a King James Bible at age twelve. His father had recently died, and his whole family felt a "radical emotional and economic insecurity"

(*RBF,* 13). In the context of this insecurity, the gift of a Bible proved too much of a temptation. The young Jack Spong read his Bible with fearful regularity, and he believed what he read. Raised by a mother "of a simple faith," and taught by a high school teacher who "believed that God had dictated every word of Holy Scripture" (*RBF,* 14), he fled from his insecurity into the fleshpots of biblical authority. Jack Spong allowed his religious identity to be rooted in the text. "There was for me," he reports, "no authority beyond the affirmation of 'the Bible says'" (*RBF,* 14). He permitted himself the security of thinking that the words he read were trustworthy, wholesome, and upbuilding; he allowed himself to believe that they were infused with the permanence and holiness of God.

How, you might ask, is this sin? How is reading the Bible and believing what it says a highway to destruction? Bishop Spong has a great deal to say about the horrors of the Bible. He decries the arrogance of biblical claims on behalf of the land of Israel, claims which, he says, legitimated invasion and genocide. He bemoans the acceptance of slavery and the subordination of women codified by the Torah. Throughout Jewish law, he writes, "womanhood was insulted in verse after verse" (*RBF,* 19). He regrets the New Testament portrayals of Jesus as "narrow-minded, vindictive and even hypocritical" (*RBF,* 21). He utterly rejects the idea that his Lord could "believe and teach that eternal punishment was an appropriate sentence to pronounce on sinners" (*RBF,* 22). But however important these passages might be, none constitute the crux of the matter. What Bishop Spong most decries is a general attitude that the biblical text encourages us to adopt, a disposition or habit of thinking characterized by certainty, security, and conviction.

Certainty and conviction add up to a sinful way of thinking. For Bishop Spong, a deep insecurity and fear leads us to treat the biblical text as authoritative, tempting us to assume that the clear dictates of the text are fixed points for faithful reflection and action. This point of view characterized his own attitudes in his youth, the simple faith of his mother, and the critical ignorance of his high school teacher. In all those cases, no matter how pure he or his mother or his high school teacher might be in action, the dominant attitude was irrational, judgmental and self-protective. For Bishop Spong, then, far from the ideal of faithfulness, such a point of view is disastrously anti-Christian. It is the sin of fundamentalism, the sin of literalism.

This sin is very much a part of the biblical world and dominates traditional uses of the Bible by Christians. The role that Bishop Spong feels that fundamentalism plays in the Bible itself is most aptly illustrated in his approach to the postexilic literature of Ezra and Nehemiah, the one part of Scripture that he seems to hate more than any other (*LS*, 28–32). Just as his own fall into the sin of literalism occurred during an insecure period in his family life, according to Bishop Spong, the postexilic literature was written after "a difficult period in Jewish history" (*LS*, 28). After their defeat by Nebuchadnezzar "the people were deeply infected with what is perhaps the most dangerous tenet of any religious ideology" (*LS*, 28). Instead of maintaining an appropriate openness to reality and tolerance of differences, the Jews responded to their insecurity by identifying unquestionable truths as anchors of certainty. Most important, they were "absolutely convinced that they were God's specially chosen people" (*LS*, 28). This sinful belief, one brought on by experience of vulnerability during the Babylonian captivity, encouraged an ethnocentric, self-protective strategy of separation and exclusion.

The way in which Bishop Spong tells the story of this period of Jewish history captures the dynamic of his view of sin. Insecurity, vulnerability, and the threat of change tempt us to look backward for the comforts of venerable certainties and clear boundaries. Returning to Judah, the religious leaders of Israel deemed the "unchosen" Gentile world unclean. The difficult experience of exile was explained as punishment for the unfaithfulness of Israel, an unfaithfulness especially manifest in a mixing of Jew and Gentile. Emphasizing the reinstitution of ritual purity in the rebuilt Temple, the leadership took the "comfortable" route of excluding the non-Jew in order to ensure the purity of the chosen people. In this way, "fear, fantasy, prejudice, and magic all fed the nationalistic imperatives of the day" (*LS*, 31). Xenophobia reigned unchallenged. "Hysteria drowned out every objection," Bishop Spong writes. "Religious zeal combined with political power to merge with tyranny. Personal liberties and individual, non-conforming values had no protection or platform" (*LS*, 31–2). The main currents of Ezra and Nehemiah typify the sin of fundamentalism. A backward-looking attitude tries to fend off change and

innovative insight by appeal to fantasies of a pure and authoritative past. Devoid of the forward-looking optimism that realizes
that change is inevitable and that difference is the fruit of God's
bounty, Ezra and Nehemiah exhibit a close-minded rather than
open-minded disposition. They encourage exclusionary judgment
rather than inclusive tolerance. They trade in easy and reassuring
certitudes rather than the hard and challenging ambiguities of all
genuine truth.

Backward looking, close-minded, full of certitude, exclusionary, and judgmental—these are the sinful attitudes the Bible so
easily tempts us to adopt. Awash with a deep fear of change,
fearful that our self-importance will be challenged by the
stranger, we seek the security of an authoritative past and will
believe just about anything in order to expel the threat of novel-
ty and the challenges of reality. Ezra and Nehemiah are unique
among the biblical texts not because other parts of the Bible are
exempt from this temptation, but rather because the dynamic of
threatening insecurity and exclusionary certitude are so close to
the surface and so dominate the text. And just as Ezra and
Nehemiah look backward to a supposedly God-given Torah, so
also do Christian teachers and preachers appeal to the supposedly infallible words of Scripture. The teachings of the Bible
become weapons against change. Favorite verses appear again
and again as bulwarks against the challenges of the modern
world. Judgment and exclusion dominate. Or at least this is how
Bishop Spong sees the matter.

The Sin in Sex

Sexual morality is important for Bishop Spong because it provides the clearest example of literalistic sinfulness. Sensitively
attuned to reality, prayerfully disposed toward change, open to
difference, Bishop Spong cannot help but notice that his children
think about sexual morality rather differently than he did as a
young man. However, he knows sin is fear of change, anxiety
about purity, and the desire to maintain dominance and chosen-
ness. As a consequence, Bishop Spong is able to see this change
in sexual mores as a sign of the times, as a manifestation of "the
fruits of the Spirit" (LS, 66).

Traditionally, Christians have thought that the purpose of sexual morality is to restrain lust. This is entirely mistaken. Sexual

morality is a tool of dominance and exclusion. Through strict sexual mores, writes Bishop Spong, "we reject that which we cannot manage" (*LS*, 23). Feeling ourselves threatened and insecure, "we condemn what we do not understand" (*LS*, 23). Our anxieties about ourselves and our place in society turns sexual morality into "a major arena in which the prejudices of human beings find expression" (*LS*, 23). For just this reason, Bishop Spong notes that his entirely sensible challenges to this system of prejudice produce "anger" and "even violence" (*LS*, 23).

Bishop Spong does not consider it surprising that sexual prejudice links arms with biblical literalism. They are branches from the same tree. Those who seek the security and comfort of an unchanging sexual morality are equally attracted to the certainty and comfort of an unchanging Word of God. "The Scriptures," he diagnoses, "when literalized and proclaimed with certainty, bring a sense of stability and security to those who resist change" (*LS*, 90–1). Sexual morality and biblical authority become mutually reinforcing prejudices. Defenders of judgmental traditionalism feel "justified, vindicated, proud, and right" when they find chapter and verse to buttress condemnations of changing mores.

However, Bishop Spong knows the sinful root of their denunciations. "They approach what they regard as the challenge to morality," he writes, "with disturbingly high levels of hostility and anger that reveal their runaway anxiety and insecurity" (*LS*, 92). The underlying dynamic is familiar. A young Jack Spong, made vulnerable by his father's death, latches onto the security of biblical literalism. Heterosexual men, increasingly anxious about their declining social dominance, take refuge in an exclusionary sexual morality. Traditionalist church leaders, embarrassed by the increasing irrelevance of church teaching, flee into the unquestionable authority of the Bible. Just as we read Scripture as the unchanging Word of God, so also we invest ourselves in an unchanging moral outlook. In the same way, Ezra and Nehemiah championed a backward-looking, close-minded, judgmental stance rooted in naive beliefs.

This basic pattern characterizes Bishop Spong's response to every hesitation and objection. Are you troubled by the pervasive acceptance of premarital sex in American society? If so, then Bishop Spong counsels you that your attitude is quite likely a concatenation of sin: a dishonest denial of reality, a sinful effort to control others with guilt, and a cowardly fear of the new insights of our own time. Are you shocked by the idea that the church should develop liturgies to bless divorce? If so, then Bishop Spong warns you that you must not close your eyes to the social facts of failed relationships. Do you harbor doubts about homosexuality? If so, then Bishop Spong denounces you as someone in the thrall of a patriarchal worldview devoted to the subordination of women and the dominance of a life-destroying ideal of masculinity. In every instance, the sin is the same. In the grip of an insecure fear of change, an anxiety about identity and insecurity about who they really are in God's eyes, many do not have the courage and honesty to recognize the essential health and truth in all change. Traditionalists in all areas simply recapitulate the exclusionary worldview of Ezra and Nehemiah.

Begin Without Apology

In the call to repentance from the literalist sin of Ezra and Nehemiah, Bishop Spong knows no limit to compassion. A great deal of the pathos of his books rests in his own image of himself as the courageous disciple who is animated by a relentless determination to grapple with Satan. Jerry Falwell never seems far from his mind as the archetype of one who sins and, in his sinning, leads so many others to sin. Falwell is a child of Ezra and Nehemiah. He wishes to cling to the permanence and certainty of God's Word amid the rushing currents of a changing culture.

However, Satan has conquered far more souls than Jerry Falwell. Indeed, among Satan's minions are all those who believe in the myth of Satan! Moreover, all those who believe in any clear and permanent difference between right and wrong belong to Satan, for just such a belief leads to narrow-minded judgmentalism. Indeed, the devil is terribly active. A great deal of the world thinks homosexuality immoral. The vast majority of Christians find divorce a scandal. Jews abound who think that they are a chosen people. Christians seem unable to resist affirming that Jesus is the risen Lord. The Enemy is strong, but Bishop Spong has no fear. He has been to the mountaintop. He knows the truth, and this conviction gives force to his denunciation of the sin of fundamentalism.

To understand his "No," we need to turn, then, to his "Yes." What is the truth that gives Bishop Spong the courage to confront so much of the witness of the Christian church, both in the present and in ages past? His courage comes from a truth that is "much more than is contained" in the "limiting narratives" of the Gospel stories (*RBF,* 226). This truth is more than our minds can grasp, or our words can capture. "The truth of Christ for us does not lie," writes Bishop Spong, "in words or images" (*RBF,* 230). No, the living Lord cannot be limited by such earthen vessels.

Bishop Spong's truth is much bigger than the mere words and images of the Christian tradition. As a consequence, "we must journey beyond words and images into the experience that produced those words"(*RBF,* 231). This is not a journey backward. For Bishop Spong, the truth is never in the past. We "must not bind ourselves," he insists, "to the maps of yesterday" (*LS,* 164). The sexual revolution is revealing new truths. With this new truth, we can now see that the older order "primarily served the dominant male" (*LS,* 66). Against this old order, Bishop Spong looks to a liberating present and future. "I dare," he writes, "to claim that a new morality is emerging that does manifest the fruits of the Spirit" (*LS,* 66). The future shall deliver us from bondage to the past.

For Bishop Spong, this forward journey is not based simply on his maxim, "Change is inevitable." His view of salvation history places God's truth in the present and future rather than the past. History, he insists, is a "movement toward freedom and inclusiveness, from the Magna Charta, to the Reformation, to the emancipation of slaves, to the condemnation of racism, to the awakening to the evils of sexism and homophobia" (*LS,* 157). However, the way forward is difficult. We must leave behind the comfort of words, the security of language. We must overcome our naive trust in what St. Paul or St. John might say. We need to unburden ourselves of the immobilizing weight of the past. We must hate "ecclesiastical claims to possess infallibility in any formulated version of Scripture or creed," for such formulations are "manifestations of idolatry" and shall place us in straitjackets that prevent any genuine exploration of truth (*RBF,* 231).

Against this temptation, we must have the courage of authentic personhood. We must "embrace the subjective and relative character" of all ecclesiastical formulations, indeed, of our own formulations (*RBF,* 232). We need to be like Jesus in his passion. We must imitate "the freedom of one who knows who he is and has the courage to be just that" (*LS,* 162). Let us not be what the past would make of us, preaches Bishop Spong. Let us greet the future with an affirmation of our own being.

For Bishop Spong, the liberation truth of the gospel is the truth of being. This involves the vulnerability of seeking rather than the security of knowing, the radiance of "intense life-giving experiences" rather than the dead letter of creedal formulations (*RBF,* 225). The truth of being is not a fact or a formula. "There are no changeless, eternal creeds or Bibles," he insists (*LS,* 163). And this is a word of grace, for "the moment that truth is articulated or codified it becomes finite, limited, and in the end falsifying" (*LS,* 163). The truth of being, for Bishop Spong, is an attitude, an approach to life, an existential disposition. He drapes himself in Tillichian gowns. Truth is a "courage to be."

The source of the "courage to be" is our experience of love, the "powerful life-affirming reality" that knows no barrier (*RBF,* 237). This love calls for openness, "for the death of prejudice, for the radical insecurity of a fully accessible humanity" (*RBF,* 238). Jesus is the image of that love, and in interpreting that image, Bishop Spong is quite consistent. The virtues of his version of faithfulness match the vices of his adversary, the sinful fundamentalist. Bishop Spong's faith is open, not closed. If we have tasted the life-affirming reality of love, then we "cannot reject or oppress or define pejoratively" (*RBF,* 239).

God affirms life. As we journey into the future, we encounter many and diverse ways of life. Some people marry. Some are single. Some cohabit. Others divorce. Still others are committed to another of the same sex. These ways of life and love are different, but all are affirmed by God's love. Therefore, reasons Bishop Spong, we must have the courage to affirm just as God affirms.

With just such a vision of faith, Bishop Spong tells us again and again of his own virtue and grace, his own courage and openness to life. "The Word of God in Jesus," he reports, "is a call to me to be myself, my whole self, without apology" (*LS,* 162). He has "walked the edges of the ecclesiastical world" (*RBF,* 239). In so doing, Bishop Spong has been a true disciple among false teachers, for God's Word "is a call to dare, to risk, and to venture" (*LS,* 162). He has taken the risk of speaking honestly and acting with integrity.

Even amidst the taunts of heresy and charges of dereliction of duty, Bishop Spong portrays himself as alive to the experience of life. Instead of hiding behind the words of Scripture or the teaching of the tradition or the decisions of ecclesiastical bodies, he has dared to be himself. Instead of enslaving himself to an obedient submission to anything or anyone, he has taken the risk of living and thinking freely, of doing and saying just what his experience of reality tells him. Instead of retreating into the security of the sanctuary, he has ventured to engage the emerging world. In all these self-descriptions we find Bishop Spong clearly bearing witness to his definition of faith: faith is being true to our experience; faith is daring to affirm ourselves; faith is risking changes rather than defending certainties. "That is what it means to me," he writes, "to worship one who is the ground of all being... to discover the courage to be the self I am in Christ" (*LS*, 162).

One illustration of Bishop Spong's movement toward faithful self-affirmation should help us grasp his vision. He has been to a blessing of divorce and has felt its truth. No power in heaven or on earth shall silence his witness to that experience. He was there. The experience was profound. "It takes courage," he reports of those he saw witnessing to their broken marriage, "maturity and a deep willingness to endure, enormous vulnerability to stand up... and confess failure and ask forgiveness" (*LS*, 192). We need no Ph.D. in theology to see the key attitudes at work. Courage, self-accepting maturity, vulnerability, openness to the realities of life: the "courage to be" is palpably present. Could this be anything, asks Bishop Spong, other than a manifestation of God's love?

The participants in the liturgy are able to let go of the dead letter of past teaching against divorce. They are able to face reality rather than allowing their lives, their experience, to be deformed by guilt brought on by first century social norms fossilized in the biblical text. They are walking on the edges of the ecclesiastical world, challenging the literalists by the very honesty and integrity of their mature acknowledgment of the reality of their parting. And further, their courage empowers those who have come to witness the ceremony of parting. Their "courage to be" overwhelms the mental reservations of observers who might worry about the past teachings and practices of the church.

Not surprisingly, "after weeks of processing feeling," Bishop Spong could not resist affirming the ceremony for the blessing of divorce as "a pastoral tool, to be used in appropriate situations to bring the grace, love, and forgiveness of God to a common human experience" (*LS*, 193). The conclusion is hardly shocking. Any ceremony, any teaching, any pastoral counseling that helps us escape from the limits of traditional faith and allows us to live and breathe the healthy air of honest engagement with the facts of life" is a word of grace. In this way, the ceremony for blessing divorce typifies a general pattern. And the pattern in turn guides Bishop Spong's interpretation of Jesus. "The experience of Jesus," he writes, "was an experience of Being," and this gave him "the courage to be himself" (*RBF*, 241). As such, "the call of Christ is an external call to the affirmation of that which is" (*RBF*, 242). Most specifically, of course, this call is for us to affirm ourselves.

In view of this general pattern of affirmation, Bishop Spong's reasoning is simple. Homosexual relations are a reality. Divorce is a social fact. Unbelief is widespread. Euthanasia is practiced. Suicide is part of our experience. Premarital sex is the norm. These are unavoidable facts of life. The call of Christ, according to Bishop Spong, is to shed the insecurity and fear that prevent us from affirming these facts and to enjoy the "immensity of human life" in all its diverse forms. "I have never met God by retreating from life," reports Bishop Spong, "I seem to meet God only when I enter deeply into life" (*RBF*, 243). And in entering deeply, Bishop Spong has trained himself to be a disciple of New Being. The message of his books is an Eternal Yes to everything that is new, everything that breaks the mold, everything that challenges the status quo.

The Great Inversion
Now that we have walked with Bishop Spong to the mountaintop of New Being, now that we have tasted something of his "Yes," we should be able to see that his view of sin has crucial implications for our understanding of faith. If we believe that God has been revealed in words rather than in our experiences, then we are, thinks Bishop Spong, ignoring reality, fleeing from vulnerability, denying our very selves. If we believe that God's presence is anchored in ancient texts, in venerable ecclesiastical traditions, then we are turning our back on what is. If we bind ourselves in any way to what has actually been said and done in the past, then we are fleeing from the present and failing to take responsibility for the future. If we assume that obedience to ecclesiastical authority encourages our own growth in love and

fellowship with God and one another, then we are trying to escape from our own freedom, from our own being. In the end, then, Bishop Spong's polemics are directed against what amounts to a single disposition, and, traditionally, Christians have called that disposition faith.

That Bishop Spong so blithely turns what the Christian tradition has called faith into the archetype of sin tells us something important about the world of ideas that animates his thought—and not only his thought, but the thought of much of the modern church. Historically, the Christian tradition has treated faith as a form of obedient submission to the lordship of Christ, a lordship that has a real presence in the ecclesial life of the Christian community. The great second-century bishop Ireneaus emphasized this real presence in the visible continuity of apostolic teachers. There is, he argues, a clear and concrete form of Christ's lordship, and that authority can be discerned in the public teachings of the church as handed down from the apostles. Ireneaus's affirmation of the objective authority of Christ found in the life of the church is built into the baptismal covenant. In baptism, we pledge to "continue in the apostles' teaching and fellowship." Because we wish to follow Christ, we submit ourselves to just that public teaching which Ireneaus identified as anchoring the church to Christ's truth.

How one understands the public teaching of the church has varied in classical Christian thought. For centuries, however, the canonical witness of Scripture has been regarded as the indisputable core of that public teaching which animates Ireneaus's vision and as the self-evident source of the apostolic teaching to which the faithful are bound in the baptismal covenant. The life of discipleship, therefore, has been understood as the process of bringing one's own sensibilities and experiences to the judgment of the text rather than the other way around. Faith is a submission of oneself to the teachings of the text.

In addition to Scripture, throughout the history of the church, theologians have struggled to give adequate expression to the role of the creeds and the liturgical tradition as additional embodiments of apostolic teaching. Judgments about this role vary considerably. Yet, however differently a Calvinist and a Roman Catholic might view the ecumenical creeds of Nicea and Chalcedon in relation to Scripture, to say nothing of liturgical

traditions, an underlying consensus dominates. Inherited forms
of prayer and reflection, however understood, should shape our
sensibilities and experience rather than the other way around. In
this way, the differences that have characterized Christian
denominations are united in a similar "dynamic of faith."
Something is present in the everyday world of language and
action that has sufficient clarity and precision to command our
obedience. Something concrete gives effective and formative
power to the lordship of Christ. And the task of faith is to allow
oneself to be formed in heart and mind by that discrete and concrete authority.

The classical view of the dynamic of faith is fundamentally at
odds with Bishop Spong's view. His work gestures toward Being
or Life or Reality as objects of obedience and devotion, but such
terms are hopelessly vague. We are to affirm life, but not a life
that is judgmental. We are to embrace being, but as Bishop Spong
says time and time again, we are not to be exclusivists. Being
would seem to be very much in the eye of the beholder! We are to
acknowledge reality, but we are to deny our desire for certainty, no
matter how real that desire might be. How, then, are we to discern true Being, true Life, and true Reality? How are we to be
faithful to the God of Being? In Bishop Spong's case, the pattern
of discernment is clear. We must consult our experiences. We
must process our feelings. We must make our own decisions. At
root, the dynamics of faith all point inward.

With a vision of a faith grounded in our own experience,
Bishop Spong quite naturally defines the impulse to turn toward
something other than oneself in obedient discipleship as the primal sin of fundamentalism. Whether one privileges the Bible or
the traditions of the church, whether one emphasizes the decisive
role of the creeds or the teaching office of the church, whether
one identifies an authoritative theological school or normative
ascetic practice, the issue is always the same. For Bishop Spong,
we might submit to a text, a tradition, a creed, an institution, a
school of thought, or an ascetic discipline because we think it
empowers us or because it serves our experience. However, we
are absolutely forbidden to submit because we think that it
bears the authority of God rather than of ourselves. A submission born of the conviction that I enter into fellowship with God
by disciplining myself to listen to the words he has chosen to

speak or by following a pattern of life he has commanded is what Bishop Spong calls sin. Just such an approach to discipleship involves the betrayal of self, which he diagnoses as the cause of our fear of change, of our ethnocentrism and sexism, of our racism and homophobia. Thus, when we take a considered view of Bishop Spong's jeremiads against scriptural faith and traditional moral teaching, we see that, for him, sin is what Ireneaus and Augustine, Aquinas and Calvin, Cranmer and Newman called faith.

The clarity of Bishop Spong's inversion of faith and sin gives a certain importance to his work. For all his reliance on the overused clichés of modern theology, Bishop Spong is new, even fresh. In the past, the Tillichs and Pittengers and Pikes wrapped their inversion of sin and faith in an earnest and soul-searching examination of conscience. Tillich huffed and puffed about his method of correlation that allowed him to preserve the verbal forms of prayer and worship even as he revised the substance of Christian teaching. Precisely because Tillich defined the essence of faith as existential, the traditional language of faith could remain unchanged. After all, that language is but the historical vessel of the timeless truth of Being.

Tillich's less philosophically pretentious successors such as Bishop Pike were less thoroughly gnostic. Perhaps because they were rather more forthright about the consequences, they felt the need to undergo the difficulties of renouncing classical formulations and beliefs. Bishop Spong, in contrast, neither dissembles nor appears torn by pains of conscience. He seems a smiling evangelical, smugly confident that he knows a sinner when he sees one, naively credulous when he reads books by scholars who support his own position. His books are full of confident declarations. He knows the truth. He knows that everything the church says is "subjective and relative" (*RBF*, 232). He knows how crudely mythological and irrelevant is belief in Jesus's virgin birth and his bodily resurrection (*LS*, 234–235). Changes in sexual behavior are "signs of the times," part of the "movement of the Holy Spirit" which Bishop Spong affirms without the slightest hint of self-doubt (*LS*, 66). But most importantly, Bishop Spong knows the truth of "experience." In his own experience, Bishop Spong rests with the fullest confidence. In his own consciousness, "in the dawning moments of a transcendent awareness" made possible by his own efforts and great courage, "by risking love, daring to live, and by having the courage to be [himself], he knows that he has "touched divinity" (*RBF*, 244).

Here, Bishop Spong is a true evangelical of experience. "I will speak of Christ," he writes, impressed with his own honesty and courage, "as I have experienced Christ" (*RBF*, 244). "I will not," we hear by implication, "submit myself to anything or anyone: not to the writer of the Gospel of John, not to Paul, not to Augustine, not to Aquinas, not to Hooker. I will not allow anyone or anything outside of me to govern my faith." Bishop Spong does not pledge to continue in the apostles' teaching, for that would entail submission. Instead, he pledges to use these teachings to enrich and inspire his experience. However, should the teachings of the apostles prevent him from accepting himself, should those teachings command faithful obedience rather than nurture the courage to be, then Bishop Spong shall cast them out. Should the Scriptures contradict his experience of "reality," then he shall throw them upon the consuming flames of the Eternal Now. Should the decisions of the church, either now or through the ages, seek to contain him as he "walks the edges of the ecclesial world," then he shall burn them on the altar of change. His mission is clear: "I shall cast out the Satan who tempts me to believe rather than to be."

Justification by Being Alone

When one sees just how much Bishop Spong appears as a living reductio ad absurdum of the theological world he represents, the interesting and useful questions flow quite naturally. How could he find so much excitement, so much drama and risk, in self-acceptance? How could he think that taking his spiritual pulse as he "walks the edges of the ecclesial world" would yield anything other than a vain proclamation of himself and his sensibilities as the gospel? How could he think that his recycling of a very tired old Tillichian theology, complete with embarrassing clichés such as New Being and the Courage to Be, is new or progressive? How could he exclaim so often on behalf of the need for change (e.g., "A Christianity that is not changing is a Christianity that is dying" (*RBF*, 230) when his own theological outlook is a dreary recapitulation of modernist myths (e.g., "Human life is evolving... into higher and higher levels of consciousness" (*RBF*, 236)? How could he portray himself as a patron of the "future" of the church when he parades about with a theology of the Eternal Now, a theology of "being who he is," an outlook that guarantees that he remain frozen in the ruts of his own prejudices and blindness?

This self-styled progressive is really rather old fashioned in his theology—an episcopal version of the father who uses the word "groovy" around his teenage children in hopes of sounding "hip." It tells us something about the theological ambiance of the Episcopal Church that Bishop Spong could even speak in the House of Bishops without generating gentle chuckles at his theological dotage, to say nothing of outright laughter. It indicates that the leadership of the Episcopal Church is living in an ecclesial time capsule in which the pious incoherence of seminary professors such as Urban T. Holmes III echoes endlessly. "Anglicanism is a mode of making sense of the experience of God," we read in the very beginning line of Holmes' little summa, *What Is Anglicanism?* Has Bishop Spong really done anything more than repeat that beginning sentence again and again in his rather more grating voice? Does Bishop Spong not rightly claim the mantle of prophet, not of God, but of the now superannuated modern theology that has dominated good old "mainstream" Anglicanism for decades? He, unlike so many, actually takes seriously what he was taught in seminary. And he is intelligent enough and energetic enough to apply that modern theology with relentless consistency.

More important, however, is what Bishop Spong reveals about the latent anti-humanism of modern theology. His treatment of literalism as the archetype of sin urges us to examine carefully all of our commitments and to cast a suspicious eye upon any trust we might have in external things. After all, we are surrounded by temptations to complacency. The very reality of the Bible as a written text, the existence of the church as an institution, the fact that our parents have the power to speak and utter to us moral principles—all these things can easily stand in the way of Being. Like a ravening and roaring lion, our common world of words and relationships threatens to absorb us. What I said in my baptismal vows closes in upon me as something to which I must be faithful. The stories of that man, Jesus of Nazareth, stare at me and gloat over the fact that my experiences are chimerical, while the words of the text are durable and sharp with their own sense.

Thus, Bishop Spong joins modern theology in petitioning God to deliver us from the affliction of covenants that bind us together in a common future, from the threats of institutions that command our loyalty, from the biblical text that refuses to be collapsed into our experience.

In just this way, the "courage to be" seems to require us to declare our independence from everything but ourselves. If we have given and received vows in marriage, then we must recognize that the words are but expressions of our love. They have no binding reality, and should our love change or die, those vows may be discarded or remade according to our present experience. If we have found life in Jesus Christ, then we must see that he is but an expression of our discovery of Being. Should our sense of life change, he may be set aside. If our faith journey has led us into the Episcopal Church, then we should acknowledge, as Urban Holmes urges us, that Anglicanism is but a mode of our experience of God. Should that experience change, we are at liberty to discard Anglicanism or remold it to fit our new experience. This pattern of treating what is said and seen and touched as so many disposable vessels for the Eternal Now runs throughout Bishop Spong's work and is typical of modern theology. Everything we encounter is but a resource for self-expression and self-discovery. To think otherwise is to be a literalist. To think otherwise is to sin.

Surely the world has been turned upside down. For Bishop Spong, what the Christian tradition has called faith is sin. And not surprisingly, what Bishop Spong portrays as a saving faith is what the Christian tradition has called sin. Turning the world into a prop for our journey of faith hardly seems a recipe for the self-giving love that runs like a red thread through the Christian vision of the moral life. Quite the contrary, by denouncing as sin any and all submission of ourselves to that which is not us, Bishop Spong has transformed self-giving into sin. Our commitments and convictions must serve our "courage to be." No features of our lives can serve God or our neighbor; no features of our lives can be given in submission. The upshot is stunningly unappealing. We must protect ourselves from the temptations of loyalty, the bondage of vows, the prison of believing that not I but something else is the way, the truth, and the life. All this we must do so that we can be ourselves.

Good News? In Milton's epic *Paradise Lost,* Satan sees his and our condition rather more clearly than Bishop Spong. Milton describes Satan as the paradigmatic "seeker." He is on the move, "walking the edges of the ecclesiastical world," unwilling and unable to rest in pious certainties. Indeed, many modern commentators have expressed no small degree of amazement that Milton the Apologist should portray Satan as so singularly interesting, so appealingly human. However, unlike Bishop Spong, who fairly vibrates with satisfaction at the accomplishment of "being," the Satan whom Milton allows such a range of character and experience is anything but satisfied.

> Me miserable! [Satan says] which way shall I fly
> Infinite wrath, and infinite despair?

"Oh," says the modern reader, "Satan merely thinks himself miserable because he has such an oppressive view of God as Judge and Jailer." But Milton is very much a modern writer, and so he anticipates the modern reader. Satan is not oppressed by God. He is oppressed by himself.

> Which way I fly is hell [Satan continues]; myself am hell;
> And in the lowest deep a lower deep,
> Still threat'ning to devour me, opens wide,
> To which the hell I suffer seems a heaven.
> *(Book IV,* lines 72–78)

For Milton, Satan has looked into the depths of his very interesting and vividly expressive soul, and though he is a great speaker of lies, Satan sees and knows the truth. To make "being ourselves" into the goal and purpose of life transforms the gift of our existence into the curse of self-love.

From this curse of self-love, Milton's all-too-human Satan very much wishes for deliverance. In the very next lines we read Satan's plea.

> O, then, at least relent; is there no place
> Left for repentance, none for pardon left?
> (lines 79–80)

Satan knows the answer to this question. There is a place for pardon. Yet it is not a place that affirms him. The hell of self-love cannot be broken by an even more intense commitment to "being ourselves." There is a place for all of us, and Satan knows the way.

> None left but by submission; and that word
> Disdain forbids me, and my dread of shame
> Among the spirits beneath, whom I seduced
> With other promises and other vaunts
> Than to submit, boasting I could subdue
> The omnipotent.
>
> (lines 81–86)

In the end, then, Satan must be true to himself. He has the "courage to be." Surely readers of Milton are entirely right: Satan is a great and interesting individualist. He is someone who will not renounce his plans, his hopes, his aspirations, his experience. And what is so striking is that, for Bishop Spong and his theology of Being, far from falling, Satan has risen in an act of faith.

Works Considered or Consulted

Dawson, David. *Literary Theory*. Minneapolis: Fortress, 1995.

Holmes, Urban T. *What Is Anglicanism?* Wilton: Morehouse-Barlow, 1982.

Lindbeck, Georg. *The Nature of Doctrine*. Philadelphia: Westminster, 1984.

Milbank, John. *Theology and Social Theory*. Oxford: Blackwell, 1993.

Placher, William. *The Domestication of Transcendence*. Louisville: Westminster John Knox, 1996.

Soloveitchik, Joseph B. *Halakhic Man*. Lawrence Kaplan, trans. Philadelphia: JPS, 1984.

Trilling, Lionel. *Sincerity and Authenticity*. Cambridge: Harvard, 1972.

Urs von Balthasar, Han. *Love Alone*. Alexander Dru, trans, and ed. New York: Herder and Herder, 1969.

From Castle to Bungalow
Bishop Spong and the Virgin Birth
Edith M. Humphrey

WHEN *BORN OF A WOMAN* hit the bookstores in time for Christmas 1992, it was sure to reestablish the Episcopal bishop of Newark as a common topic of dinner conversation in Christian homes beyond the boundaries of Anglicanism. This was the third of what might be called "The Bishop Rethinks" series. The subtitles declare quite openly the stance of John Shelby Spong as bishop, and his major interest, which is, as it should be, the church. However, Spong's ideal audience is rather more narrow than the church as a whole. This is surprising in a day when even academic biblical scholars are attempting, en bloc, to inform the religiously "naive" about contemporary currents in scholarship. So, while Polebridge Press (the offspring of the California-based Jesus Seminar) concerns itself with educating the public in the area of "the Fourth R" (i. e., religion), Bishop Spong is rather less optimistic about such noblesse oblige, and does not direct his books primarily to the rank and file whom he knows will find his ideas disturbing. He declares in the introduction to *Born of a Woman,*

> Long ago I decided that I could no longer sacrifice scholarship and truth to protect the weak and religiously insecure. I see another audience that the church seems to ignore. That audience is made up of brilliantly educated men and women who find in the church a god too small to be the God of life for them, a knowledge too restricted to be compelling or a superstition too obvious to be entertained with seriousness. My now-grown daughters

are part of that audience. I want them to find in the
Christian church a gospel that takes seriously the world of
their experience, that does not seek to bind their minds into
premodern or ancient forms, that is not afraid to examine
emerging truth from any source whether from the world
of science or the world of bibilical scholarship (xv).

Despite the explicit elitism expressed here, we must applaud
the bishop's desire for a faith robust enough to examine truth
from any source. However, it is highly unlikely that any of
Spong's "church alumni association" (i. e., those who have left
the church, xvi) will find in *Born of a Woman* a compelling repre-
sentation of the One who is Truth. Their return to the church
may just possibly be aided by hearing again, in the bishop's
undeniably eloquent voice, those *few* parts of the gospel that he
has not totally reshaped. It is hoped that in the event of their
return, they will discover in their local Anglican parish a gospel
less marked by predictable rationalist reduction and more
touched by the glory that is the inheritance of the faithful.

Romancing the Stone
Bishop Spong argues that liberals do not take the Bible seriously
enough and that fundamentalists distort the Bible through literalism. Along with other academic and popular construction
workers in the biblical field, he is engaged in a large-scale effort
to fit the figure of Jesus into an overall picture of a first-century
milieu, the writing of the gospels, and the life of the church
today. The figure of Jesus remains, for many in the church
(including Bishop Spong), the cornerstone that must not rejected. It seems, however, that he, along with other carpenters and
construction workers, has taken on a second profession—that of
the jewel-cutter or fabricator, who changes the shape of the stone
so that it will fit into a building more congenial to late twentieth-
century sensibilities. Of course, this is not a new calling; we could
think of ancient jewel cutters such as the second-century Marcion,
who shaped the ethical and theological teachings of Jesus by
removing whole sections of the New Testament and editing others. This side of the Enlightenment, however, the procedure is perhaps more complicated. In the time of Marcion, everyone agreed
that the agenda was a thoroughly theological one; today many

builders and stonecutters will insist that they are not driven by theological concerns, but that they are working dispassionately, and that they simply follow scientifically sound principles as they do their work. The emotive quality of Bishop Spong's appeal to his daughters and his obvious distress with fundamentalism should be strong indicators that such neutrality simply is not possible.

Upon a careful study of Bishop Spong's arguments, I am not quite sure why the building he has erected should be taken seriously, except as an example of great rhetoric and passion. While he "grieves" outwardly that he will be causing pain to "simple believers," he boldly and fearlessly sets up a new edifice, cobbled together from various works of such unlikely partners as the radically feminist Jane Schaberg and the rather conservative Roman Catholic scholar Raymond (called affectionately "Ray" by the bishop) Brown. What Schaberg thinks of Spong's indebtedness I do not know; as for Raymond Brown, he himself comments, "Spong is complimentary in what he writes about me as a NT scholar; ...I hope I am not ungracious if in return I remark that I do not think a single NT author would recognize Spong's Jesus as the figure being proclaimed or written about" (*The Birth of the Messiah*, 704). Nor do I think that Brown may easily recognize himself in Spong's writing, for under the bishop's pen the Roman Catholic scholar's ideas have been trivialized and metamorphosized as radically as the figure of Jesus himself!

It's in the Details

Please join me in this chapter, as we engage together in a building inspection of this construction site. We have already considered the question "For whom is this home being built?" That is, for whom is he writing? What is his audience? As thorough inspectors, let us go on to follow a checklist of three basic questions. First, why the building in the first place? What are the builder's reasons for his work, both explicit and implicit? Second, what does the building as a whole look like; that is, what is the general picture of first-century society and of the New Testament Gospels sketched by Bishop Spong? And finally, how does the central block or cornerstone fit into this building; that is, what picture of Jesus emerges in his presentation? En route we will need to consider also the various tools used in the erection of the edifice. As a conclusion to our building examination, we will move on to talk more particularly about the desiderata of a faithful Christian and Anglican approach to the cornerstone, Jesus, and the question of history.

Our purpose, then, is to understand more carefully the work of this popular episcopal figure (work about which we may have been viscerally uneasy), to consider the dangers and issues presented here, and then to move on to apply what we have learned to our own fond ideas of Jesus. Critique should never be one-sided, and this inspection should help us to see what we can do to avoid building on the wrong foundations, or erecting eccentric wings or rooms that must inevitably be pulled down for the Spirit to do his authentic work in our midst. If my remarks on Bishop Spong's work appear rather rigorous, I hope it will become clear that all of us need to allow the illuminating light of the gospel to flood our shadowlands as well and lead us, sometimes gently, but sometimes painfully, into truth and health and luminosity.

Know Your Enemy

The first question, "*Why* the building?" has already been partially answered. We have noted the bishop's fear of what he calls fundamentalism, his concern for the state of the church, and his projected audience of "brilliantly educated men and women." Connected with this rejection of fundamentalism is an even more unequivocal denunciation of "biblical literalism," which he declares to be "not even a benign alternative for contemporary Christians," but rather "an enemy to faith in Jesus Christ" (*BOW,* 11). In *Born of a Woman* he also tackles yet another enemy, the well-known foe of patriarchalism, although (ironically) he makes judicious use of his position as bishop to combat this ill through copious personal references and the inscription of his position in the titles of his books. Bishop Spong is quite clear about the nature of his enemies: fundamentalism is a *distortion* of the Scriptures, while patriarchalism at least finds its beginning *in* the biblical writings themselves. Fortunately, he feels, we have been led beyond abusive power in our time, but need to take heed that the more patriarchal parts of the Scriptures do not lead us back into less enlightened times. He launches his challenge,

Can the church surrender its defining prejudices of a per-
sonalistic, masculine, and patriarchal worldview?... Can
we escape the stereotypes of the past that define gender,
sexual orientation, and sexual morality in a way that has
always violated women and now is seen increasingly to
violate everyone? Can the church get out of the behavior-
control business and into the business of calling people
into being the holy and complete selves God has created
them to be?... Can the Christians be freed to explore the
sacred writings of our faith story without being bound
inside the prejudices, worldviews, and emotional pitfalls
of another era? Can the Christian church at the dawn of
the 21st c. be called out of the literalism that if not escaped
will finally be the cause of its death?" (*BOW*, 12–13)

There is an illustration in the writings of C.S. Lewis that is an
apt response to the bishop's words. Lewis speaks of a sinking
ship, in dire straits and filling fast with water, being ministered to
by a well-meaning attendant with—a fire extinguisher. It is clear
that Bishop Spong speaks from conviction, and from revulsion to
his childhood experience in a very narrow church, for this is how
he portrays himself. And it is certainly true that all of us, males
and females included, need to repent of authoritarianism, of
pride, of the desire to sit at the right and left hands of Jesus. We
need, rather, to follow the delivering pattern of our crucified and
resurrected servant-Lord and use whatever "power" comes our
way to free, enliven, serve, comfort, and encourage others. This
impulse is commended by the Scriptures to women, as well as to
men! Yet it is curious that the church is in fact languishing most
dangerously in those very churches that are following the course
of action prescribed by the bishop. Notably, too, many orthodox,
evangelical, and charismatic churches that Bishop Spong
(though not everyone) would classify as "literalistic," even "fundamentalist" and "in the business of behaviour control [sic]" are
becoming places of healing and worship for people of varied
backgrounds. Certainly the church must be preoccupied with
"calling people into being the holy and complete selves God has
created them to be." These communities of faith believe that
when the Bible speaks explicitly about holiness or sets before us
examplars of full humanity, these words and pictures are to be

considered very seriously indeed and not dismissed as "the prejudices, worldviews, and emotional pitfalls of another era." It
seems that the worldview presented by the sacred writings is not
so completely bankrupt as the bishop thinks—perhaps the problem with the church lies elsewhere.

Biology and Theology

At any rate, this is Bishop Spong's diagnosis of the present situation
of our twentieth-century-old edifice, coupled with his challenge to
"get out of this business" and into another. He is convinced that
our "male-dominated church" has been bolstered by the unfortunate cover-up story of a virginal birth. In this death-dealing story,
the ideal woman (Mary) set before the church exemplifies an
unreal and unattainable modesty for Christian women; so too
the specter of a celibate Savior tacitly suggests that sexuality, contact with women, is an unfit state for the Holy One of God.
Spong's argument includes both a tendentious rehearsal of the
development of Christology in the Scriptures and patristic times
and a rather inaccurate account of Mary's career (BOW, 167), in
which the title of *theotokos* is portrayed as a development *subse-
quent* to the immaculate conception! This "progress" is, of course,
not borne out by church history, since *theotokos* was established
as an important patristic doctrine to safeguard the integrity of
Jesus' nature, whereas the immaculate conception was a nineteenth-century mariological proclamation of the Roman Church,
and it depends on a view of original sin that became common in
Western theology. For Bishop Spong, both the Gospel stories and
the later developments reflect "the residue of that deep Christian
negativity toward women that still infects the church"(BOW,
189). Instead of a virginal conception and a "passionless" Jesus,
Bishop Spong revises: a moving story of the man for others, the
one who dies for us, but whose birth had the humblest beginning as an illegitimate child (perhaps the offspring of rape), who
was tenderly rescued by the much-forgotten adoptive father,
Joseph, and whose adult years might well have involved him in
intimacy, even marriage with Mary Magdalene, or Mary the
Great, as he prefers to call her.

   What makes this work so difficult to analyze is that the bishop constructs his edifice with different tools, at times calling
strongly for "straight reason," at other times speaking playfully

about the imaginative possibilities of ancient Scripture, if only we will not be bound by our previous theological prejudices, and at still other times calling with the voice of the revisionist for a reading that will suit the ethical and ideological demands of our day. Thus, we may see the author as modernist, uncovering the most plausible explanation for mystery and scoffing (in the classic attitude named by C.S. Lewis as "chronological snobbery") at those who can still accept the mighty acts of God ("miracles") in our twentieth-century world. So, he pronounces, "From the second century... until the nineteenth century, the church viewed the literal virgin as an undoubted fact of history.... Biology and theology were inextricably bound up together. That is no longer so today" (*BOW*, 111). The title of his book itself suggests this perspective of cool reason, as the bishop "rethinks" a classic doctrine. In this vein, the bishop categorically declares, "No recognized New Testament scholar, Catholic or Protestant, would today seriously defend the historicity of these [birth and infancy] narratives" (*BOW*, 44–50). He might have considered the carefully nuanced summary of scholarship and treatment in I.H. Marshall's commentary on Luke or even the words of his mentor, Brown, who writes of "the probable presence of items of historical value" (*Birth of the Messiah*, 362) in these stories. No wonder Brown characterizes the "realist" bishop's treatment of the Bible and his secondary sources as "highly quixotic" (*Birth of the Messiah*, 702)!

Imaginative Speculations

Alongside this "serious and scholarly" stance (*BOW*, 188), Spong engages, at times, in a breathtaking speculation worthy of the postmodernist who declares that meaning is created by the reader, and does not reside at all in the text being read. A fascinating example of this is his interpretation of the Cana wedding as Jesus' *own* wedding to Magdalene (although this fact is, of course, suppressed by the narrative.) The major clues to this revelation come from the bishop's own late twentieth-century experience of weddings, rather than from a serious study of wedding customs in the first century C.E.: "The only time my mother and my closest friends were at a wedding together with me was my own wedding"; "why would [the lack of wine] have been a concern to the mother of Jesus?" (*BOW*, 192). But what were weddings like in small Palestinian villages where everyone in the whole town knew each other?

Another example of such speculation is to be found in an odd argument based on Magdalene's address "my lord" to Jesus on Easter morning. This is, suggests the bishop, a telltale sign of Magdalene's marital relationship in a time when wives so addressed their husbands. A more sober explanation of these words would be to note the unusual nature of the Fourth Gospel, which often explicitly supplies the theological implications of stories and events in a manner unlike the synoptics. It is in John, too, where we hear Thomas's unequivocal assertion, "My Lord and my God," and the shocking use of the divine "I AM" in a controversy with the Pharisees. How ironic that a writer who appeals to the unusual genre of the nativity narratives would ignore the special nature of John so completely!

In both the reference to Cana and the treatment of Magdalene's words, we see that the bishop is following his own goal: "Reading these texts with a new consciousness brings new possibilities into the imagination" (BOW, 194). In fact, the reader is invited to join in the "interesting speculation," as Bishop Spong paints the scene in the garden, noting that Jesus and Mary both address each other with intimacy, and then suggests, "Try to imagine what happens next. The text simply has Jesus say, 'Mary, do not hold me'" (BOW, 194). Here, the bishop's free-ranging imagination finds insight through anachronistic parallels and through a playful filling in of the story along Hollywood lines. This tendency has been encouraged by his new freedom "from the straitjacket of literalism." Through powerful rhetoric, the bishop encourages his hearers to join in the exercise, in a move beyond that of cold reason. The unsuspecting reader, moved by such exhortation, may not notice that the bishop has encouraged fantasy, rather than the discovery "in...the gospel" of "treasures beyond our most fanciful imagination" (BOW, 112).

A Bungalow for a Castle

So, then, the bishop's tools are mixed, as he wields the axe of hard, cold reason but adds the material of imaginative speculation, combining his bricolage with the glue of magnificent rhetoric. His argument is strongest where he tells again the authentic story of the Christian family and does not improvise.

So, he speaks movingly about Jesus' strength, which lay in his willingness to "sacrifice himself to his enemies" and about "his life [as]... a call to reverse the standards of the world"—that is, our fond ideas of privilege and power. So, for Spong, "Jesus reflected a new image of God, an image that defied the conventional wisdom, an image that called into question the exalted king as the primary analogy by which God could be understood" (*BOW*, 38–39). It is at this point that the argument makes a subtle shift to a revision of the gospel. In this telling of the story, the real Easter moment is not the resurrection per se , but the *internal* realization, the "mind-boggling revelation" that our image of God must change, and that we must see God in the experience of a weak man: "God was [to be] seen not as a king ruling life but as a power within life" (*BOW*, 40). This is the version or revision of the Christian gospel recommended by the bishop, who does a disservice to his readers and a violence to the richness of Christian explanations of the death and resurrection of Jesus. Yet again, the less well informed may not be aware that he has prefaced his telling of the story by a careless dismissal of atonement theology. He presents the reader with a cartoon of Anselm's satisfaction theology, gives no other traditional views of the atonement, and implies that any acceptance of these doctrines leads inevitably to "religious imperialism" (*BOW*, 36).

Thus, the crucifixion (as reinterpreted) is key to Bishop Spong because it exemplifies divine power in weakness; the resurrection story, however, is read as an unfortunate attempt to recapture humanity's fond idea of of a glorious and victorious God. Both the turnaround of the resurrection and the hierarchy of the early church are seen as betrayals of the radically "leveling" words and acts of Jesus. Interestingly enough, in so arguing the bishop parallels the thinking of Crossan and others in the Jesus Seminar but does not follow them in seeing the crucifixion as irrelevant to this message. The problem for Spong is not the crucifixion, as revised by him, but the putative later reversion to a pattern of God as Imperial Ruler, extended onto the figure of Jesus (and church leaders!), first through the resurrection story and then by the infancy narratives. This is, I think, where the problem lies: not in what the bishop affirms about the nature of God, but in what he thinks must be denied. For he has, in one fell swoop, taken away the grandeur of the Christian temple or castle, and replaced it with—a bungalow. Where is the drama in realizing that God is not exalted as we thought, but a weak friend? But *here* is drama: in the unretouched story of the Scriptures, the story of that One who was rich, but for our sake *became weak*, who tinged with an ineluctable glory the womb of his mother and our whole world, who suffered the inevitable fate of the meek and obedient in this life, who took the most ignominious route of all, dying as a criminal, who plumbed the depths of hell—and *then* emerged in an unexpected and before-time resurrection, showing to all with eyes to see that God's new age, God's intimate dwelling with humanity, has in fact begun and will be brought to completion. From such a perspective, the bishoply washing of feet, the tender compassion and humility of those set in authority over the church, the mutual respect of each member of the community of God, may dramatically bespeak God's own great act of kenosis, or self-emptying: if only the whole church will continue to heed the model of Philippians 2:5–11.

Midrash Mismash

But Bishop Spong will not have it so. For any touch of partriarchy is for him death to the church, and the mighty acts upon which the Christian story turns smack to him of literalism. Instead, he works on the edifice and the cornerstone with various tools, creating a new building. It is clear that this man has had not a little exposure to various sorts of biblical criticism, which he uses in a sometimes cavalier way to complete his task. His favored method of approaching the more wonderful stories of the Bible is by reference to "midrash" and "midrashic technique." It may be that Bishop Spong is not entirely aware of the complex ways in which the term *midrash* has been used in scholarship. He has made some steps in a more recent tome (*Liberating the Gospels*) to clarify his use of the term, which still remains (in my opinion) unadvised. In *Born of a Woman*, however, it seems that he has picked up the idea from the atmosphere of biblical scholarship, and not by an actual reading of *midrashim* (pl. of *midrash*). Usually, when biblical scholars speak of midrash and midrashic technique, they refer to the ancient conventions of the Jewish rabbis who studied and commented on scriptural texts, often in a line-by-line commentary on a book: "Rabbi A said… such and such" and "Rabbi B said… this and that." Sometimes the term (*haggadic*) *midrash* is used for a loose, homiletic explanation or interpretation of a difficult scriptural passage: the difficult passage is interpreted or brought to life by retelling it in a fanciful or folklore-like manner. Always, however, midrash is tied to the text being interpreted: it is "a literature about literature" (A. Wright, *The Literary Genre Midrash*, 74).

So I stop, puzzled by the suggestion that the birth narratives of Jesus are midrashim, and by Spong's easy use of this term for other stories involving what we call the miraculous. Raymond Brown, from whom (among others) Spong borrows the term, says himself that "midrash, taken in its strict sense, is not a term that describes well the literary genre of either infancy narrative... [because] the birth stories were composed, not to make the Old Testament Scriptures more intelligible, but to make Jesus more intelligible" (*BOW*, 561.) That is, *midrash* suggests a kind of writing that explains other sacred writings—and the New Testament is *not* written as a *commentary* upon the Old, although it is interconnected with it, quotes it, and makes allusions to it throughout. If we were to look for midrash in the New Testament, the book of Hebrews might be a good candidate since it retells details and events from the Torah that deal with the tabernacle. Other candidates might include Paul's allegory of the two mountains of Zion and Sinai (Gal. 4:21–31) or his intriguing reference to Christ as "the rock that followed" (1 Cor. 10:4).

The infancy narratives are, however, another story. When careful scholars use the term *midrash* to explain the nativity accounts, they do so advisedly because

1. There are similarities in the atmosphere and images of these Gospel accounts to Jewish midrashim on Exodus 1–2 and

2. They see clear connections between the canticles and figures (especially in Luke's account) and important Old Testament stories and personages.

However, it is quite clear that the nativity stories are not expositions on the stories of Moses, Hannah, Sarah, and so on. Thus, they are not in themselves midrashim even though their style of writing bears some similarity to works that would qualify for this title. Unfortunately, Bishop Spong seems to lay hold of the term *midrash* not because of these factors, but because the narratives bother our twentieth-century psyches with wondrous signs. To be sure, the flavor of the narratives, both in Matthew and in Luke, is very different from the rest of the Gospels: the stories are shaped and poignantly told in ways that recall key figures and highly symbolic passages in the Old Testament. This does not mean that they were created from whole cloth, however, nor that they have no bearing on events such as historians research. As presented by the bishop, *midrash* becomes an escape hatch against believing "100 impossible things before breakfast." It is thus a new way of demythologizing, so that the "symbolic" meaning of the text may be preserved while denying any connection to history. This rescue attempt may be difficult, however, considering that for the bishop the key symbols themselves, "virginity," "father-God," and the like, are vicious in a twentieth-century milieu. Left alone to speak, the traditional symbols conjure up "a tale of divine sexual aggression, acted out upon a compliant Jewish peasant girl" (*BOW*, 179). Left to the church, they have, he says, been applied so as to cause every oppression known to women in the Western world. Do we then need the ministries of this wise bishop to release their true power and grant them new life left for today? In fact, it is not the gospel story that is granted new life, but a replacement narrative that is commended to his late-twentieth-century readers. The bishop seemingly becomes the mediator of a new midrash, filled with new characters bearing the traditional names.

Revising the Story

In positing an atmosphere of creative midrashim for the genesis of the Gospels, Bishop Spong makes room for his own creative midrash on Jesus' birth—and other aspects of Jesus' life as well. He argues that "Matthew [and Luke] neither suggested nor believed that everything [they] wrote was factual" and that the original readers, too, would not have "viewed" the infancy narratives "literally," but rather as a "beautiful...pageant"and "interpretive drama." Hence, the bishop drives a wedge between history and meaningful interpretation, claiming that "readers... must realize that [this] work is not history or biography, it is a proclamation of a living faith." The latter statement is true, but are our only options "literal history," which turns "truth into either nonsense or fantasy" or a legendary reading such as that offered by Bishop Spong? Is there no other category, where symbol and event may reside together, to speak to the reader? In fact, Raymond Brown, upon whom the bishop leans, has suggested one alternative, viewing the nativity stories as "a mélange of items of history or verisimilitude, of images drawn from the Old Testament or Jewish tradition, of images anticipated from the Gospel account of the ministry" (*BOW*, 361). In considering these options, we need also to be aware that the bishop is not content simply to critique *the way* that readers have, in his view, "misinterpreted" the pageantry. In the very seeds of the nativity pageant, as well as in the story of the resurrection, lurk dangerous elements, he insists, that need correction today for the life of the church. Thus the stories, and not simply their (mis)interpretation, are at issue here, requiring the bishop's revision.

It needs to be strongly established that "midrash" cannot be used as a convenient method for sidestepping the awkward elements of the Christian story or as an antidote to what Spong calls "literalism." The proper antidote to literalism is to come to appreciate the Scriptures in their fullness, to search them not simply as quarries to buttress doctrines we have already learned, but to allow them to engage us at all their different levels, whether biographical, symbolic, typological, or theological. It is certainly true that the Gospels are not sheer biographies of Jesus, but that they are written "so that we might believe," as the Fourth Gospel puts it. When we see symbolic sophistication, the use of literary allusion to Old Testament events, details that remind us of Hannah or Moses or Samuel or Elijah, does this mean that the Gospels are not intended to speak historically? This would only be so if the two alternatives were flat reportage (i. e., lists of events and dates) and fable. In fact, the inclusion of such elements in the Gospels means that they contain much *more* than a flat record of "what happened"—as though any good narrative could be written that way! "The gospels are not *less* than biographies," as N.T. Wright reminds us (*Who Was Jesus?* 74), but they do contain a good deal more. Those who are committed lovers of the Word need not be afraid to note the careful, theological shaping given to the telling of the stories. These nativity narratives are designed to ring bells, to resonate with other stories we know about God's dealings with his people. Why should it be otherwise? For the God who created our minds also gave to us hearts and memories and imagination, and the Gospels seek to move the whole person to worship and belief and repentance.

Sex on the Mind

The bishop is himself obviously moved by some of the deeper mysteries of the story, but in the interests of the modern day, cannot go the whole way in hearing it. In and throughout his concerns about literalism and fundamentalism, and woven into his own creative "midrash," or retelling of the Gospel stories, we find a very curious preoccupation with sex and sexuality. It may be that in this author's experience, conservative theology was mingled with "gnostic" or repressed ideas of sexuality. Certainly this is his take on the development of the doctrine of Mary and the call to celibacy in the priesthood. As for his understanding of Jesus' own sexuality, he argues that people are appalled by the idea of a married Jesus because of their rigidity, and that they assume "marriage is not appropriate for one who is defined as Holy, as the God-man" because "even marriage is a compromise with sin" (*BOW,* 189).

Surely this is all beside the point. For the One who came among us as fully human is also the Lamb to whom the church, as a whole, is to be, in some mystical sense, married. We find this complex idea not only in the strange book of Revelation, but also in the epistle to the Ephesians, where marriage is called a great "mystery" because it mirrors the sacrament of Christ and his church.

We know from our own time what kinds of things happen when a religious leader brings together this mystical concept with his own private life. For example, we can see in the writing of David Koresh, the "sinful messiah," that he believed his unions with young women were part and parcel of the bringing together of heaven and earth—a kind of sympathetic magic. (See, if you doubt my interpretation, Koresh's own views in "Eden to Eden," the poetic frontispiece to his posthumously published and incomplete *Exposition of the Seven Seals,* Phillip Arnold and James Tabor, editors, Reunion Institute, PO Box 981111, Houston, TX 77098). The Gospels do not, however, show Jesus as taking such steps. The bishop, along with others in our sexually oriented world, has been intrigued by the marked presence of Mary Magdalene at key points in Jesus' ministry, death, and resurrection. There may well be, however, other more compelling explanations for the Gospels' emphasis on her, which Bishop Spong never considers. For example, Magdalene was accorded the status "equal to the apostles" (a technical term) in the early church, and so her presence might have been of real importance for this reason. (Here is a bone fide encouragement to women, which is, admittedly, not as titillating as the scenarios of Schaberg and Bishop Spong.) At any rate, Jesus' marriage and intimacy with a particular woman is not inconceivable because it is sinful; it is a problem because it obscures the place of the Son of God as the man for others, for all others, and it would usurp the great intimacy of which the Scriptures speak between Christ and his people. Part of Jesus' self-giving, we may now see, is the self-denial of this great delight and good in human life because of his devotion to God's people, and *to us.*

Do we begin to see the difference? On the one hand, there is Bishop Spong's edifice—"rational" Scriptures, purged of all hierarchy, and well pleasing to a society of well-informed, well-adjusted people who claim that God is in their world, but not over them. On the other hand, there is the heartbreaking and heart-changing story of the One who *became* like us so that he could enliven us and so that we could *become* like him. In Bishop Spong's view, as soon as the experience of the divine achieves form it is distorted; as soon as the writers of Scripture begin to put into word and story the way God meets with his people, the intense experience is falsified. So the ignominity of Jesus' birth is rescued (and thus obscured) by stories of a virgin birth, and the plainness of his death is overladen again with visions of resurrection, exaltation, and kingship. Always, he tells us, the human experience of God is primary; when we seek to express the experience in words, the original mystery is distorted (*BOW,* 33). But what if, instead, it is *in* the enactment of the story, *in* the telling of the story, that God's being, God's grace, God's love, comes most powerfully to us, confirming our best hopes but shocking and surprising us in ways we had never imagined? Jesus was the great storyteller; it seems, then, that Jesus is God's great story. The great surprise is, he tells it to us in our own world, in the world of flesh and blood and time and

space, not in some never-never land of mythic truth, abstract
meditation, or abstruse midrash. The Gospel does not tell us,
"In the beginning was the experience," but rather, "In the beginning was the Word." It is the deep, rich, and challenging role of
the Gospels and of our own lives in the church to show forth
more and more what that means.

What to Do with the Building:
History, Theology and the Church Today

And so, having done our building inspection, we need to consider
our own house. We see, I think, the limitations and near-bankruptcy
of a house built on reaction—reaction to fundamentalism, literalism, and patriarchalism. Reaction does not make a good foundation. What begins as revision in the bishop's mind seemingly
finishes on the margins of revenge. This is clear in the sometimes
too-personal tone of his argument, as in his memory of a debate
with Carroll Simcox, which he retells and then comments (in
perhaps an ill-considered phrase), "History reveals that he, with
his point of view, found life inside the bounds of the Episcopal
Church no longer possible, and so he departed" (BOW, 177). The
issue that is most pertinent here is, it seems, the change in ECUSA
in the last two decades, not the state of his interlocutor's mind.
The bishop has obviously had much trouble with those of a
more conservative stance than his own, an allergy that began, by
his own account, at a very early age. Those who retain a faithful
stance toward the Scriptures and Christian tradition may well
have something important to learn from Bishop Spong, although
not the lessons that he has in mind.

In noting some of the eccentric features of this builder, it may
be that we are tempted to scrap or ignore the building project. If
we do not share the bishop's drive for reconstruction, if we see
major problems with the edifice he has erected, if we are appalled
at the route he takes to ensure the humanity of Jesus, why engage
in the question of Jesus and history at all? Why not just read the
Bible as we always have done? The fact is that none of us *simply*
reads the Bible: each of us, consciously, or unconsciously, stands
within a tradition of interpretation and sees the stories, the words,
the events of the Gospels through a certain set of spectacles. So
"doing history" is not an option: we either do it consciously or
unconsciously, badly or well, just as we all "do theology" and

"interpretation" whether we are aware of it or not. We cannot, after all, escape this, because the Bible is a book that brings together theological and historical concerns, not to mention ethical and social concerns as well. Perhaps we do well to consider some of the challenges of Bishop Spong—especially the charges of literalism—and seek to read the Bible with our whole heart and soul and mind. Again, as we have seen that no one does historical or theological work in a vacuum, that no one works from an entirely neutral stance, we should beware of our own unexamined assumptions. We each work from a particular perspective. The danger is not our viewpoint, but the unacknowledged smuggling of that viewpoint into a portrait of Jesus that we sketch or reformulate in our reading of the Scriptures. The historical questions are not irrelevant, and the nature of the New Testament itself is such that it calls us to ask, "Who was—and is—Jesus?" rather than simply to ask in personal isolation, "What does Jesus mean to me?"

Jesus and History

Our talking and thinking of Jesus takes place within the context of the church, in the sight of God, and in the power of the Holy Spirit, but also in the public sphere. It is not good enough to throw up our hands at the absurdity or contradiction of some of the pictures of Jesus created in our time, and say, "So much for historical research!" Rather, we can evaluate, and appreciate each picture by asking questions about the edifice built: why, what kind, and how does Jesus fit into this. We may be surprised to find ourselves challenged to rethink certain passages or certain ideas we have about Jesus and his life because of light shed upon them, even by the torch of a Bishop Spong. I was surprised, for example, to discover that Bishop Spong, despite his talk of the "feminine side of God" is not a champion of "Mother Goddess" worship, but that he recognizes that "mother-goddess worship stands in inverse relationship to high secular status for women" (*BOW*, 219, quoting James Freeman, "The Cross Cultural Study of Mother Worship," in *Mother Worship*, James Preston, editor, University of North Carolina Press, 1982). More recently, the bishop is to be commended for his emphasis upon the Jewish nature of the Gospels, even if we may not be convinced to follow his championing of the British scholar Michael Goulder.

Together, then, as a community, we need to do hard thinking

about Jesus and history, not simply because we worship a Christ principle or pay lip service to the Christ of faith, but because we believe that God became a human at a particular place and time in first-century Palestine to speak to his own people and to reconfigure his community so as to include us. We see in the Scriptures a beckoning and bewildering figure, the keystone that the builders rejected, a person who fulfills but also explodes convenient or congenial molds, a Lord who was also a "dying man for others." The advent of this One for others opened the door for full humanity and eventual glory in his creation as well. It is of this glory that the nativity speaks: the Lover of Israel, and of the whole world, came to dwell with us, and the creature is glorified by intimate contact with the Creator. Despite the contention of Bishop Spong that in the Gospels the figure of Mary is dehumanized and flattened, we may see in her person an obedience, a courage, an experience of God's intervention, a human anguish and conflict (Luke 2:35 and elsewhere), and a humility mingled with strength, that remains a potent model of the servant in this arrogant age. The more we understand about the world into which Jesus came, and the more deeply and sensitively we read the Gospel stories, the more we will understand about God's purposes for his people and about the actions of Jesus on our behalf: this is our heritage, a richness that the Gospels call us to explore and enjoy.

Jesus did not come proclaiming an internal experience of the divine, as grist for the antipatriarchal mill. He came announcing a new beginning, a new era of God's rule, to be found concretely in himself. In his preaching, healing, and living with others, in his death and astonishing resurrection, and (yes, even!) in the "mythic"-sounding story of the ascension, we see the drama unfold. *Here* is the answer to Spong's fear of patriarchalism, because the One who came to us reversed the old order and made provision for all, together with him, to be glorified with him. God's glory does not avoid humility and service, but comes *through* this very unlikely route.

Jesus and First-Century Israel

Since we have been speaking of midrashim and stories, let us close with two interpetations of the primary gospel story. First, a story in the mode of historical narrative, inspired by the teaching of N.T. Wright (*Jesus and the Victory of God*, 1996). Israel, as a nation, had enacted (not surprisingly, because she was made up of humans) the general stance of human rebellion against God rather than embracing her destiny to become a light to the world (Isa. 49:6). The earthly ministry of Jesus, concentrated in Galilee and Judea, called attention to the problem of Israel as a messenger who had not fulfilled her destiny and implored God's people to join in God's new way to reach and enlighten all of humankind. As a creative and compelling prophet, Jesus spoke in such a way that recalled two strains in the Hebrew prophetic writings: he spoke as the mysterious Son of Man from Daniel who would receive power and authority from God and would be recognized by God where the shaky structures of other nations who did not know God would ultimately fail; and he spoke the language of Isaiah's Servant, who must face suffering. Bringing together these two prophetic pictures, Son of Man and Suffering Servant, Jesus indicated his expectation and understanding of his own death. *He* was to face the trial and suffering meant for Israel, a tribulation at the hand of the Romans but sent by the hand of God. Such a death would issue in the long-awaited reversal of fortunes for God's people: "Oh, that you would rend the heavens and come down" (Isa. 64:1). This reversal began, in fact, with the surprising resurrection of the One who had died but was to continue in another surprising way. God's people were themselves to be reordered into a community that included outsiders as well as insiders, Gentiles as well as Jews, misfits as well as the pure. And so Jesus came, confirming the hopes of many but also disturbing their expectations, speaking in bizarre and intense ways about the destruction of God's house and the building up of a new one. This story has its roots in Israel, in the long saga of God's dealing with a particular people—but it is our history, if we have been engrafted into the new Israel of God. We need to be challenged to reclaim our story, and live within it, and tell it, for we have lived too long without roots (the bishop is right about the Jewish foundation of the Gospels!), and we have spoken too freely about the Christ of faith without understanding the actual Jewish Lord who came to be with us.

Listen to the story again, using the theological mode of Garrett Green ("The Gender of God and the Theology of Metaphor," 60):

[There is a God who] does not jealously hoard his power. As a husband he does not beat his unfaithful wife but cries out with the pain of a jilted lover and redoubles his efforts to win her back (Hos. 2). As Father he "did not spare his own Son but gave him up for us all"(Rom. 8:32). As Son he did not claim the prerogatives of power and lord it over his subjects but "emptied himself, taking the form of a servant.... He humbled himself and became obedient unto death, even death on a cross" (Phil. 2:7–8) As Spirit he incorporates us into the mystical body of Christ, in whom "there is neither slave nor free, there is neither male nor female" (Gal. 3:28). As king he does not isolate himself in heavenly splendor but wills to dwell with his people, to "wipe away every tear from their eyes" and to deliver them from all that oppresses them, even from death itself (Rev. 21:4).

From Narcissism to Worship

The reader will have to judge between these stories and those told by Bishop Spong. I am convinced that the story of the gospel, as retold by a community seeking to be faithful, still has the power to speak the story. The problem, then, is not with the story. The problem is not with the building. It is in not hearing the story, in not exploring the original building thoroughly enough. The story of the gospel, related first by the apostles, written in our Gospels, read in our churches—*this* story is full and deep and incisive enough to cut through mere wooden legalism and literalism, to chase away patriarchalism and to create a people of love, humility, service, and freedom for God. The building has vistas, hidden courtyards, towers, and secret rooms enough to keep us busy for eternity—and it is still being built, for we are being added to it daily. The Gospels of Mark and Matthew spend the entire first half of the Gospel leading up to that critical question of Jesus, "Who do you say that I am?" Peter answers, "You are the Christ of God," upon which Jesus replies, "You are Peter, and on this rock I will build my church." But the Gospel doesn't end at this recognition: it moves on for another complete half, explaining what it means for Jesus to be the Messiah of God and telling the compelling story of one who died and rose again for us. We need both halves, the half that leads us to recognize who Jesus is and the story that explains and presses home to us what that means. The story is not over, nor the building finished—for we are a part of it, and Christ is building his church. The Stone that the builders rejected has become the head of the corner. This was the Lord's doing, and it is marvelous in our eyes.

Works Considered or Consulted

Brown, Raymond E., S.S. *The Birth of the Messiah: A Commentary on the Infancy Narratives in the Gospels of Matthew and Luke.* New York: Doubleday, 1992.

Crossan, John Dominic. *Jesus—a Revolutionary Biography.* San Francisco: Harper, 1994.

———. *The Historical Jesus: The Life of a Mediterranean Jewish Peasant.* San Francisco: Harper, 1991.

Goulder, Michael. *Luke: A New Paradigm.* vols 1 and 2. JNT Supp 20, Sheffield: JSOT, 1989.

Green, Garrett. "The Gender of God and the Theology of Metaphor," *Speaking the Christian God: The Holy Trinity and the Challenge of Feminism,* ed. A. Kimel. Grand Rapids: Eerdmans, 1992.

Marshall, I. H. *Commentary on Luke.* Grand Rapids: Eerdmans, 1978.

Schaberg, Jane. *The Illegitimacy of Jesus.* San Francisco: Harper & Row, 1987.

Wright, A. *The Literary Genre Midrash.* Staten Island: Alba, 1967.

Wright, N. T. *Jesus and the Victory of God.* Minneapolis: Fortress, 1996.

———. *Who Was Jesus?* Grand Rapids: Eerdmans, 1993.

Turtles All the Way Down
Did Jesus Rise from the Grave?
George R. Sumner Jr.

THOMAS AQUINAS, ONE OF THE GREATEST Christian thinkers, would begin to answer any theological question by listing the opinions contrary to his own. When he provided his own solution (*sed contra,* "but on the other hand"), "the angelic doctor" of the thirteenth century did not merely attack his opponents' views. On the contrary, his method consisted in large part in showing how erroneous or even heretical views could be seen as half-truths. Their real merit could be perceived only when they were returned to their natural habitat in the orthodox faith whence they had been torn.

I offer this essay in the same spirit. I come not to bury Bishop Spong's arguments on the resurrection of Jesus Christ, but to redeem them. Spong's writings have appealed to a great many people because they answer questions that lay people really ask—and that in itself is something of value.

John Spong's basic argument is this: Children love fairy tales of long ago, and they also need the rules that parents lay down for them. But maturity requires putting aside fantasies and overcoming repressive barriers created by rules, so that one can live and love deeply.

Spong argues that the Christians of the first century possessed a "naive worldview" (*EM*, 100). They had no choice but to think unself-consciously in terms of miraculous legends. During their time with their teacher, Jesus of Nazareth, the disciples misunderstood his efforts to teach them how awareness of the eternal could open them to live and love more fully.

At last Jesus realized that his followers would see his point only if he accepted death at the hands of the Roman and Jewish leaders, who insisted on making religion an instrument of state control. The disciples fled in terror when he died. Only afterward, gathered to share their grief around a meal of remembrance following their day's labors on the shore of Galilee, did these disciples suddenly understand his call to live and love, for he was "more alive dying than those around them were living."

Thus Spong believes that though the eternal cannot enter this finite realm, for a moment those disciples did enter into a vivid experience of God-consciousness, which he calls "the Easter moment," or as Paul Tillich called it, "the Eternal Now." This is the new truth by which the disciples are transformed and which they return triumphantly to Jerusalem to share.

The Sin of Literalism

Why, in this view, do stories in the New Testament speak of empty tombs, angels, and a risen but still scarred body of Christ, if the experience of the eternal takes place in a silent realm beyond all words? The explanation favored by Spong is that though the experience of the eternal is beyond all words, we humans are bound to affix words to it. The first Christians were Jews who were prisoners of the inherited words and images of their tradition (*EM*, 2). They were bound to express what had happened to them by embellishing their experience with allusions to stories from traditions of the Hebrew Scriptures.

A popular current concept among scholars, which Spong applies to the resurrection, is *midrash*, which is Hebrew for "interpretation." He believes that the early Christians borrowed from traditions, popular in their time, of speculating about the coming end of the world (often called "apocalyptic" thought). But in so doing they pinned the butterfly of experience down and killed it. The writings of the New Testament are in fact a gradual witness to this murder by words, which Spong calls "literalization."

Thus, he believes that Paul knew nothing of a physical resurrection, only visions of a heavenly, ascended Christ. Mark adds the story of the empty tomb, which Matthew in turn embellishes. Luke adds yet more literalized stories, such as the risen Christ eating a piece of fish. John shows Jesus walking about, carrying on conversations. Spong argues that believers have latched onto the literal stories and not to the ineffable experience of which the stories are mythological expressions. In this regard, he goes so far as to say that "Jesus is the name given to a life of ultimate, transcendent meaning" (*RMR*, 291).

Bishop Spong makes no claim to be a New Testament scholar, but he has been doing his homework. He has read many of the great modernist figures in New Testament research: Bultmann, Raymond Brown, Reginald Fuller, and so on. He has been struck by the fact that the resurrection stories are truly varied, written over a whole generation at the end of the first century, with details that are sometimes in tension. He also believes that clergy have intentionally failed to make this fact clear to lay people and that if the lay people find it out, their faith will be crushed. So his reconstruction has a clearly apologetic purpose; he wants to make the resurrection believable to us moderns and so enable us to withstand the shock waves when we "grow up" and see the problems with the Bible.

But Spong believes that his mission is more significant than that. Literal belief in the resurrection is not benign as far as he is concerned. It is in fact a "sin" (*EM*, 101), a form of idolatry that "leads to slaughter" among human beings obsessed with control. The roles of Pilate and Caiaphas are nowadays played by "fundamentalists," by which he means anyone who assigns literal meaning to such stories. Such people are seen as motivated by anxiety and a desire to control. In short, the reinterpretation of the stories, getting behind them, or "scraping off their veneer" (*RMR*, 182) is itself seen as redemptive, as a means of participating in the "Easter moment." Once the impediments of the tradition itself are removed, we too can attain for ourselves the consciousness of eternity, even in the face of death, which was the core of what Peter, Mary, and John experienced long ago.

On the Cutting Edge of the Nineteenth Century

Bishop Spong understands himself to be a popularizer, that is, one who lays bare what the argument really means, which more careful (or wily) professional theologians may conceal. What may seem surprising to readers who have not followed debates in theology is that virtually nothing about Spong's thesis is new. The sense of excitement and surprise that Spong himself, his readers, and his opponents experience is based mainly on the fact that Anglican theology in our day has not really kept up with or assimilated the controversies of European theology of decades ago.

As far back as the 1830s, David Friedrich Strauss believed that he was saving the accounts of Jesus' resurrection from literalizers and debunkers by reading them as edifying myths about religious consciousness. In fact, what Spong calls "midrash" is virtually synonymous with what Strauss called "historical myth." At the turn of this century, Kirsopp Lake had advanced a reconstruction of resurrection events that focused on the disciples' experience in Galilee. More recently, Rudolf Bultmann declared that Christ is risen in the proclamation, which Spong has emended, in effect, to read Christ is risen in the experience of the Eucharist. Both of these statements mean that the resurrection is an event that occurred only in the minds of the disciples.

Now, the well-worn nature of an argument does not in itself prove that the argument is wrong. But it does make Spong's claims to be an intrepid pioneer of the new millennium a bit much to take. I am thinking, for example, of a comment like the following: "My readers will be able to see new possibilities, some threatening and some exhilarating... [to] live in dramatic new ways in the challenging future of the human enterprise"(*RMR*, xv).

It is helpful at this point to rehearse briefly some of the orthodox responses to this type of argument over the past century. To do that, we have to recall the historical circumstances in which the argument first began to be made. In the early nineteenth century there was an onslaught of "historical" criticism of the Bible, as a result of Enlightenment thinking. Many theologians tried to find out what lay "behind" the text in order to find some shards of meaning amid what they regarded as superstition and fantasy. They wanted to take these shards of meaning to construct a secure and separate "religious" realm, protected from the onslaught of science and modern philosophy. Most often they sought to locate religion in the recesses of experience that lie before or beyond words, recesses that cannot involve testable claims. A classic example of this trend may be found in the theology of Friedrich Schleiermacher.

In the face of the onslaught of modern philosophy, Jesus of Nazareth was a particularly embarrassing figure. Efforts were made to see him as an illustration or prime example of a religious experience about which no particular concrete claims could be made. Perhaps because many churches resisted their views, post-Enlightenment theologians tended to locate their main theological problem in the calcified, concretized, authoritarian tradition itself, rather than in any internal problems with their views. Overcoming the Christian tradition became their goal, in the pursuit of which they have tended to see themselves as heroes.

An interesting fact about the liberal theological trend that grew out of the Enlightenment is that its heightened awareness of historical context, historical relativities, and change never extends to the period in which the theologian actually lives. Spong is a good example of this. He is aware of historical context in Matthew or John, but shows little insight into his own assumptions and methods, derived from the Enlightenment. Although this stance is contradictory, it is not surprising. Enlightenment thinkers believe that their knowledge is objective, certain, and scientific, in contrast to earlier ages, which have "naive worldviews."

To be sure, Spong does protest against the inadequacy of terms like objective and subjective. But he then proceeds to reconstruct "the facts," or "what really happened," and to peel off the "legends," with unabashed Enlightenment gusto.

The result is not hard to predict. "Legend" turns out to be whatever an Enlightenment thinker cannot fit into an approved pattern. And when the body of material that an Enlightenment thinker can accept is examined, the pattern emerges clearly. At the beginning of this century, Albert Schweitzer noticed that those who searched for the "historical Jesus" were peering down a well, only to realize that the face perceived in the murky waters below was their own. This tendency is also evident in Spong's book. There, the "fact" or "reality" of the resurrection (viewed as a wordless experience) occurs when the disciples gather to share their feelings and "do grief work" over a meal, in the service of overcoming barriers. To an observer, it looks surprisingly like the bishop's own conception of his ministry. Yet Spong reveals not a glimmer of self-consciousness about his own imposition of modern ideas on ancient texts.

To the extent that Spong's picture appeals to a reader, the reader may not happen to notice that it is a contemporary one that may have nothing to do with what Jesus' disciples did after their master's death. But the purpose of this argument is not simply to criticize Spong. We must avoid falling into these same traps, of constructing a version of events that we believe simply because it suits our own modern prejudices.

Who's Afraid of Doubt?

There is another way in which Spong typifies the liberal approach to theology during the last two centuries. He believes that New Testament accounts of Jesus literally doing remarkable things are based on a pathological or immature need for certainty, for something to hold onto—the same impulse that he believes leads religion to oppress and control. Given such a view, you would think that Spong would not be particularly anxious to achieve a great deal of certainty himself. But there you would be mistaken. Spong's analysis of the evidence regarding the resurrection tolerates little doubt about what happened. On the contrary, he "knows," for example, that no one knew where Jesus' tomb was and that the visions of Jesus after his death centered in Galilee. And he tolerates no uncertainty about all the things that did not happen.

Again, when Spong turns to the meaning of Easter, he insists that Jesus' death proves that we should live and love deeply. We soon realize that such a cliché does not require a resurrection, nor even a Jesus at all. By contrast, listen to St. Paul (in 1 Cor. 15:14, NIV): "If Christ has not been raised, our preaching is useless and so is your faith." Paul admitted the possibility that he might be wrong, and he drew the correct conclusion—that Christianity would then be an illusion. Spong, on the other hand, unwilling to risk the possibility that we might be wrong, has attempted to sanitize the faith of the risk involved in claims based on what happened. In so doing he has redefined it in such a minimalist manner that it certainly cannot prove illusory or wrong—indeed, it cannot prove anything. That is the ultimate penalty of a frantic need for certainty.

The Nature of Realistic Narrative

Yet the problems with the modernist approach to the resurrection are deeper than that. Not only does the modernist want to prove that the resurrection did not happen, he also wants to prove that the New Testament matters even without the resurrection. But, as we shall see, this flies in the face of the central witness of the New Testament writings themselves.

William James recounted a student narrating a native American story of the creation according to which the earth rests on a turtle. When James predictably asked, "What's under the turtle?" The student replied, "It's turtles all the way down."

The New Testament does not merely recount the fact of the resurrection. Every account assumes the risen Christ as its starting point. In fact, every line of the New Testament is saturated with the assumption of the resurrection, even when that event does not appear in the foreground. This puts the modernist thinker in a quandary. The only source of evidence for what happened behind the text are these writings. But to mine them for historical fact, treating the accounts themselves as so many layers of myth, is to use these writings in pursuit of a purpose quite different from the one for which they were designed, namely, to engender faith and settle issues of doctrine and morals.

We, like Spong, are moderns, and we too would surely like a little more certainty, perhaps in the form of independent accounts quite free of the perspective of faith by which the Christian claim could be proved or disproved. The reality of the texts we have in hand is messier. The Gospel stories of the crucifixion and resurrection of Jesus are realistic narratives, intended to render for us, in their retelling, a character—the crucified, risen Jesus Christ. The stories are artfully, powerfully, and diversely structured to do this. But just as it is insufficient to look at these stories as legends to be uncovered for historical evidence, it would equally truncate the truth to suppose that Christianity rests on mere literary effect. The texts do refer to a reality beyond themselves, namely, the risen Christ, but in such a way that the stories make him present in their retelling.

What role is left then for historical-critical research, particularly of the sort that attempts to dissect the stories and ascertain behind the text "what really happened"? These attempts have a limited, yet necessary, role to play. Their criticisms, if sustained, could conceivably negate orthodox beliefs about the risen Jesus Christ. However, the failure of their objections cannot in itself prove the opposite: that the claims made in the New Testament are true. Passing such a critical test is a necessary condition, but not a sufficient one for Christian faith. But the test *is* necessary, for only when these questions are met can thinking people take seriously the risen Christ as the real referent of these stories.

Facing the Critique Head-On

Like Bishop Spong, my specialty is not New Testament scholarship. But I have read some of the same books as he has. With that in mind, let us look at specific objections raised to the claim that Jesus Christ rose from the dead, as well as come of the more hopeful scholarly conclusions that he ignores or soft-pedals.

1. Paul's account, which is the oldest, lacks any mention of the empty tomb. Doesn't this show that the idea of an empty tomb is a later, "literalizing" addition?

This is an argument from silence. It is weak because the cause of the silence is merely conjectured. Paul may have assumed that his readers knew the story or that Jesus' tomb was not relevant to the issues he addresses. At any rate, Paul's omission cannot mean, as Spong would have it, that Paul did not believe in a physical resurrection. Paul, as a first century Jew, assumed that any resurrection is a resurrection of the body; hence his discussion of the nature of the "spiritual body" of resurrected Christians (See Brown, *Virginal Conception and Bodily Resurrection*, p. 81ff.).

On the whole, it is hard to see why Enlightenment critics are concerned to prove that the story of the empty tomb is fabricated. There is good reason to suppose, from any one of a number of points of view, that Jesus' tomb was empty. Mary Magdalene feared at one point that his enemies had stolen his body. In turn, those enemies accused the Christians of taking it. No faction could benefit from pretending that the tomb was empty if it wasn't. Their contention could be publicly disproved. The only plausible reason for the stress in the Gospel accounts on the fact that the tomb was empty is that it really was empty. The important question is, why was it empty? Did Jesus rise, as the New Testament witnesses say, or did someone steal his body?

Some scholars argue that the evidence about Jesus' burial is mixed. For example, Mark says that Jesus was buried by a man named Joseph of Arimathea (Mark 15:42 ff.). But Paul in Acts is said to imply that he was buried by hostile persons ("When they had carried out all that the scriptures said about him, they took him down from the gibbet and laid him in a tomb" [13:29, NEB]. Thus, they assume, Joseph of Arimathea must be a legend.

A straightforward reading reveals no contradiction: one version says the Jews buried Jesus, the second provides details about the Jewish leader who took the initiative to do so. Certainly, contemporary "shock" scholars who contend that Jesus was left as carrion or thrown in an open and common grave have no evidence in support of their views (e.g., Luedemann, *What Happened to Jesus?*, p. 23).

2. The New Testament sources are contradictory—some locate Jesus' appearances after his resurrection in Galilee, and some in Jerusalem. How can both accounts be true?

Each of the New Testament authors was concerned to emphasize an aspect of Jesus' resurrection in keeping with his own emphases and perspectives. To expect the accounts to purge all such perspectives in favor of an abstract objectivity is again to assume an Enlightenment prejudice. For example, the mission to the Gentiles starts in Gentile Galilee in Mark, but it moves from Jerusalem (eventually to Rome) in Luke. When we have considered all the accounts, we are left with a tangle of appearances in both locales; the evidence can be tied into no neat bundle. But the underlying theme itself is the same: the resurrection is the commencement of the Gentile mission. In each story, as C. H. Dodd argues in his *Studies in the Gospels*, the same elements—recognition, the message of peace, joy, and a missionary mandate—are the backbone of the story. Would we really expect news of the resurrection, the shattering and unprecedented beginning of the new creation, to present itself in a neat bundle?

3. The accounts differ in detail, rendering them suspect as historical sources.

In some cases the differing details are in direct tension. For example, in one account, the risen Lord may not be touched (John 20), while in another he eats broiled fish (Luke 24:42–43). None of the New Testament accounts is an extended historical study in the modern sense. Rather, each author wants to emphasize a critical fact about the risen Jesus. For example, where a disciple would cling to the earthly Jesus, John 20:17, JB ("do not cling to me") emphasizes that Jesus now exists in a new way. But Luke, concerned perhaps that Gentile Christians might view the risen Jesus as a mere apparition (of the sort common in Greek stories of the day), recounts an incident in which he shared a meal. We are too prone to misunderstand the realities of the risen Christ, and these stories can serve for us the same role of protecting again such errors.

4. But aren't Jesus' appearances better understood as visions than as a physical resurrection?

Paul claims that in one appearance after his resurrection, Jesus was seen by five hundred people at once. What does it mean to say that this was a vision? The sociological or psychological explanations that are offered to account for it are nowhere hinted at as possibilities in the text and are distinctly modern impositions.

A question-and-answer litany like the preceding one may rebut the contentions of an author like Spong. But what is gained? Have we then proved the truth of the New Testament accounts of the resurrection of Jesus Christ? Hardly. What I hope I have shown is that the resurrection accounts cannot be dismissed out of hand, even with respect to the narrow question of "historical" veracity in the modern critical sense. In the end, the question of what to make of the resurrection cannot be decided in this arena. Early in the century, Kirsopp Lake had this to say about the traditions of the empty tomb: "The historical evidence is such that it can be fairly interpreted consistently with either of the two doctrinal positions... but it does not support either. The story of the empty tomb must be fought out on doctrinal, not on historical or critical grounds" (See Michael Ramsey, *The Resurrection of Jesus: An Essay in Biblical Theology*, p. 53). Nothing substantive has changed since that time to alter such a judgment.

A Providential Complexity

We can go a step further and offer a theological assessment, from an admittedly Christian point of view, of such an ambiguous result. Historical-critical investigation of the sort championed by Spong offers neither a knockout punch nor a proof. To paraphrase Reinhold Niebuhr's defense of democracy, it provides just enough to make faith possible and just little enough to make it necessary. Furthermore, the very mixed nature of the evidence preserves the mystery of the resurrection even while it blocks the way to false interpretations. For example, it insists on those elements that are necessary, such as Jesus' continuity of person and the connection of the resurrection with the witness of the Old Testament. At the same time, it is significant that the witnesses to the resurrection in the canonical Gospels offer no description of the event itself. (There are accounts in the apocryphal gospels, whose untrustworthiness is in part demonstrated by this very inclusion of florid accounts of the event.)

The account of the empty tomb makes clear that a bodily resurrection occurred, which prevents us from spiritualizing the event. But the accounts of Jesus' appearances prevent us from making an easy equation between Jesus' resurrected body and our own present bodies. Together, they define subtly the contours of our knowledge of the resurrection so that we can talk meaningfully about it without encroaching on its mystery. There is a providential dimension in the very complexity of the evidence itself.

What Difference Does the Difference Make?
Another way in which Spong's views prove edifying is the light they shed on the key issue: Was Jesus bodily raised?

The most obvious reason that the notion of a bodily resurrection is offensive to Spong is that it is miraculous, and so his Enlightenment assumptions are offended. But there is more to it than that. Spong assumes that God's timeless eternity cannot act directly in the temporal order. He associates the claim of a bodily resurrection with the process of literalization, which, he believes, is also tied to an oppressive way of thinking and acting. In other words, his resistance to the idea is linked to an array of highly debatable related ideas.

Some may ask, what difference does it make which view is right? The claim that Jesus was raised bodily, though it does create an element of mystery as to the way in which his body now exists, is necessary to the Christian tradition for three reasons. First of all, you and I know what death is. Even across lines of cultural difference, amid diverse beliefs about life after death, dead is dead in any language. The New Testament clearly means to assert that the resurrection is the decisive victory over death, one in which we too will come to share. Only a bodily resurrection can offer hope for our mortal bodies; St. Paul makes just this point vigorously in 1 Corinthians 15. On our contemporary scene Caroline Bynum, in her magisterial work, *The Resurrection of the Body in Western Christianity,* which is an extended study of the resistance of Christian faith toward false spiritualization, stresses that "analysis of current philosophical discourse and of contemporary popular culture suggest that Americans, like medieval pets and theologians, consider any survival that really counts to entail survival of the body" (p. 15). On this one count at least, our culture is in line with the scriptural sense of the matter.

The second reason is linked to the first. The body makes individual identity and particularity possible. For this reason, the bodily resurrection of Jesus affirms that he is the primary focus of God's act and that we are recipients of the effects of the event at a second remove. Otherwise, it is easy for the resurrection to be seen as something that happens primarily to us, with Jesus as a mere illustration.

By now it should be clear that if the resurrection is an event like no other, we cannot separate the question of whether Jesus could have been raised from the question of who Jesus was (and is). The two questions must be answered together. Which brings us to the third affirmation, which is inextricably bound to the bodily resurrection of Jesus. To affirm that God brought Jesus back from the dead is to attribute to God something only comparable to the act of bringing the world out of nothingness in the beginning of time.

Creation and End

The word *resurrection,* as used in Jewish tradition at the time of Jesus, was an event expected at the end of time, in keeping with the prophecies of Daniel. In the language of theology, the term *resurrection* is "eschatological," meaning that it has to do with the end of the world. Spong attempts in each of his books about the resurrection to peel away the apocalyptic or eschatological dimension, but one might as well peel an onion. In other words, to claim that Jesus was raised from the dead is to link this moment in the closest theological way with both the Creation and the new creation, with the beginning and the end, with the bringing of the created, bodily world into being, and with its consummation destined by God. So in the book of Revelation we hear the risen Jesus say, "Fear not, I am the first and the last, and the living one. I died, and behold I am alive for evermore, and I have the keys of Death and Hades" (1:17–18).

To say that Jesus was not bodily raised is to disconnect the God of the Old Testament from his action in creating the world. Likewise, to think of the resurrected Jesus as a mere apparition has implications for the vision one has of God's consummation of the world. For as the body of Jesus exists in a resurrected state, so we must think of the glorified bodily status of the redeemed in the kingdom of God. If Jesus is not bodily raised, then we cannot understand God's final intention for the world to include the healing of the created, "bodily" order. The implications, for example, for contemporary efforts in ecological theology are not hard to fathom.

We must, again, emphasize that Spong understands his own motive to be apologetic in the sense that he hopes to defend the faith from scoffers by way of revision. But Spong is not proposing a different, weaker version of the resurrection. Rather, he is proposing no version of it at all. It is incontrovertible that the writers of the New Testament assumed that a resurrection must be a resurrection of the body. To speak intelligibly and coherently of resurrection entails, at least implicitly, a bodily aspect. Otherwise, as we have seen, the weave of claims that Christians make about creation, redemption, and the final consummation unravels rapidly.

Valentinus Back from the Grave

Spong is not the first thinker who has longed for a spiritual version of the Christian gospel, one that could make the message of Christ intelligible and palatable to his contemporaries. Long before John Spong, there lived someone who was offended by the coarse literalism of the Scriptures, who meant to find the real message beneath the text. He too wanted to bring the good news to searchers turned off by the institutional church. His name was Valentinus, and he was a Gnostic Christian. At the time, his ideas were viewed by many as progressive, but in the long run they were deemed heretical. For in the end, the church saw that the Gnostic attempt to rewrite the faith so as to include a bodiless resurrection cuts out any real hope of redemption we might have. Such is the "cruelty of heresy" (C. FitzSimons Allison). (The irony here is, of course, that Spong sees himself as a champion of a renewed sense of the Hebraic nature of the gospel even while he is excising the very "embodiment" that has usually been considered quintessentially Hebraic!)

Operations to reverse the fleshliness of the covenant are rarely successful, and Spong's is not an exception. The interesting thing is that those who would even attempt such an operation often champion causes that appear to be a liberation of the body—in the case of John Spong, sexual liberation, for example. But there is a surprising link between denial of a bodily resurrection and support of such causes. Despite its guise of affirming the body, sexual liberation politics involves a refusal to see the disposition of our bodies as truly integral to our spiritual lives. That refusal involves a denial, not an affirmation, that our bodies are ourselves, even before God.

By contrast, the traditional theology of marriage takes the union of bodies as heavily freighted with spiritual significance. It is a true theology of "embodiment." Likewise, Spong's facile advocacy of the now fashionable right-to-die movement reveals the same disregard for the spiritual significance of our bodies. The reason that we Christians are not free to do as we please with our bodies is that they are the locus of God's work in us. They must be conformed to his crucifixion and resurrection, for the sake of our being "reclothed" for eternity (2 Cor. 5:1 ff.). Spong's attack on the bodily resurrection raises far-ranging questions about the context and consequences of his other pet projects.

Slouching Toward Jerusalem

A striking fact about Spong's work is that, interspersed with all the modernist reinterpretations, doubts, and debunking, he struggles to give some substance to the reality of the "Easter moment." Perhaps those attempts are only homiletical vestiges, flourishes he has retained from the tradition in spite of himself. For example, he writes that "Jesus is alive in the heart of God," and that "death could not contain him" (*EM*, p. 257, 156). Perhaps these are only meant metaphorically, as if to say that the memory of Jesus is irrepressible, in the same way that some revolutionary might insist that "Che lives!" Perhaps. But it may also be that for all his revisionism, Spong is driven by the problem of explaining what New Testament scholar Martin Dibelius called the "X," the something that transformed the disciples. This drives him to say some things that undercut his whole revisionist project, if indeed one is to take his words seriously. In the process, Spong, in spite of himself, points us back toward reclaiming the orthodox affirmation of the resurrection of Jesus Christ.

If it is true that death could not contain Jesus, then God can enter into time and space even as he remains God. And once one has affirmed this, one is halfway down the road to the orthodox doctrine of the Trinity. If Jesus, once dead and now risen, is in God, then the relationship of body and soul, the destiny of the human person, and the relationship of time and eternity must all be radically rethought. This rethinking is what we call Christian theology.

If Jesus was raised from the dead, then to assert as Bishop Spong does that humans live in time but God is timeless—as if that were an impenetrable wall between the two—must be incorrect. The wall, it turns out, is penetrable, though only from God's side. The great twentieth-century theologian Karl Barth puts the matter this way: "[Jesus] was the concrete demonstration of the God who has not only a different time from that of man, but whose will and resolve it is to give man a share in this time of His, in His eternity" (*Church Dogmatics,* III/II, p. 451).

The entrance of God's eternity into time is expressed in the New Testament in terms of the invasion, or the anticipation, of God's kingdom. It prefigures here and now the consummation of creation under the manifest lordship of God. For this reason, in the twentieth century theology has been characterized in large part as reflection on Christian eschatology. In other words, the rethinking of time and eternity consequent to the resurrection must take the form of a rethinking of the relationship of the present (and past) to the future. And this rethinking is incumbent on Christians only because Jesus Christ, who lived an earthly life and died an earthly death, is now alive, the New Testament says, in the very mode in which the whole world will exist in the kingdom of God.

The kingdom of God has begun to dawn in the midst of this dying world: who can express exhaustively what that means? John Spong is quite right when he emphasizes at the outset of his works that God is more wonderful than human words can express. But this does not mean that God remains an unknowably numinous blank, which we fill in with talk about ourselves, our experience, or our consciousness, as if we were chattering nervously with the Sphinx. No, what makes God wonderful is precisely what God has done and revealed, namely, Jesus risen from the dead and standing among his followers.

Theology, in other words, does not start at a loss for words and use Jesus as an illustration. On the contrary, it starts with the resurrected Jesus bringing the shalom of the Kingdom into our world. It tumbles over itself, struggling for words and concepts to describe that wonderful event. In short, Christian theology, in contrast to efforts like Spong's, is always, to use Karl Barth's term, "thinking after" (literally, Nachdenken), following along in our minds after the event, redefining terms in the wake of what God did in Jesus of Nazareth. So, though we may find occasional overlaps, Spong's project moves in the diametrically wrong direction. The popularity of his conclusions may be seen (again profitably) as God's chastisement of a church that too long sloughed along without the rigor of theological "following after."

Thinking in the Wake of Easter

Reflection on the resurrection cannot be confined to scholarly scrutiny of a few passages at the end of the Gospels, as if the rest of the New Testament were about something else. Every word is an exposition of the resurrection, for every word shows how past events, present hardships, and future hopes appear to the first Christians in the light of the fact that Jesus rose bodily from the dead. Jesus is not a dead man they remember fondly. He is viewed as present, among other things, in the reflecting and the writing itself. Bearing that in mind, we can see more easily how seemingly contradictory and diverse passages all convey, each in its own context and answering its own question, the one reality of the risen Christ. In other words, to believe that Jesus rose from the dead and to believe that the scriptural accounts are inspired are implications one of the other. And neither survives scrutiny if the other does not.

To the extent that the resurrection permeates the New Testament witness as its premise, power, and purpose, then in contemporary defenses of the resurrection, we require nothing short of an interpretation of reality, a reconstruction of the world. Far from being one subject among others, the resurrection is the starting point for a systematic exposition of all the subjects with which theology concerns itself: Who is God? Who are we? What is the church? What is the Christian hope?

The resurrection also requires an ongoing engagement with secular thought. Can we as followers of the risen One believe, for example, in a cooling, dying, random universe? If creation is the arena for such an act of God as the resurrection, what concepts of time and space might we expect? Interestingly, the new physics, with its more expansive, open, mysterious view of the material universe, would seem for the Christian to be a world that accords with the reality of the resurrection better than the (apparently exploded) nineteenth-century materialist view. In this regard the modern reformed theologian Thomas Torrance, for example, has endeavored to show precisely how modern notions of space and time in the theory of relativity can be useful in helping us to imagine how the resurrection is a "new kind of historical happening which instead of tumbling down into the grave and oblivion rises out of the death of what is past into continuing being and reality" (*Space, Time and Resurrection*, pp. 88–89).

This does not mean that we should expect proofs of the resurrection to emerge, for we have begun with the resurrection as a premise. But we can expect an array of suggestive analogies and convergencies from a wide variety of sciences and arts.

Back from the Future

No "facts" will render superfluous the faith from which Christian understanding moves. One can perhaps speak of proof, or "verification," in the eschatological sense: before the throne of the Lamb slain who lives, the whole created order will offer self-evident confirmation. But to speak, as the contemporary theologian (an apologist for the truth of the resurrection) Wolfhart Pannenberg does, of "eschatological verification" is rather to commit oneself to an ongoing process of radical redefinition and openness to agreements especially with philosophy and natural science.

Does the fact that we do not look for proof mean that faith in the resurrection is irrational? Only if we suppose that we can know only those things that the natural sciences can prove. It would be safe to say that the history of philosophy in our century has been one long and multifarious demonstration of the foolishness of such an idea. A cursory survey of personal truths (e.g., of the reality of love, or of the existence of one's own mind) that we believe but cannot prove will attest to this. No, belief in the resurrection shows itself to be altogether rational just in those repeated, hopeful, searching forays in conversation with the other disciplines I have just mentioned.

Christian theology, the science of the resurrection, is a rational and credible enterprise in this dying world that is also the real world in which Jesus was raised. The supposedly strict Enlightenment dichotomy between proof and irrationality offered by figures like John Spong is merely quaint.

To diagnose the trouble, to represent a bygone era, to punish a theologically forgetful church, to call us to historical-critical work without fear, to lay bare the central issue, to illustrate a tempting false path, to suggest, even in spite of himself, a real solution, and in doing so to highlight the nature of Christian theology as a whole: for all these services, in all these respects, we should thank John Spong. The church, however, has always looked to its bishops to be defenders and teachers of the faith. It has traditionally hoped for more from them than mere hints of truth.

Works Considered or Consulted

Allison, C. FitzSimons. *The Cruelty of Hersey*. Harrisburg: Morehouse, 1994.

Barth, Karl. *Church Dogmatics*, III/I. Edinburgh: T & T Clark, 1960.

Brown, Raymond. *The Virginal Conception and Bodily Resurrection of Jesus*. New York: Paulist, 1973.

Frei, Hans. *The Identity of Jesus Christ*. Philadelphia: Fortress, 1967.

Jenson, Robert. *The Triune Identity*. Philadelphia: Fortress, 1982.

Pannenberg, Wolfhart. *Jesus—God and Man*. Philadelphia: Westminster, 1977.

Ramsey, Michael. *The Resurrection of Jesus: An Essay in Biblical Theology*. Philadelphia: Westminster, 1946.

Torrance, Thomas. *Space, Time and Resurrection*. Grand Rapids: Eerdmans, 1976.

The Joy of (Newark) Sex

David A. Scott

BISHOPS SHOULD BE TEACHERS OF THE FAITH, and Bishop Spong should be commended for being an active teacher. Through his writings— but also through speeches, debates and sermons— he has sought to fulfill the teaching office of the bishop. Clearly, he has the courage of his convictions, because he speaks out even when he knows that his views will provoke anger and rejection.

However, when it comes to the doctrines he is actually teaching in the area of sexuality, I must identify two fundamental weaknesses.

First, Bishop Spong's thought about sexuality is marred by fatalism. According to his book *Living in Sin? A Bishop Rethinks Human Sexuality,* my primary resource for Bishop Spong's beliefs on the subject, technology and social change act as controlling forces that neither the church nor anyone else can resist. In terms that recall Karl Marx, he insists that the church must adjust and accommodate—or be destroyed. In Spong's universe, the most powerful force does not seem to be God or the church, but social and cultural change.

As a result, it is not always clear whether Spong advances his ideas about sexuality because he believes that they are in accord with God's will or because he believes that the church will be rejected and die if it does not attune its teaching to modern assumptions. Assuring the church's survival as an institution seems to be Spong's chief goal. I will return to this point later.

The second and more serious criticism of Spong's teachings on sexuality is that his understanding of the Christian message which underlies his teaching on sex is not truly Christian. He uses Christian terminology; indeed, he invokes the language of the Christian dogma of the Holy Trinity and the incarnation of the Word in his teaching about sex in this book. But he reduces the meaning of the Christian message to mean "life is good, that everything that is shares in the divine origin and must therefore be celebrated and affirmed" (*LS*, 156). In my opinion, this is a heretical statement of the Christian message, since it leaves out the themes of sin and redemption that are part of the Christian creeds and all traditional summaries of Christian faith. Further, it is hard to take his statement of Christianity's message at face value, since many things that are, for example poverty, illness and injustice should not be "celebrated and affirmed." Indeed, a reader of Spong's statement of the Bible's message must wonder how he understands that statement, because he finds so much in the world that cannot be "celebrated and affirmed."

For example, his central teaching is that there needs to be an affirmation of life, an expansion of life, and a surpassing of imposed limits. This is actually reminiscent of the beliefs of that great modern critic of Christianity, Friedrich Nietzsche. The Nietzschean flavor of Spong's work is not in itself very surprising. Nietzsche's views are deeply imbedded in the fabric of modern thought. They are widely held in one form or another, even by people who have never read a word of that brilliant philosopher, poet, and social critic. Even many people who claim to disapprove of Nietzsche actually hold views substantially similar to his.

A third issue is that Bishop Spong denigrates those who hold views different from his own. I will substantiate that charge later in this chapter, but let me give an example of Spong's "put-down" rhetoric from the opening paragraph of the book's first chapter. There he says his book is not about sex but about prejudice, the prejudice of those dominant groups who use sexual attitudes, taboos and practices to keep others subordinate. "The guiding principle is to ensure the comfort, the convenience, the happiness and the well-being of the dominant ones" (*LS*, 23). The obvious rhetorical intent of this paragraph is to imply that anyone who contradicts Bishop Spong's views on this subject is motivated by prejudice, i. e., a desire to protect a position of social dominance and to subordinate others. I submit that the actual effect of this "put-down" rhetoric is to poison waters of Christian dialogue and to hurt people who disagree with Bishop Spong.

What Spong Actually Teaches on Sex

Changing Moral Norms Are Inevitable

As I mentioned earlier, for Spong, changes in the sexual beliefs and practices of the society around us are normative—that is, they tell the church what it ought to think and do. Thus, he believes that the church should affirm new patterns of sexual attitudes and relations because secular society is doing it.

Bishop Spong asserts that contemporary patterns of sexual behavior are here to stay, that there can be no return to earlier patterns of sexual relating. "The alternative of returning to the sexual patterns of the distant past, however, is no longer open to us," says Spong (*LS*, 52). Perhaps because he believes this, Spong's views about sexuality are curiously pervaded by the language of the law and inevitability. For example, when Spong cites Genesis and God's calling created life good at Creation, Spong immediately transforms the divine affirmation into a moral law of affirm your life, enhance your life, actualize your potential (see *LS*, 156–160).

For Spong, the most important recent shift in sexual attitudes is away from "the patriarchal mind-set" toward a new appreciation of the value of the feminine. When Spong speaks of this shift, which he calls "the sexual revolution," he means to imply a basic change in human consciousness—or, to use an overworked expression, a paradigm shift. For example: "At the heart of these swirling tides of change there is a primary shift in the understanding of the proper balance of power between men and women. The organizing rule of life in the past has been the patriarchal mind-set" (*LS*, 41).

Spong believes that human culture as a whole has been shaped for millennia by the patriarchal mind-set, by a "male mentality," a "masculine spirit," or the "reign of male domination." This patriarchal mind-set may have been culturally useful in human cultural evolution at one point. But now, Spong says, humanity is aware of the lethal potential of that mind-set and everywhere it is being rejected. (*LS*, 42.)

It is important to grasp that for Spong the cultural rejection of the patriarchal mentality is not so much a prophetic moral insight as it is the inevitable result of social evolution and the instinct of species survival. "The quest for survival of the human race has brought all of these definitions [of the patriarchal mind-set] into question. As the need to change becomes more urgent, every sexual pattern based upon these definitions will begin to fall" (*LS*, 24).

Like Nietzsche, Spong views society and history as ruled by the evolutionary drive for survival; the moral values of any epoch reflect that struggle. Spong seems unaware that the evolutionary struggle for human planetary survival functions in his theology in the same way as divine providence does for Christians, that is, as the final guiding principle of history.

Spong is, in fact, a fatalist in relation to cultural trends: humans are helpless before them; we must accommodate or die. For example, when the biological age of sexual maturity for girls decreases, he decrees that traditional Christian norms of abstinence before marriage must change. "Moral law must be in harmony with nature" (*LS*, 50).

With the rejection of the patriarchal mind-set comes the rejection of all patriarchal sexual norms, norms that described the man as dominant, as the breadwinner, the warrior, the protector of hearth and home, and women as submissive. According to Spong, these roles denied woman almost all her strengths, restricting her role to that of wife and mother. These norms denigrated homosexuals as well and privileged male definitions of values.

All such norms are doomed, he writes, no matter how hard the forces of patriarchy, acting from fear, the desire to control and contain, want to retain those values. "The tide [of the sexual revolution] became inexorable" (*LS*, 51).

Spong's conclusion is clear: There can be no return to the moral values of the patriarchal age. We live in an era when men and women are redefining who they are, with a new consciousness and new knowledge. The church must not fight for the values of the patriarchal era but must undertake the contemporary quest for new moral values that "will engage the lives of all people."

Why should the church do this? Only in this way will the church have credibility as a relevant institution. Here emerges Spong's underlying motivation: the survival of the church in the modern age. The church must change its moral teaching so that it won't be rejected by modern people: "The time has come for the church, if it wishes to have any credibility as a relevant institution, to look at the issues of single people, divorcing people, post-married people and gay and lesbian people from the point of view removed from the patriarchal patterns of the past, and to help these people find a path that leads to a life-affirming holiness" (*LS*, 53).

Divorce Is Not Always Evil

The change in commitments that Spong wishes the church to undertake is very great, and it is important to understand the implications of what he is asking for. For example, when he says that divorce is not always evil, he does not mean merely that it can be the lesser of two evils. Rather, he means that divorce is actually neutral in itself. It may be a positive good if it is the means by which one partner—he usually has the woman in mind—can attain a fuller life. This observation indicates Spong's deepest moral commitment: enhancement of life, understood as individual self-actualization, together with species survival.

The high incidence of divorce, Spong teaches, is a price we must pay for the emancipation of women in our society. He believes that women's emancipation is a good thing. But whether we like or don't like it is actually irrelevant. Because it is a component of a shift in the sexual power balance in culture and society, and it will happen whether we like it or not, it is a law to which Spong believes we must submit.

In addition to believing that the emancipation of women requires freer access to divorce, Spong also thinks that the church's teaching against divorce was actually intended to support male domination of women. "For the church not to recognize that its traditional moral codes rise out of, enforce and interpret a system of male oppression of women is irresponsible" (*LS*, 66).

Not only should the church stop condemning divorce as wrong, Spong devotes a chapter to the idea that it should develop liturgies to be used by and for divorcing persons. Such a service is "needed by the church as a pastoral tool, to be used in appropriate situations to bring the grace, love, and forgiveness of God to a common human experience of brokenness and pain. [Such a service] would also be a symbol of the church's willingness to surrender its power position as the dispenser of moral judgment and the custodian of community standards" (*LS*, 193).

It is worth noting in passing that Spong is oblivious to an observation made by many feminists today: Jesus' (and the church's) traditionally strict teaching against divorce have tended to protect women from the impact of divorce on them. While granting with Spong that church teaching has often been sexist and hurtful to women, the teachings about divorce are not a particularly good example of that problem.

Homosexuality Is a Part of Life
Spong believes that sexual orientation is "part of the essential nature" of a person and that 10 percent of the world's population is homosexual. The expression of shared love, even between two persons of the same gender cannot, says Spong, be wrong, "if that experience calls both partners into a fuller state of being." That important phrase, "a fuller state of being," points yet again to Spong's most fundamental moral standard: will to being, will to life.

He asserts that homosexual orientation arises, probably biologically, in the very earliest stages of a fetus's development. Thus, homosexuality is like left-handedness, not something abnormal but "a reflection of the rich variety of human life."

Because couples of the same gender can express love through their sexual relating, Spong argues that the church should bless their commitments. Indeed, he devotes a chapter to arguing for the blessing of gay and lesbian commitments. Thus, for Spong, the solemn act of church blessing aims at supporting, stabilizing, and undergirding "life" (*LS*, 200).

Marriage Is the Ideal and Celibacy Is an Option
Spong holds that marriage is the single most important human relationship (*LS*, 167), the standard against which every other relationship should be measured (*LS*, 170). Marriage should be marked, however, by mutuality between the partners, not the subordination of wife to husband. Spong also believes that the church should serve as a larger family into which the besieged nuclear family might fit. He endorses celibacy as the right choice for some, so long as it is freely chosen.

Of course, Spong would not restrict the marriage bond to heterosexual couples. But he believes that the goals sought in marriage should be the norm for other relationships. For him, the "primary ethical commitment is directed toward nurturing the fullness of life in individuals as well as society at large within whatever limits life places before them" (LS, 175). Again, the primary concern is the affirmation of "life."

Betrothal Is an Idea Whose Time Has Come

By betrothal, Spong means a relationship that is faithful, committed, and public but not legal or necessarily lifelong. Spong thinks many young people are practicing betrothal already. They live together with full sexual intimacy, are not legally married, and may break up, but while they are together, they are sexually faithful to one another.

He has high hopes for the social effect of church support for his notion of betrothal. "The radical suggestion that the institution of betrothal should be revised and offered by the church as a symbol of responsible commitment will send shock waves through a generation that is quite sure that religion in general and the church in particular has nothing of substance to offer their lives" (LS, 187). Spong is very anxious that young, progressive people should stop rejecting the church.

Spong says, however, that couples in a relationship of betrothal should not have children, because children morally deserve "the nurture available in and the security provided by a legal bond of marriage with permanence of commitment being the expectation of both the father and the mother" (LS, 178). Spong believes that this limitation on betrothal is easily dealt with through contraceptive technology because" conception [is now] safely separated from sexual activity" (LS, 182). We will return to that claim later.

In developing his ideas about betrothal, he castigates the church's sexual teachings as a "control system" that uses guilt as its weapon (LS, 181). Spong's main reason for advocating betrothal is to "uphold the goodness of sexuality and affirm responsible and discriminating uses of that godly gift."

There Is Holy Sex for Post-Married Singles

Another sexual relationship Spong wants to encourage is between older persons who never married, who have divorced, or who lost their partner through death. Wherever sex "enhances life," Spong wants to call it good (LS, 210). Virginity is, for him, an expression of an evil system of oppression (*LS*, 211). For economic reasons, older persons may not want to enter a legal marriage. Yet they may wish to express their love sexually with another single adult. He argues that the church should affirm the moral rightness of such sexual relations under the right circumstances: when the relationship is one of love and caring, when relations express a prior love and caring, and when the sexual intimacy remains very private and exclusive.

Throughout his discussion of holy sex between post-marrieds, Spong castigates the church for refusing to step down from its moral superiority and arrogance in claiming to define morality and in not affirming that such sex can be holy. Further, he reiterates his theme that the church's failure to abandon its irrelevant moral judgments is not only futile but risks discrediting the church. His greatest anxiety, as we have seen, is that the church will not be respected by modern people.

Spong's Asssumptions

The Authority and Interpretation of the Bible

Bishop Spong devotes the whole of the second part of his book on sex to the Bible. His remarks indicate his awareness that the Bible continues to be an authoritative guide for Christian teaching and life. He opens the section by portraying those who consider the Bible an authority as "frightened religious people" who quote the Bible "in support of their opinion [to be] justified, vindicated, proud and right." He paints them as inerrantists who use the Bible to give themselves a sense of stability and security against change. He describes them as filled with hostility and anger that "reveal their runaway anxiety and insecurity" (*LS*, 92).

Since this is the way he believes the Bible is used on matters of sexual morality, he needs to tell the reader what it is really about. The Bible is "a sacred source" that needs to be freed from its "literalistic imprisonment." He wants to attack a "literalistic and magical view of Holy Scripture that [he believes] imprisons the real truth of the Bible" (*LS*, 93).

The Bible, in his view, is a collection of stories written at different times by different people for different reasons. Stories were collected in opposition to opinions that needed to be contended against. Each writer of the Bible writes from his or her own assumptions; we don't understand a passage in question until we understand those assumptions and the opposition the biblical writer had in mind.

Spong illustrates this view of the Bible and its interpretation by discussing biblical views on women. The whole Bible is biased against women, Spong says. The reason is that the Bible reflects a struggle between a male-dominant religion, Yahwism, and a female-centered religion, Baalism. Out of this struggle, "the biblical writers adopted their pervasive anti-female bias that permeates every page of their Scriptures" (*LS*, 120). This bias passed into Christianity. Since, says Spong," we do make God in our own image," Christians have accepted the anti-woman bias into their theology and morality.

Spong's understanding and interpretation of Scripture is the subject of another chapter in this book. Here I wish to focus only on how he uses the Bible on the topic of sexuality. We have seen that, in general, he assigns himself the task of rescuing the Bible from the hands of those who misuse it out of base psychological motives.

The rescue attempt employs the strategy of showing the reader that the Bible was not dictated by God but is the result of a human religious movement, Yahwism, which opposed another human religious movement, Baalism. Knowing this, the reader will presumably be freed from reading the Bible literally or believing it is inerrant. And the reader will understand that the Bible is controlled by a patriarchal, anti-woman bias.

The Word of God in the Words of the Bible

Does this mean that the Bible has no truth for us at all? Not at all, says Spong. Rather, one must discern the Word of God in the words of the Bible (*LS*, 156). Spong identifies three such words of God. He describes them, in a way reminiscent of the Christian doctrine of the Trinity, as the word of God in Creation (*LS*, 158); the word of God in Christ (*LS*, 160); and God's word "seen and heard through the Spirit" (*LS*, 162)

The Word of the Father is the Word of God, the Creator. That word is that creation is good; life is good. Life is to be cherished. The Word of the Christ, who is God's Word, is to make that goodness real and apparent. Jesus reveals God as the giver of life. The Word of the Son is really the moral imperative to "live fully, freely, and openly, scaling the barriers that inhibit life, escaping the straitjacket of someone else's or my own stereotype of who I am" (*LS*, 160).

To say that Jesus is the truth means that Jesus was free to know who he is and had the courage to be himself (*LS*, 161–162). The Word of God as Jesus, therefore, is a call for an individual to be his or her whole self, without apology, without boasting.

The Word of God the Holy Spirit is a call into community. God's Word as Spirit calls each creature into community because "a sense of corporate identity... enhances and enriches our individuality" (*LS*, 162). The Holy Spirit is the life-giving breath of God that animates and vitalizes the creation. The holiness of the Holy Spirit is the wholeness of human life to which the Holy Spirit calls each person in community.

According to Spong, those who can discover these Words of God in the Bible will be able to change and grow in the realm of sexual relations and in every other realm.

The underlying assumption behind Spong's teaching on sexual ethics and the Bible is that the Words of God, as described here, can be discovered in and through the words of the Bible, but they are not the literal words of the Bible.

However, we can identify one word as expressing the fundamental value, the basic norm, of Spong's theology. That word is *life*. By *life* Spong means creaturely vitality and especially human vitality unfolding in history. Included in human vitality would be the fact of biological life. But Spong especially means that fullness of life that comes through each person actualizing all his or her potential in community.

Thus, Spong's core commitment is to what might be called personal vitalism, the sheer phenomenon of life, especially life appearing as human persons. Anything that encourages created life and its flourishing is good. Any idea, group or institution that in any way questions, opposes, or challenges a person's life or style of life is evil.

Assessing Spong's Teaching on Sex

The Demeaning of Those Who Disagree
The style of a person's argument, which includes how he or she describes those who might hold a different opinion, is a moral issue in itself.

As I indicated earlier, Christian moral dialogue should be marked by respect for those who might hold another opinion. But Bishop Spong's teaching on sexual morality in his book *Living in Sin?* unfortunately lacks any trace of this respect. I have quoted enough statements to demonstrate Spong's dismissive and abusive comments about those who might disagree with him. It is surely significant that nowhere in his book does Spong cite a source to justify his imputation of the evil motives in those who differ from him. Spong describes those who disagree with him in two abusive ways. First, he describes those against whom he writes as driven by a need to control and impose their moral views on others (see *LS*, 23). Second, he "psychologizes" their condition by saying they are driven by fear (*LS*, 23) or even by a more pernicious motive: to instill inappropriate guilt in others (*LS*, 180–181).

Further, he employs an unworthy rhetoric in protecting himself against possible critics. According to him, if his book is read "only by the faithful remnant and those ecclesiastical persons who work to keep that remnant secure, then it will face attack, ridicule, and deliberate misrepresentation" (*LS*, 228). In other words, Spong implies that his fellow Christians, bishops, clergy and laity, are incapable of reading his work objectively and charitably—and that they simply could not have objective disagreements with him.

Maybe he meant to say only that some persons in the church will subject him to uncharitable treatment or be unable to listen to what he is saying. But as he does not nuance his statement, it is either insulting as it stands or careless writing.

For anyone in the least acquainted with the proper methods of intellectual exchange, not to say the norms of civility and respect required of Christians talking to others, Bishop Spong's "put-down" rhetoric makes me embarrassed for the church and angry.

Spong's Reading of the Bible on Sexuality
We saw that for Spong, the Word of God, Father, Son and Spirit, was the affirmation of life. The whole biblical witness, Spong says, is the affirmation of life; life is good and we are morally obliged to serve the development of life.

There are two major shortcomings with this reading of the Bible. The first is that it abstracts the biblical witness of God's affirmation of his creation from the rest of the biblical story. That God calls his creation good is certainly true—in the Genesis creation stories. But the Bible does not stop there. The story of the Fall follows, and then the stories of God's passionate and suffering engagement with sinful humanity. For, as we all know, the Bible also teaches that human life has fallen from its original right relation to God. One result is that human vitality is distorted and self-contradictory.

To say that the Bible teaches us to "affirm life" either is so abstract as to be meaningless or it invites the question: whose life, whose vitality should be affirmed? Suppose a cash-starved city council must choose, for example, between funding a care home for Alzheimer victims, a support program for abused women, or a sports stadium for promising young athletes? Has the Bible no specific guidance to give apart from the shallow platitude that we should "affirm life"? The Bible would hardly rank as a book of even ordinary wisdom if it did not acknowledge the inescapable difficulties in affirming life that are created by mortality and human limitations.

And if the concern is that modern people will not take the church seriously if it maintains its traditional witness, consider this. A message as simplistic as "affirm life" also makes the church vulnerable to repudiation by anyone over thirty who knows that "life"—human life, individual life, social life—is extraordinarily ambivalent and ambiguous.

The richness of the Bible's teaching about life is wholly absent from Spong. The true life that the Bible speaks of is Jesus' life in relation to the Father, made available to us only at the cost of Jesus' death on the cross and resurrection by the Father. The rich, deep, paradoxical portrayal of human life in the Bible, culminating in the life of Jesus, cannot be crudely reduced to the maxim: "Affirm Life." That simplistic message robs the Bible and the Christian message of its rich, attractive, dramatic depth. Men and women have been drawn to the Bible partly because it speaks of life and death; hope and despair; fullness and emptiness; resurrection and the cross.

The most likely explanation, in my opinion, for the naïve and shallow rendition of biblical teaching that Spong offers is that he has ruled out the Bible's specific teachings on sexuality as valueless in principle. We saw that Spong tries to show that the whole

Bible is simply a reflection of a conflict between Baalism and Yahwism, resulting in a teaching that denigrates women. If that is all the Bible is and has to offer, at least in the Old Testament, then one wonders why Spong seeks any word of truth at all in the Bible. For that matter, if the Bible's teaching on sex is so driven by an evil ideology of Yahwism, it is unclear to me why Spong calls it a "sacred source" and turns to the New Testament for a Word of God. Spong's use of the Bible is discussed by others in this volume, but I am left with the question whether his appeal to the Bible coheres with his portrayal of it as suffused with the ideology of patriarchy.

However much Spong may want to enlist the Bible as an authority for his beliefs, to sum up its teachings as "affirming life" is wholly inadequate to its actual teachings about life. But if we are seeking a source for Spong's root value of affirming life, there are several likely sources from our popular contemporary culture.

One source is evolutionary biology, which describes all life as the dynamic, forward-moving process of competition and adaptation of life forms. In this context, "affirm life" is not a divine command or a moral norm but simply a fact about all forms of life on earth.

Another source is nineteenth- and twentieth-century romantic philosophies of life. Examples are Bergson's concept of the *élan vital*, Schopenhauer's concept of the world as will and manifestation, Bernard Shaw's "Life Force," and Nietzsche's idea of reality as the will to power, as well as his notion, developed in *The Birth of Tragedy*, of "the Primal Mother, eternally creative, eternally impelling into life."

Another strand comes from modern humanistic psychology, which speaks of unconditional regard of others in the therapeutic relationship and of self-actualization. "Do your own thing," "I gotta be me," and "Be yourself" are all slogans summing up the contemporary secular ideology of human-centered self-affirmation. Various New Age movements also speak of the divinity suffusing all of nature as the immanent life force.

Spong refers to the Bible and uses the traditional Trinitarian language of Father, Son, and Holy Spirit. But in content, his teaching is identical to these modern philosophies of "affirmation of life." I call them "sub-Christian" because their response to the nature and problem of evil is typically poorly developed or nonexistent.

One outcome of importing the pagan wisdom of modernity, the modern "affirmation of life," into his plan for the church is that Spong has nothing new to say to modern secular people; all he has to say is that God agrees with them in their affirmation of life.

Keeping It Simple

Spong questions the Bible as a resource for specific teaching on sexual ethics because he believes that the whole Bible is controlled by Yahwism, which is patriarchal, sexist, and homophobic. Nevertheless, he wants biblical authority for his own teaching, which means that he must reduce the Bible's meaning to "affirmation of life." But such a reduction is really the importation into the Bible, or the imposition on it, of modern views about the self-assertion of human vitality.

The result, as we saw earlier, is that Spong's views on marriage, homosexuality, divorce, and living together are driven by the simplistic maxim "Life is good, affirm life, actualize life."

Because he dismisses what the Bible actually teaches about sexual morality, Spong can appeal only to his own authority when he commends some sexual relationships over others. For example, he says that marriage is the "ideal" relationship, the one against which all others should be measured. Presumably he considers marriage the ideal relationship because he believes it has the most potential for affirming or enhancing human life. But in that case his affirmation that celibacy is the right choice for some becomes problematic.

Further, Spong's loss of the Bible as a resource on marriage closes off to him the richness of the biblical teaching about marriage. For example, the creation stories portray marriage as an institution of creation, which means that marriage does not exist just for the joy and satisfaction of the partners but for the replenishment of the earth. Indeed, the biblical creation stories could provide a foundation for Spong's observation on the potential of marriage to satisfy deep human needs. But because he ignores the specific biblical teachings on marriage, Spong is left only with the option of asserting his views dogmatically on his own authority.

Another important biblical teaching on marriage is that it is a sign to the partners and to the people of God of God's fidelity to his people. This idea, richly reflected in the prophets and in Ephesians, is the basis of the Christian teaching that marriage is a sacrament or sacramental rite. All this richness of traditional Christian teaching on marriage Spong loses with his dismissal of the Bible's specific witness and his substitution of the abstract law: Affirm life.

In the Bible, the primary argument against the rightness of homosexual relations is not the specific prohibitions against them. It is true, of course, that wherever homosexual relations are mentioned, they are rejected as contrary to God's will. But the main issue is that the creation stories portray God's intention for human sexual relations as heterosexual and procreative. Spong's approach to the Bible rules out acceptance of the primary biblical basis for affirming heterosexual relations over homosexual.

Further, Spong's discussion of homosexual relations is marred by a failure to consider the seriousness of scientific evidence concerning homosexual practices. I am not concerned here with his claim that 10 percent of the population is homosexual, a figure contradicted by a plethora of scientific studies. I refer, rather, for example, to Spong's failure to acknowledge the physical dangers of anal intercourse, which is a primary form of genital-sexual relations between male homosexuals. Since Spong typically appeals to modern science as a warrant for his views, I would expect a more balanced use of scientific and medical evidence than Spong gives in his discussion of homosexual practices.

Anal intercourse greatly increases the possibility of sexually transmitted diseases, including, of course, the HIV virus. Spong's failure to acknowledge the specific dangers related to this form of sexual act results in an unrealistic treatment of homosexual genital expression, an unrealistic treatment that is morally wrong because it endangers people's health.

A similar oversimplification mars Spong's treatment of betrothal. Studies show that living together before marriage does not improve but rather decreases the chances of a successful marriage. Women often enter live-in relationships hoping they will become permanent, while men characteristically feel no compunction about living with a woman and then ending the relationship and starting another.

And what about the children conceived in such relationships? Spong asserts that artificial contraception successfully separates intercourse from conceiving new life. He writes as though he has never heard of "contraceptive failure." At times one wants to tell him to "wake up and smell the coffee!"

Spong Domesticates the Church...

As noted earlier in this chapter, Bishop Spong wants younger people and people who have rejected the church's traditional teaching to renew their interest in and respect for the church. He wants his ideas to be debated, and even if they are rejected, to get people thinking about sexuality in relation to the enhancement of human life here and now.

Bishop Spong does not eschew the role of gadfly for the complacent in the church. But his deepest yearning, I think, is that people who have given up on the church, especially the younger, responsible, thoughtful people in society who ignore the church, will renew their interest by learning that he, a bishop of the church, is teaching the ideas outlined in this chapter.

One must affirm his desire to reach out to those who have left the church or who have no interest in the church. But we are left with two obvious questions.

First, is Spong offering anything in the name of God and Jesus Christ that people outside the church don't already believe and affirm? The answer is no. The ideology of "affirm your life" and "enhance your life" is a basic moral assumption in our wider secular culture. Bishop Spong is saying, "Christianity, properly interpreted, teaches affirmation of life."

But the obvious next question is, why should thoughtful secular people care? They don't need the church to teach them what they believe already or to give them permission or authority to believe it. Perhaps some people will have a renewed respect for the church when they learn that it teaches what they already accept as true. Maybe some of those people will rejoin the church for some reason. But it gives one pause to think that the Christian community, its Scripture, its gospel has nothing to say that is different from what intelligent, thoughtful people outside the church already believe.

Further, I think that Spong has too great a concern for the institutional survival of the church. While I understand that a bishop would be concerned about the survival of the church as an institution, and while all Christians should want to commend the authentic Christian faith and the Christian community, institutional survival should not be such a preoccupation of Christians as it is for Spong. Over and over he repeats his worry that traditional thinking about sex will push people away from the church and he hopes that if people outside the church will hear his views, they will have a new respect for the church. Survival of the church as an institution seems to be an overriding concern of Spong.

The only legitimate reason for the church to be teaching is that the Christian message is true and good news; that it is a saving message about God. The purpose of teaching is not what Spong repeatedly says, to maintain the viability of the church as an institution, but to teach God's truth. The Christian teacher primarily serves not the church as an institution, but God. It is embarrassing for me, as a professor in the church, to see a fellow Christian teacher, Bishop Spong, presenting the purpose of Christian teaching as trying to get people interested in and respectful of the church again.

This tendency in Spong's volume on sex—to see his task as teaching about sex to regain the respect of thoughtful, responsible people who ignore the church—is all the more surprising, considering that Spong seems to aspire to the role of a prophet. True prophets are aflame with a passion for God's cause, God's truth, not with trying to engineer the survival of an institution by getting it to update its thinking.

...and Trivializes the Gospel!

This brings us, of course, back to the most important point, the—in my opinion—sub-Christian character of Spong's approach to sexual teaching. Spong's discussion of the Word of God in the Bible makes it clear that for him the church's message is summed up by the idea of enhancing individual and social life. In one sense the church's message is about enhancing individual human life. But at a deeper, more authentically Christian level, the church's message is about God's actions in Christ to overcome sin in order that humans may share and be blessed by God's eternal life. This deeper, authentically Christian message is reduced by Spong to the vague idea of "Affirm life." Spong's presentation of the Christian message involves a loss of Christian substance.

But think what this means. Spong's "gospel" (and note how quickly his message, "Life is good" turns into a law that says, "You must affirm your life and the life of others") makes religious language and ritual into a resource and supply for human self-actualization. God is reduced to a legitimizer of the modern human project of self-actualization, here and now in history. Christianity, in Spong's view, is no different in character from Marxism, scientific humanism, personalist psychology, or any other ideology or "ism" of secular modernity: it is merely the self-affirmation of human life or even of life and vitality generally.

From a biblical and classically Christian perspective, Spong's basic message is a massive domestication of God, the church, and Christian teaching to serve the needs of the modern project of human self-expansion. The meaning of God's goodness and power is defined within the horizon of enhancing human life. God's goodness is that he gives us ourselves; that is Spong's gospel.

That, however, is neither the Bible's message nor classical Christianity's message. The Bible's gospel is that in Jesus Christ and the Holy Spirit, God draws us into his life and blesses us with the fullness of his life as Father, Son and Spirit. God's goodness and power are demonstrated in his sharing his life with us, not in being a resource for the human project of self-enhancement or self-actualization in nature and history.

In the end, Spong's teaching on sexuality should evoke more sadness for Christians than anger. It is sad to see a popular spokesperson for the church offering nothing different from what the secular world already teaches and believes. Second, it is sad to see a spokesperson for the church so anxious about the survival of the church that he appears willing to reduce its message to whatever he believes will reawaken disaffected people's interest. Third, it is sad to see someone speaking for the church who appears not to know the difference between the classical teaching about God's goodness and power, on the one hand, and the domestication of God-talk and the church to humanity's self-affirmation, characteristic of so much of modern Christianity, on the other.

For Spong to write as he does, and to find a strong resonance in the Episcopal Church and perhaps other churches, illustrates the distortion of much teaching in the church today. It is a judgment on the modern church's loss of its own center in the God witnessed to in the Bible and in its glorious gospel.

Works Considered or Consulted

Avis, Paul. *Faith in the Fires of Criticism: Christianity in Modern Thought.* London: Darton, Longman and Todd Ltd, 1995.

Brown, Harold O. *The Sensate Culture: Western Civilization Between Chaos and Transformation.* Dallas: Word Publishing, 1996.

Hanigan, James P. *Homosexuality: The Test Case for Christian Sexual Ethics.* Mahwah. N.J.: Paulist Press, 1988.

Hefling, Charles, ed. *Our Selves, Our Souls and Bodies.* Boston: Beacon Press, 1997.

Sapp, Stephen. *Sexuality, the Bible and Science.* Philadelphia: Fortress Press, 1977.

Schmidt, Thomas. *Straight and Narrow: Compassion and Clarity in the Homosexuality Debate.* Downers Grove: InterVarsity Press, 1995.

Inside the Whirlwind
Christian Theism and the Monism of John Spong
Stephen M. Smith

THERE IS A "GREAT GULF FIXED" between religious monism
in its Christian guise and classical, creedal Christian orthodoxy.
Their first principles are diametrically opposed and lead to opposite conclusions at many key points. This chapter will attempt to
achieve a measure of conceptual clarity. I would like to think that
Bishop Spong would agree with my description even though his
commitment is clearly to the other side of the gulf.

Monism asserts that reality is ultimately one, no matter how
differentiated it is in appearance. Generally, this means that the
universe is to be seen as a sort of emanation from Being (God) to
the realm of beings, that is, an eternal flow from a sort of fullness
and *necessity* within the divine. Religious monism is the "discovery" and experience of this unity. All religions find their identity
in the meanings they project onto this unity. Philosophical
monism says, "All is one"; religious monism says, "All is one—
praise to the divine."

Classical theism needs no definition except to note the importance of the doctrine of creation *ex nihilo*. Langdon Gilkey, not
one to describe himself as a conservative theologian, nevertheless
considers this doctrine as "the indispensable foundation on
which the other beliefs of the Christian faith are based" (*Maker of
Heaven and Earth*, p. 4). This doctrine is a defining principle of
theism. It, at least partially, answers the question, what sort of
God would send his Son for our salvation? This doctrine denies
ultimacy to anything else but God. It roots creation *not* in the
mystery of the divine *nature* (monism's *necessity*) but in the divine
will. Worshipers in heaven exclaim, "By thy will they [all things]

existed and were created" (Rev. 4:11). Theism establishes the fundamental distance between the Triune Creator and the creation. But note, this is not a distance of space, for God created space. It is a distance in being, no matter how hard this is to conceive. The God of the Bible "inhabits eternity" (Isa. 57:15) but deals with us in space and time. Karl Barth has said that "we must be astonished at the fact that there are ourselves and the world alongside and outside Him. God has no need of us... He is rich in Himself" (*Dogmatics in Outline*, p. 53).

This chapter will attempt to show that Bishop Spong is a committed religious monist, though he rarely uses the term. His proposal and all its ramifications call to us from the other side of the great theological "gulf" that is creating so much tension in Western Christianity at this time. In this chapter I will attempt to display how the bishop describes his theological foundations and how this radically shapes his theology and ethics. My hope is to show that his project is as compatible with authentic Christianity as night is to day.

The Bishop's Project

Bishop Spong has a rather remarkable media persona. He may well have been on more talk shows than any other religious figure in the last decade. His rhetorical skill is remarkable and both respected and feared in the church. He is a man with a mission—to deliver the church from its so-called biblical and creedal "literalism" and bring it into the twenty-first century, ready or not.

The bishop is very helpful in aiding the alert reader who is trying to locate him theologically. In the preface to the second edition of *This Hebrew Lord*, he describes himself as standing "in a place very similar to that occupied by John A.T. Robinson... whose works the reader will soon discover were powerfully influential on my own development as a priest and as a scholar. I am a bishop who dares to be a scholar, [and] who welcomes theological controversy" (*THL*, x). Robinson's *Honest to God* created an enormous furor when it was published in 1963. Its task was to both declare that the theistic Christian worldview had lost its plausibility and to propose a monist alternative. God must no longer be seen as the transcendent creator *ex nihilo*, but rather as the ground and source of all being to be encountered *only* in and through creation, especially humanity. In his first two chapters

Robinson attempted to replace Christian theism with an alternative monist worldview and show why it still should be called Christian. This book was a bestseller in the Sixties and is still important to read.

At first Spong did not consider Robinson's book terribly significant. But as he reread it, he said it "put together many of my own doubts and questions.... It was no longer possible for me to play the role of the believing person with the same certainty" (*THL*, 10). He pored over the book three times. "I have never been the same since. I was driven to my roots and forced to think again about everything I believed" (*THL*, 11).

To grasp the significance of this formative encounter we must proceed to analyze the particular shape of Spong's religious monism as it plays itself out in several of his works. As we proceed we will note how his monism shapes the various issues he addresses. We will also be interested in the way he understands and articulates the irreconcilability between his position and traditional Judaeo-Christian theism.

Facing the Wind

Consider one of the least read, and yet in my opinion, one of the most substantive books the bishop has written—*Into the Whirlwind*, published in 1983. Talking about prayer, the bishop clearly explains his concept of God and the influences that brought him to his present conviction.

Spong sees a problem in the traditional concept of God assumed to be there when we pray. He is quite clear in what he rejects. "[A] divine king on a heavenly throne who must be praised by his subjects [who are] begging for mercy, asking for a boon.... [This is] a God I cannot worship, a God in whom I cannot believe" (*ITW*, 49). Further, he says that Charles Darwin radically reshaped our perception of God so that "the deity we [now] perceive at work in this continuing creation is not the traditional deity" (*ITW*, 50). Moreover, Freud's understanding of religion and psychic projection "challenges traditional religious thinking at its very core" (*ITW*, 51). In other words, the discoveries of science have shown the very idea of a transcendent deity, who can intervene in this world, to be essentially implausible.

The bishop's deep sense that contemporary culture determines what can be believed is reflected in the following litany of theological collapse: "Gone is the God up there or out there. Gone is the sense of human depravity, the literal fall from grace. Gone is... the substitutionary atonement of Christ, that strange vision of a God whose justice had to be served by punishing his son.... Gone is the God who plays favorites," and so on (*ITW,* 52). These ideas are declared "largely dead in theological circles." What is remarkable is that he so totally and consistently ignores the vast influence of Karl Barth at the scholarly level and C.S. Lewis at the popular level, both of whom eloquently reasserted these very ideas against the nineteenth-century liberalism that had denied them.

So what does Spong say is to be done? "The first task... is to move beyond the personal images of God" (*ITW,* 54). Then, we must side with Paul Tillich, who was among the first to popularize the concept of God as the "Ground of All Being." Today, by "almost common consent" God has been, shall we say, relocated. He is no longer "separate from the world [but God is] the source and ground of all... the final depth of matter... the source of all meaning... [and] the holy, mysterious, ultimate power never separated from life [and is]... transcendent only in immanence" (*ITW,* 57). God can be experienced as "that infinite power who calls our humanity into ever-increasing expansiveness" (*ITW,* 60). In these abstract, impersonal, and all-unifying terms we have a clear, forthright affirmation of religious monism: God and the universe are essentially inseparable. This remains an underlying assumption throughout Spong's works, even if certain unspecified distinctions between God and the universe are said to be still true. In an earlier chapter this idea is specified by this sentence: "God has become for me power that is deep within this world but always more" (*ITW,* 45).

We now see how the bishop would speak of God. He has moved beyond all personal images. Spong finds nonpersonal words "not as limiting" as he once thought (*ITW,* 57), though it is clear they pose a challenge to his concept of prayer. Words adequate to this impersonal and all-embracing reality must reflect God as present when "consciousness is expanded and personhood is enhanced" (*ITW,* 61). Spong meets this immanent God deep within life as "the Divine Energy that is a force for wholeness and healing" (*ITW,* 61).

We soon see that this radical departure from historical theism, which undergirds biblical faith, affects our view of authority, particularly our view of Christ. We end up with what might be called a "degree Christology." Jesus is but one channel for our awareness of the indwelling life of God. He is not unique. He is different from others only in degree as the decisive presence of God by which all others must be judged. He is "the perfect channel by which all other manifestations of God's *ruach* [spirit] must be judged" (*ITW*, 44). This is indeed a strong claim, when you consider that no objective evidence has been adduced to elevate Jesus to such an exalted position.

Spong's thesis in *Whirlwind* is that the church must face the great challenge of modernity by embracing a theology with "no discernible fixed points," by giving up the "narcotic of religion" that offers certainty, and by embracing the "relativity of all truth" (*ITW*, 15). This, of course, leaves the puzzling question of how Christ can possibly be what the bishop claims, namely "the perfect channel" by which all other manifestations of the divine "must be judged." It is obvious that the bishop has a difficult time himself giving up a Christianity with fixed points—and facing his own rules.

Let us now see how Bishop Spong's monism plays itself out in three of his recent books, *Living in Sin?*, *Rescuing the Bible from Fundamentalism*, and *Born of a Woman*.

Deconstructing the Bible

Living in Sin? is indeed a radical book, not just for its proposals on human sexuality, but for its theology. Bishop Spong's proposals that the church bless a time of living together for young couples (which he calls betrothal), bless faithful homosexual unions, and bless cohabiting elderly for whom formal marriage would be too expensive are rather modest when compared with some of the more aggressive advocates of the sexual revolution within the church (for example, Professor Carter Heyward's advocacy of "sexual friendships" and the "Beyond Inclusion" Conference at All Saints' Episcopal Church in Pasadena, California, at which monogamy for gays was said to be unnecessary)

What is truly radical is Spong's linking of his monist proposal to an approach to biblical analysis that deconstructs the very possibility of there being truth in Scripture. To him, the issue of sexuality is finally "a debate over the authority of Scripture and over the role of both Scripture and the church in sustaining the ignorance that is the basis of prejudice" (LS, 116). It is well known that there are ways to deconstruct any text. First, one challenges the text's message by showing its inner tensions, ambiguities, and contradictions; and second, one ascribes whatever concepts remain to the writer's social, cultural, and economic circumstances. A text is thus silenced, in that it is no longer able to communicate on its own terms. Instead, the interpreter now has a relatively free hand to imaginatively interact with whatever strikes his or her interest. The text, in effect, becomes inspirational mood music for the interpreter's own creativity and imagination.

We see an example of this in the bishop's two-pronged strategy: first, he challenges Scripture as a reliable witness and source for the faith, and second, he "unmasks" the Bible's patriarchal prejudice.

The first prong of Spong's strategy aims to free us from the normative claims of the Bible and its "literalistic imprisonment" (LS, 93). Unless "fundamentalist interpretations of the Bible are discredited," he says, "the Bible itself will be rendered impotent and valueless" (LS, 93). As others in this volume have pointed out, Spong's crusade against literalism seems almost a consuming passion. While literalism is never defined in Living in Sin?, it is generally clear what is meant: an approach to Scripture that attempts to discern the mind of the author and then holds such insight in its proper context to be binding truth.

To read the Bible literally, for Spong, is to read it assuming it has a coherent witness to reality and its diversity is complementary, rather than contradictory. Spong sees contradiction to be of the essence of Holy Scripture: "In the Bible there are conflicting accounts of creation, conflicting versions of the Ten Commandments, conflicting understandings of who Jesus is and was, conflicting details concerning what happened on the first Easter" (LS, 111–112). Starting with the assumption that no author is really objective, and that all authors have their own agendas, Spong insists that every writer distorts what he or she writes (LS, 112). One can't help wondering whether this applies equally to bishops! So, "Who is literally correct?" (LS, 110). Clearly no one is, according to the bishop's logic. The Bible is unreliable and contradictory at its deepest theological levels—in its teachings about creation, Christ, the resurrection, and a great deal more.

By breaking out of the "prison of literalism" the bishop is able to see the Bible as a purely human document reflecting little more than the struggles and ideologies of its time. It offers no timeless binding truths to aid and instruct God's people through history. Perhaps some truths can be seen behind the ancient texts, but the process of uncovering them can only begin once one has been delivered from the "bondage of literalism." The net effect of this project is to make the Bible self-contradictory and unworthy of enlightened confidence.

The second prong of the bishop's strategy is to propose a social location for the biblical writers that accounts for why they say what they do about God. He builds his case first by saying that humans "*always* form their understanding of God out of their own values, needs, and self-understandings. We *do* make God in our own image" (*LS*, 122—italics mine). This starting point is necessitated by Spong's commitment to the nineteenth-century idea of projection, developed by Feuerbach and then Freud, who contend that all our religious ideas are mere projections of internal needs, hopes, interests, and drives. Applying this insight to the Old Testament, Spong sees a "pervasive anti-female bias that permeates every page of [the] Scriptures" (*LS*, 120).

In prehistoric times, he conjectures, people lived in a sort of undifferentiated world of nature/goddess worship, As the male began to become more isolated from the family matrix, he began to create more male-type deities. The Old Testament represents the ideological triumph of male hegemony. We are left with one true masculine deity. He is Lord, King, and Law-giver of Israel. For the bishop this means that the Old Testament represents a stage in human consciousness—the projection of male interests onto gods (see *LS*, chapter 8).

Since the Old Testament God is merely a male projection, it cannot have enduring value and moral authority for our church or culture. We are at a different stage of development and thus recognize how deformed the Old Testament, and by extension the whole of biblical religion, really is. Its emphasis on God's sovereignty and difference from creation is but a reflection of the male quest for control and domination over women.

Bishop Spong puts a very interesting spin on his case against the Bible. Since all religion at the cognitive, conceptual level is projection, we must be relieved of the need to read the Bible or any religious document as either coherent at face value or binding. We are delivered from this need by exhibiting its contradictions and revealing its projections. This leads to the conclusion that although religion is some form of participation in the divine, no religion can be literally true. In particular, since the Bible's basic theological content posits a male deity who is Lord, Judge, and King, we must put this all behind us, for we have transcended that stage and have seen more truly the nature of religion and life.

At the conceptual center of *Living in Sin?* is the argument that the Bible can have no binding authority. One would be a fool to read it in search of any coherent, binding content. Indeed, if read literally (as traditional Christians have read it) the Bible is nothing short of evil, since an "anti-female bias... permeates every page" (*LS*, 120).

It may be instructive to observe what else Bishop Spong does to the text in order to discredit it. He claims that "the law of Sinai was addressed only to men" (*LS*, 129), though nothing in the narrative in Exodus 19 and 20 suggests this limited application. Spong tells us that since the tenth commandment (against coveting) mentions a wife along with an ox, the Old Testament degrades women by reducing them to property. Doesn't the bishop remember the fifth commandment? How can the "mother" who is to be honored by all her children be treated as property? There is no basis in the Old Testament for simultaneously honoring someone and treating that person as property. (For further discussion, see *God's People in God's Land*, C. J. H. Wright, pp. 200–210.)

Spong goes on to claim that "women were defined in the Bible almost entirely in terms of their sexual function" (*LS*, 130), yet Genesis 1 gives to both men and women dominion over the earth (1:26, 28). Also, Proverbs 31:10-31 is a poem of praise for the virtuous wife without one direct reference to procreation. And what does one make of the Song of Solomon? In *Rescuing the Bible* Spong claims that "in a patriarchal age, nations did not seem to have mothers" (*RTB*, 41), yet in Genesis 17:16 Sarah was explicitly called "a mother of nations." The bishop's zeal to challenge Scripture seems to have moved way beyond the facts.

Salvaging Salvation

If the Bible is full of contradictions and sexism, and if the biblical rendering of God expresses a stage in the movement of consciousness no longer ours, an age in fact we now see as evil, can *anything* be retrieved from its ancient pages? Like a magician reaching into his top hat, Spong surprises us with an emphatic yes. He insists that he takes the Bible seriously, though not literally, and that he can see a Word behind the conspicuously flawed words, a transcendent truth behind the all-too-human projection. That Word is that "God is the ground of all being" and "the source of life" (*LS*, 160–161). Creation is good and to be valued. We see the God who is the source of life in Jesus, who as God's Word makes creation's goodness real and apparent. That is what salvation is all about (*LS*, 160). Monism can be miraculously seen shining through the cracks in Scripture! All is one; all is good.

Try to understand the logic here. As we have seen before, God is the depth or ground of all creation and is not separate from or above creation. The creation's goodness derives from its participation in God. That goodness has become manifest in Jesus. Because each of us is rooted in the ground of all being, we too are good. Thus the call to salvation in Christ is simply the call to be "like" Jesus, to cast aside all that hinders, restricts, and discourages and to follow the call to be what one is. In the words of the bishop's friend and popular mythologist Joseph Campbell, we are called "to follow our bliss." Not only is the gospel for our new emerging consciousness pure religious monism, but the self becomes the center since it is empowered by nothing less than the ground of its own being. It is not empowered by anything that transcends its self.

To follow this vision the bishop is "willing to live fully, freely, and openly, scaling the barriers that inhibit life, escaping the straight-jacket of someone else's own stereotype of whom I am" (*LS*, 160). Indeed "the Word of God in Jesus is a call to me to be myself, my whole self, without apology, without boasting... That is what it means to me to worship the one who is the ground of all being" (*LS*, 162). It is hard to reconcile this with Jesus' call to self-sacrifice, turning the other cheek, taking up one's cross, or even loving one's neighbor. Religious monism leads to expansion, not obedience, to self-fulfillment, not sacrifice. One recent culture analyst uses the phrase "the unencumbered self" to describe American culture (see Richard John Neuhaus, *America Against Itself*, Chapter 4). The bishop's words are an excellent description of this contemporary desire to be rid of all obligations and commitments other than those that are self-generated.

It is worth remembering that the habit of seeing Scripture through the eyes of some "ism" is not new. More influenced by monism than they were willing to admit, liberal German theologians in the earlier part of our century wrote political speeches for Kaiser Wilhem. They had given up any transcendent objective stance by which to challenge the German war machine. Karl Barth remembered that betrayal as a "black day." Later the German church had all too little backbone to challenge Hitler. Critical liberal theology had again confused the voice of culture with that of Scripture. Stanley Hauerwas and William H. Willimon observed that "Nazi Germany was the supreme test for modern theology." The issue was, then as now, whose voice will prevail? (*Resident Aliens*, 1990).

Alister McGrath has noted, "The authority of Scripture is... something profoundly liberating. It frees us from the slavish cultural demand that we follow each cultural trend, and offers a framework whereby *we* may *judge* them" (*A Passion For Truth*, 1996, p. 62, italics mine).

The point I am suggesting is that the freedom the bishop celebrates gives no critical leverage by which to evaluate one's personal passions. It should not surprise us that the bishop's Jesus looks strikingly like a New Age guru through whom the divine "light" shines. This is the Jesus of monism, but neither the Jesus of the Gospels nor the Eternal Son of God.

When we finally come to examine what the bishop says about homosexuality, we should not be surprised to discover that he finds Scripture to have no binding power. He admits that the two texts in the Holiness Code in Leviticus do condemn homosexual acts, but argues that the authors of this document were not possessed of "sufficient knowledge... to make an adequate judgment for all ages" (*LS*, 145). In fact, he says, "The Levitical condemnation of homosexuality is a pre-modern illustration of ignorance" (*LS*, 147). In Paul's case, we have no more than "ill-informed, culturally biased prejudices" (*LS*, 152). Indeed, we discover that this converted Pharisee, who claimed after his conversion to "delight in the Law in his inward parts" (Rom. 7:22), was actually "anti-Semitic!" (*LS*, 152). In *Rescuing the Bible*, the case of Paul is taken a step further, and it is hypothesized that he may have been a self-loathing, repressed "gay male" (*RTB*, 119).

In examining Romans 1 and its teaching about homosexuality as a practice that distorts the order of creation (this is the widely acknowledged meaning of "against nature"), Spong notes that Paul sees homosexuality as "a punishment meted out to those who rejected the God of creation" (*LS*, 149). Since this text assumes that God is the separate author of creation, and that there is a real, objective moral order with real universal standards, it must be rejected. Spong sees the whole argument as reflecting an outdated worldview and therefore simply unacceptable. Here we see an approach to the text that would discredit it if it challenges prior assumptions (see Richard B. Hays, "Relations Natural and Unnatural" in the *Journal of Religious Ethics* 14 (1986): 186–95; C.E.B. Cranfield, *Romans 1–8*, p. 104; and James Dunn, *Romans 1–8*, pp. 53, 74–75).

Search for the Hidden Truth

The bishop, as we have seen, appeared poised over the abyss of nihilism in *Living in Sin?* He came perilously close to dismissing every aspect of the faith as nothing more than a tool for cultural hegemony and a projection of male self-interest and neuroses. In *Rescuing the Bible from Fundamentalism*, he tries to return to more positive themes. The Bible is not to be considered evil, with its every page laced with sexism; rather, the biblical writers were simply naive and uninformed, sharing the prejudices and prescientific world pictures of their intellectual and cultural environment.

The task of this more recent book is "to rescue the Bible from the exclusive hands of those who demand that it be literal truth, and second, to open that sacred story to levels of insight... that literalism never produced" (*RTB*, 10). His project is to achieve in his rereading of Scripture what "no one seems ready to invest the energy [in]... the task of reforming the Christ story" (*RTB*, 38). Here we see a now familiar pattern, beginning with the Enlightenment, of seeking the "hidden truths" of Jesus behind the plain meaning of the text.

Positioning himself in a rhetorical *via media*, Spong proposes to give us a view of Scripture that takes it seriously but not literally, somewhere between that of ignorant literalists and skeptical liberals. He describes the fundamentalist or literal reading of Scripture as absurd and mindless (*RTB*, 247). But his challenge to liberal Protestantism is equally clear. He sees liberalism's message as fuzzy, imprecise, and relatively unappealing. "They have no real message. They tinker with words, redefine concepts... behind... a few psuedoradical thinkers" (*RTB*, 35). While he writes the fundamentalists off, he is deeply concerned to inspire the Protestant liberals with a love and understanding of Scripture.

But here is the irony: it is Spong who takes a more literal view of the Bible than most literalists. He writes that Genesis 1 gives us "a vision of the cosmos that no educated person could today assume... namely that the earth is flat, surrounded by water, [and] the sky is a dome over the earth into which a sun has been placed" (*RTB*, 27). God is "living just above the sky [and] would intervene in the life of this world to effect a cure... or deliver [someone] from peril" (*RTB*, 32). Thus by depicting the world picture of the Bible as conveying prescientific pictures, Spong dismisses the worldview as hopelessly premodern and irrelevant. But, clearly, this will not work. Anyone can easily see the difference in Genesis 1 between the picture given and the meaning proclaimed. Genesis 1 was given to tell us not that there is an ocean in the sky, but that there is one transcendent Creator and that we are valued members of that creation. There is no reason to confuse the world picture with the theological revealed meaning.

But the bishop wants us to get beyond this limited worldview. We moderns "must think about God in the light of our perceptions of divinity" (*RTB*, 33). We must accept the "dawning realization that God might not be separate... but rather deep within... the sum of all that is, plus something more"(*RTB*, 33). With this emerging realization he reconstrues the faith and attempts to restore its plausibility to the contemporary skeptical mind. This is not an optional task, but one that is required because of the monist view of God as "deep within... the sum of all that is, plus something more."

Spong has told us that we must get behind "the ancient world with its narrow focus, its limited embrace of reality, its pre-scientific mind set of miracle and magic" (*RTB*, 37). We must enter "the experience out of which the text came to be written"(*RTB*, 245). But how could one possibly get behind the text and enter the experiences that produced stories of the burning bush, the deliverance through the Red Sea, the thunder of God on Mt. Sinai, the victory of Yahweh on Mt. Carmel, the feeding of the five thousand, and the appearances of the risen Christ? This is essentially impossible for three reasons: first, both the experience and the report are inextricably interwoven (we weren't there); second, there is no "mechanism" for engendering such experience (we can't go back); and third, these events were depicted as uniquely grounded in the transcendent will and action of a Sovereign Creator God (they are sui generis, that is, one of a kind). We simply cannot create burning bushes or the experience behind them any more than we can manufacture elation at a Super Bowl victory that happened in the past. From the traditional perspective, God is simply not available in that way. He makes himself available to us on his own terms through the text of Scripture. I say this, of course, because I am not a monist.

What is fascinating is Spong's optimism that such an experience can be entered. How would one ever know that one had truly entered into Moses' experience, that is, the experience that produced the story of the burning bush? To this insoluble problem his monism comes to the rescue. When Spong reads his Bible his worldview tells him that he is in touch with the same reality "out of which the literal text came to be written" (*RTB*, 245). Thus we should assume that whenever, like Jesus, one has the "courage to be himself," whenever one experiences a "call to love, to live [and] to be and to work for those things that create life"(*RTB*, 243), one is entering into an experience *in principle* that is in continuity with that of the biblical writers. Of course, a modern person would describe this experience in terms of self-actualization rather than transcendent intervention, because people know God "only when [they] enter deeply into life" (*RTB*, 243).

Viewed this way, the words of Scripture and the creeds no longer offer a "sterile choice between literalism and nothing." Beyond these dated words expressed in an outdated worldview is "the same reality that I am in touch with today at the edges [depth?] of my human limits.... Then suddenly the ancient biblical story becomes my story.... I know then that I have touched divinity... that is the same yesterday, today, and forever" (*RTB*, 243–244). Confidently, he describes his response: "I breathe that divinity in and I worship its source and I commit myself anew to live... as one is transformed by the infinite and eternal presence of God" (*RTB*, 244).

The intrinsic absurdity of the whole proposal is not hard to see. First, the claim of fundamental continuity between the modern monist's awareness that life is to be actualized and the descriptions of an encounter with God in the biblical narrative beggars the imagination. To propose continuity between the experiences of generic self-actualizing optimism and an encounter of the holy God of Scripture leaves one breathless.

Second, over the case hangs the universalizing call to "embrace the subjective and relative character of everything [the church] says and does" (*RTB*, 232). But surely this "everything" must apply to the bishop's own proposal. If it does, then why should his monism be seriously embraced? This is not a trivial objection. The claim that "God is the sum of all that is plus something more" is *not* a relative claim. It is a first principle, which if not absolutely true means that everything else the bishop says is no more than merely a subjective venting against traditional Christians. First principles are not offered, nor do they function, as a relativistic subjective guess. Spong does not offer his proposal as a relativistic subjective hunch. He is a committed religious monist who means business—even as he inconsistently contends that all knowledge is relative!

The Divine Within the Human

In the final book we will describe, *Born of a Woman*, we see the same familiar themes we have noted in the others. Again Spong places his proposal between "the two sterile camps of believing literally or rejecting all" (*BOW*, 15). Again he sees the biblical world picture as destroying the literal plausibility of the text. Again he makes an intense case against literalism, as "an enemy to faith in Jesus Christ" (*BOW*, 11). Again he salutes his heroes such as J.A.T. Robinson, Rosemary Radford Ruether, and Matthew Fox, all committed monists. Again he is committed to the monist first principle that the "divine essence [is] not separate from and not identical with but incarnate within humanity, emerging from the heart of life in self-giving love" (*BOW*, 40).

What is new in this book is the attempt to ground the monist first principle in the New Testament witness to Jesus' resurrection. The truth of Easter is not "a supernatural miracle but... the dawning internal realization that this life of Jesus reflected a new image of God" (*BOW*, 40). The truth behind the mythological depictions of the empty tomb and the appearances of the resurrected Jesus was the realization that the "divine essence [is] not separate from... but incarnate within humanity" (*BOW*, 40). One wonders what other "new insights" are to be seen behind the reports of Jesus' resurrection!

In his handling of the virgin birth Spong gives much insight into the narrative structure of the text. Clearly, his enjoyment of the story shines through in his well-crafted descriptions. Yet this event cannot be understood as literally true: "Virgins who give birth without a male agent exist for us only in legends and fairy tales" (*BOW*, 84, also 59–60). The bishop deals with the key texts in Matthew and Luke, showing their inner tension and improbability. Matthew "created this birth tradition out of the whole cloth of the interplay between his imagination and the Hebrew Bible" (*BOW*, 84).

The new aspect of Spong's argument is his use of midrash to explain why the text cannot be taken literally. He defines midrash as the attempt by Jewish rabbis to probe the Torah (Old Testament) in order to discern its truth and apply them to the present situation. Midrash, he says, was aimed at interpreting the present by the past. Since the New Testament writers believed Jesus was the "key to the Jewish Scriptures," they retold and invented "stories out of the Jewish religious past to illuminate a new experience" (*BOW*, 18). The birth stories become a case in point. The New Testament writers appropriated Old Testament stories to interpret the life and significance of Jesus. This means that "there was nothing objective about the Gospel [birth] tradition" (*BOW*, 19) and to read these stories as literally true is to "violate" the author's intention. "The only obvious historical fact beneath these narratives is that Jesus was born" (*BOW*, 21). In *Who Was Jesus?* Anglican New Testament scholar N.T. Wright responds by charging that the bishop "has grabbed this word (midrash) out of the air.... He misunderstands the method itself, and uses this bent tool to make the gospels mean what he wants... The gospels are not midrash" (*Who Was Jesus?* pp. 72, 73).

The value of the idea of midrash to Spong is that it enables him to solve a serious problem with biblical skepticism as it relates to the idea of a creative first century church. To be truly plausible, skepticism has to dismantle the surface tradition as a web of improbabilities and contradictions and recover the "real

Jesus" behind the text. Then (this is crucial) it has to describe how we get *from* the "real" Jesus *back to* the text we now have. For example, if we show that the resurrection accounts are contradictory and implausible, and believe we have recovered something of what really happened, we still have to go on to show why the text says that Jesus died and rose again. It is this second task that has been most difficult for skeptics. If the resurrection never happened, if there were no empty tomb and appearances, if what "really" happened was a new monist awareness of God, then why did the evangelists write all those resurrection stories? Why did they not simply give a monist rendering of Jesus' life? Later Gnostic writers certainly tried something like this. This has been the problem. Midrash is the answer, since it explains the creative impulse that generated the New Testament narrative we now have—at least as Spong uses it.

This is a remarkable, though highly implausible, achievement. Spong can explain what really happened back in the first century in terms of the plausibility structures of the twentieth century. Thus he can give it a religious depth and explain why the story exists in its present form. He knows the "real" truth, can explain the appearances, unmask literalism, and show forth the original intention of the biblical authors. Quite an achievement—if you can believe that cats like to swim. If you can't, then we have nothing more than the speculations of a skeptical but fertile imagination.

Concluding Observation
I have surveyed several recent works by Bishop Spong to find the conceptual first principle of his theology, which I have called monism, and to explain how it works itself out in his view of Scripture, Christ, salvation, and sexual ethics. First, although he continues to affirm his monist principle and identify himself with Bishop Robinson, Spong's understanding of monism does not seem to have blossomed or developed. Surprisingly, one finds the same collection of phrases used almost liturgically over twenty years of writing. They may shed light in new areas, but there doesn't seem to be a great deal of ongoing reflection. Perhaps this is because whenever much reflection is given there is always a movement to the divine as impersonal. No matter how much development one might wish to show, an impersonal deity is always static—and boring!

Second, there is a strange reluctance on the bishop's part to look long and hard at his first principle. Is this reluctance because there is a fear that behind the verbiage one finds only superficial metaphysical speculation? Ought not one's first goal be to examine one's first principle?

Third, the concept of God the bishop uses seems more to elevate the self than to move anyone to worship. Indeed, with his theology, *can* one worship? The categories of obedience and living unto the praise of God's glory are noticeably absent in his writings. Instead, we have the "unencumbered, expanding" self who with Jesus can say "I AM." This makes us all potential little "godlets," if you will. In the end the monist God becomes nothing but a means to reinforce the absolutization of the self. The bishop's worldview is really no more than a way of giving religious legitimacy to the life style the authors of *Habits of the Heart* called expressive individualism. It was their conclusion that "romantic individualism is remarkably thin when it comes to any but the vaguest prescriptions about how to live" (p. 81). The exaltation of the self is ultimately the death of the soul. As the Psalmist said, "He gave them their request but sent leanness to their soul" (Ps. 106:15).

I conclude by again referring to the Oxford theologian Alister McGrath as he comments on Bishop Spong's theology. "Spong constructs a fantasy world, in which his own vision of a politically correct culture leads him to impose stereotypes upon the New Testament with a fierce and uncritical dogmatism and a lack of scholarly insight" (*A Passion for Truth*, p. 65). As a point of fact, Spong does speculate that future bishops will be "taking part in defining God... [and] reinterpreting creeds" (*LS*, 223). The question I cannot shake is this: Is a church that expends its energy defining and reinventing itself really something that any "normal" Christian would want to be a part of?

Works Considered or Consulted

Barth, Karl. *Dogmatics in Outline.* New York: Harper & Row, 1959.

Bellah, Robert N., et al. *Habits of the Heart.* Berkeley: University of California Press, 1985.

Gilkey, Langdon. *Maker of Heaven and Earth*. Lanham: University Press of America, 1959.

Hauerwas, Stanley, and William H. Willimon. *Resident Aliens*. Nashville: Abingdon, 1990.

McGrath, Alister. *A Passion for Truth*. Downers Grove: InterVarsity Press, 1996.

Macquarrie, John. *In Search of Deity*. New York: Crossroad, 1985.

Wright, N.T. *Who Was Jesus?* Grand Rapids: Eerdmans, 1992.

Euthanasia and the Newark Way of Death

Daniel A. Westberg

THE EVANGELICAL CHRISTIAN who is scandalized by Bishop Spong's beliefs about miracles or the Bible may support him on euthanasia. Strangely enough, conversely, institutional experts who are more liberal on social issues than the average lay person tend to be more conservative on euthanasia.

One reason for this disparity may be this: the public is influenced by arguments based on pity, fear of death, costs of health care, and the like, and thus is attracted to a liberal position. But physicians, theologians, and even government officials who have explored the legal and social implications and moral analysis of euthanasia are more aware of its dangers.

For example, the Michigan juries that routinely acquit Dr. Kevorkian probably represent the general public. But the recent overturning of the law allowing for physician-assisted suicide in northwest Australia is more typical of the position of moral theologians (including Christian ones), doctors, and public officials. The American Medical Association has likewise adopted a very cautious position.

In their statements in support of euthanasia, Bishop Spong and the Diocese of Newark seem to capitalize on public perceptions of the issue rather than on the positions taken by those who have studied it carefully.

An Anglican Point of Reference

According to Spong, the traditional position on assisted suicide comes from a premodern worldview that has been essentially changed by modern medicine. In a typical rhetorical ploy, the bishop implies that he has light and modernity on his side, while his opponents have their heads filled with fear and darkness.

In fact, most of the relevant arguments against euthanasia among Anglicans were developed in the last twenty-five years, for the express purpose of taking into account changes in medical practice. For example, a very carefully thought-out document was issued in 1975 by the Church of England's General Synod Board for Social Responsibility, entitled On Dying Well: An Anglican Contribution to the Debate on Euthanasia.

The conclusion of the task force writing just over twenty years ago was that a change in British law with respect to euthanasia would create greater evils than it would prevent. In summing up their reasons, the task force noted that:

1. There are very few exceptional cases [where euthanasia might be justified], and there would be even fewer if medical practice were sounder;

2. Allowing euthanasia would reduce the incentive to improve such practice;

3. There would be pressure on patients (both terminal and non-terminal) to allow themselves to be "put away";

4. This would result in recourse to euthanasia in cases where it was not justified morally;

5. Even in such rare cases ["if such there are," they wrote], medical practice should do "all that is necessary to ensure peaceful dying";

6. There would be a weakening of confidence in doctors.

Later we will see how the recent experience of legal euthanasia in the Netherlands justifies the British task force's concerns about an increase in the number and type of cases in which euthanasia is resorted to.

Some distinguished physicians and academics served on the task force, including moral philosopher R.M. Hare (not known for conservative views), theologian Peter Baelz, and the founder of the modern hospice movement, Dame Cecily Saunders. The convictions and clinical experience of Cecily Saunders led her to believe that much of the problem of pain in modern health care came from the fact that the needs of dying patients were not a priority as compared with the needs of patients who were expected to recover. Her perspective gave the members of the task force confidence that the traditional opposition to suicide and euthanasia was still justified. But the task force also insisted that a great deal more could be done in medicine to alleviate pain and suffering.

Today the hospice movement and palliative care procedures in general are much more widely known than in 1975. But the training and practice of physicians in pain management is still inadequate; this problem fosters public sentiment in favor of euthanasia.

The Position of Bishop Spong

Bishop Spong's views on euthanasia and assisted suicide, like the rest of his revisionist agenda, are not based on careful analysis but on the alleged need to change traditional attitudes imposed by rapid social change and modern technology.

The bishop is right in thinking that the possibility of extending life through modern medicine has given us a degree of control over the occurrence of death, and that we need to respond with some new thinking and constructive approaches, rather than with ostrichlike stalling tactics. No one familiar with the issues would dispute his view that the debate must be engaged and Christians must be part of it.

But in his article preparing the Diocese of Newark for policy recommendations, Bishop Spong tells us that "after much internal wrestling" he now favors "both active and passive euthanasia" and that "assisted suicide should be legalized" ("In Defense of Assisted Suicide," THE VOICE, Diocese of Newark, Jan./Feb. 1996, p. 3). In the following section we will consider the slightly more careful formulations recommended and voted on by the Diocese of Newark; but here we can summarize the widely shared concerns expressed by Bishop Spong that put the Newark enterprise into motion.

1. *The problem of pain.* Pain is hardly a new feature of the human condition, of course. Before the development of anesthetics, nothing much could be done about it. But the very success of modern

medicine produces some situations in which people who would once have died quickly from severe injury or illness now cling precariously and often painfully to a life of dubious quality. "Is life sacred when pain is intense and incurable?" the bishop of Newark asks.

However, as methods of treatment become increasingly sophisticated, intractable pain is not the main problem. Rather, the prolongation of life involves other forms of suffering, such as incontinence and difficulty in breathing. Yet more significant to Bishop Spong, as we shall see, is the loss of awareness caused by the aggressive treatment of pain: he asks, "Is it a value to drug a patient into insensibility while continuing to keep him or her alive biologically?"

2. *Cost of health care.* When health care resources are scarce, does it make sense to prolong life at great expense with little benefit? The bishop reminds us that we already spend 80 percent of health care funds on the last year of a person's life. The strain on the public health system, not to mention the resources of individuals and their families, must be taken into account.

3. *The problem of mere "biological continuation" or "extension."* There is a disjunction between our real selves, our identity as full human beings and children of God, and the kind of marginal existence produced at the end of life by artificial clinical support. This is indeed a fruit of modern medicine, a complexity of life that our forebears did not need to consider.

The public wrestles with these issues, as do many Christians. While some fear intractable pain (and perhaps their fear is heightened by sensationalism in the media), most of us fear suffering of a more general kind: helplessness, immobility, loss of control and faculties, and difficulty in breathing, swallowing, and eating. These conditions cannot be cured by treatment, and they are sometimes aggravated by it. Tubes and IVs that are meant to help can make patients even more immobile and isolated.

We have an understandable dread of spending our final days of life at a distance from loved ones, cared for by harried nursing staff who have an ever increasing number of patients to look after because of hospital cutbacks, in a system that sees the dying patient as a burden. We do not want to be a burden. It seems irrational to waste a modest nest egg that might be of much help to a young family starting out in life on useless treatment at the end of life.

Here the bishop tries to resolve the issues that euthanasia raises by arguing that we must separate true human life from biological life. He couches his argument in the theological language of the image of God:

> The sacredness of my life is not ultimately found in my biological extension. It is found rather in the touch, the smile and the love of those to whom I can knowingly respond. When that ability to respond disappears permanently, so I believe, does the meaning and the value of my biological life ("In Defense of Suicide," THE VOICE, Diocese of Newark, Jan./Feb. 1996, p. 29).

Here, many Christians would probably agree with the bishop. Of what earthly value is a permanently vegetative life, in which awareness of others is totally lacking?

But Bishop Spong takes this further. He describes the vegetative state as one in which there is no longer a relationship to God:

> Even my hope of life beyond biological death is vested in a living relationship with the God who, my faith tradition teaches me, calls me by name. I believe that the image of God is formed in me by my ability to respond to that calling Deity. If that is so, then the image of God has moved beyond my mortal body when my ability to respond consciously to that Divine Presence disappears ("In Defense of Suicide," THE VOICE, Diocese of Newark, Jan./Feb. 1996, p. 30).

This is where the bishop's argument treads on thin theological ice. Many would agree with him that there is a problem in seeing a merely biological extension of life as reflecting the sacredness of life. But he goes on to imply that (1) the image of God is not related to our being but to our function, (2) the image of God disappears when our ability to respond to it ceases, and (3) our personhood exists in *our* ability to respond, not in *God's* character and unchanging relationship with us.

In other words, in his view, the image of God is constituted not by God's view of us but by our ability to respond to God. Instead of seeing us as objects of God's love and faithfulness, no matter what our condition, Bishop Spong seems to believe that once we slip below a certain threshold of awareness, we are no longer to be treated as bearers of the image of God. Such a notion of personhood excludes many who are at the beginning, end, and margins of life.

Christians who are concerned about the issues surrounding death who share many of the bishop of Newark's concerns should beware the implications of his argument. It directly contradicts the view of human life expressed in both the Old and New Testaments. For example, in Psalm 139 God values human life before birth while it is still in an early stage of development. Human life is there portrayed as a life in the image of God, not because of our love or plans for it, but because of God's. And in Romans 8:35 St. Paul encouraged countless Christians with the reminder of the depths of Gods's love, insisting that persecution, famine, peril, height and depth, nothing can separate us from the love of God.

But can failing health, Alzheimer's disease, failing memory, and declining faculties separate us from the love of God? Apparently, yes, according to the bishop's argument. There is a fundamental Pelagianism in Bishop Spong's thinking—our ability to respond is made the basis for our worth as persons. By contrast, the whole argument for grace, as understood by Paul or Augustine, is that it comes from God's love for us. God's love is not a response to our own desire or effort or capacity. Thus Bishop Spong's argument is a clear antithesis to this central biblical teaching that the basis of our confidence lies in the steadfastness of God, not in the quality of human effort.

Especially at the end of life, it is important that this fundamental Christian teaching be made clear. Precisely when our powers fade and our energies and mental capacities erode, our confidence must be in the faithfulness of God and not in our capacity to respond.

The Newark Resolution

Both Bishop Spong's surprising theological views and his concerns about pain and the extension of life have been written up by a task force into resolutions adopted by the 1996 convention of the Episcopal Diocese of Newark. The summary resolution of the 122nd convention of the Episcopal Diocese of Newark reads as follows:

> Resolved: That we affirm that suicide may be a moral choice for a Christian when: a person's condition is terminal or incurable; when pain is persistent and/or progressive; when all other reasonable means of amelioration of pain and suffering have been exhausted; and when the decision to hasten death is a truly informed and voluntary choice free from external coercion. Assisting another in accomplishing voluntary death under these circumstances may be an equally moral choice.

The use of language in this resolution seems slack. According to moral theologians, a "moral" action is any action that is the product of reflection and deliberation; it is a choice that expresses one's values. The fact that a choice is "moral" doesn't prevent it from being bad or wrong. It is any choice for which the agent is morally responsible. What the resolution actually wants to argue is that suicide may be a justified, legitimate, or correct choice.

Let us consider the conclusions of the bishop's task force; it seems to put into the form of resolutions the concerns that he expressed, and that many people would share. Let us consider the relevant conclusions:

1. Christian theology demands respect for human life and recognizes that human life is sacred.

2. Modern science has created a situation in which biological existence may be extended far beyond the point where a reasonable quality of life exists.

3. There are circumstances in which involuntarily prolonged biological existence is a less ethical alternative than a conscientiously chosen and merciful termination of earthly life.

4. In such exceptional cases, assisting a suffering person in accomplishing voluntary death can be morally justified as part of the dying process, because it enables the person to die well.

Should Christians find the Newark propositions and the reasoning behind them acceptable? Let us look at the evidence from our
faith and tradition.

The Distinction That Matters

The term *life* is being used by the Newark body to mean two different things. In one case, life means the extension by artificial
means of a life that would naturally end ("involuntarily prolonged biological existence"); in such a case, a Christian may
wisely accept death. But in the second case, the task force statement above refers to "earthly life," that is, the life available to an
individual human being that may have come to seem undesir-
able because of pain or limitation.

The task force propositions confuse accepting death with taking steps to end life. Simply put, the authors equate the legitimate Christian concern that life not be extended beyond its proper boundaries with an acceptance of suicide. "Ending life" in
these two situations is not the same type of action at all. In the
first case, one is terminating an existence that is unnaturally
extended, where there is no purpose for the extension except, perhaps, postponement of the inevitable. This has the appearance of
an unwillingness to face death.

Sometimes this unwillingness is an expression of defiance, the
desire to exercise human control over nature, the kind of will to
mastery that many feel is the expression of contempt and arrogance for natural forces that is part of the technological mentality that is responsible for environmental damage. This attitude is
not only unfortunate in a Christian, but spiritually dangerous.

Yet our Newark friends want us to go further than this. They
want us to accept "a conscientiously chosen and merciful termination of earthly life." There is, however, a fundamental distinction between refusing to lengthen one's life by technological
artifice and deliberately shortening one's natural life. To the
extent that we believe that God's providence controls our life, we
accept that there is a natural course to it, dependent on genes,
constitution, and circumstances. Thus, a distinction can be
made between accepting the boundaries of one's life and
attempting to circumscribe them.

If we accept the view that human life has its appointed
boundaries that arise from its natural circumstances, we will

immediately see that there is an ethical similarity between need-lessly prolonging life and willfully shortening it. Both points of view manipulate the natural course of life to serve questionable purposes. This is well put by William May: "Nature has already drawn a line between a death that nature brings about—if we only let it—and a death that we wreak on ourselves or others" (*Testing the Medical Covenant*, p. 17).

He expands on this point:

> Our ambition to conquer nature has tended to render nature invisible to us. Increasingly, we focus only on human motive and intent, and nature slips from view.... In allowing to die, the physician, the nurse, and the family simply step out of the way to let a host of natural forces aggressively bring a life to its end. In active euthanasia and in assisted suicide, a human being does the killing. We ought not to conflate the two" (ibid.).

Some try to obscure the distinction between killing and letting die by saying that the motive, compassion, is the same and there-fore the acts are equivalent. But the acts are not equivalent. Letting the dying patient die is a way of accepting the natural course of human life. Killing the patient banishes nature from view and reduces all events to options under human control.

What about the issue of the "living will"; is it a valid option for Christians? The legitimate purpose of such a will is to empower another person to assist one's own judgment so as not to stand in the way of nature, but to let it take its course. It should not be the purpose of a living will to give instructions that one is to be put to death in the event of extreme pain or incompetence. This distinction is maintained by the medical and legal professionals and by a solid majority of ethicists, Christian or otherwise.

Blurring the distinction between killing and letting die, as the Newark resolution does, is dishonest. It may enable the desired conclusion to be reached, but it is conceptually wrong and philo-sophically harmful. The importance of this distinction between killing and letting die, and of the public's coming to understand and accept it, is critical. There is a natural course to one's life, and to extend one's time in a hospital bed on a resuscitator is not truly prolonging life but fostering an illusion. But shortening one's life is also a refusal to accept the life that one has been given.

No doubt, Bishop Spong and the Diocese of Newark will receive a great deal of attention for their proposals. Therefore we should look at the troubling experience of the Netherlands, where assisted suicide was legalized, so that we can establish what the outcome is likely to be if their proposals are adopted. Then we can then try to articulate a theological response.

Do We Want to Go Dutch?
The experience of the health care system in the Netherlands in applying the practice of euthanasia is instructive, because its rationale for legal approval is similar to the qualifications sought by Bishop Spong and by the Newark resolution. One is the emphasis on incurable pain, and the other the importance of voluntary choice—that the patient is in complete control of his or her destiny. But what actually happened, according to the first-hand experience of Dutch Christian physician H. Jochemsen, is not encouraging.

In order to secure acceptance for euthanasia, the principle of patient choice was built into the very definition of legal euthanasia: "The active killing of a patient, at his or her request, by a physician." The conditions that legitimated a discussion of assisted suicide included terminal illness, intolerable pain, last resort, and the clear request of the patient. In practice, however, the application of these criteria has expanded, causing genuine erosion in the safeguards and raising fundamental questions about the practicality, not just the morality, of legalizing assisted suicide.

Despite this turn of events, the pressure to expand the range of cases in which euthanasia is an option is enormous. We can see this in the reasons for euthanasia given by doctors in a recent survey—no prospect for improvement, futility of therapy, relatives' inability to cope, and low quality of life.

In a number of cases the request of the patient is not even possible, because he or she has passed the point of competence and there is no living will. In these cases, the doctor may appeal to urgent necessity to justify his action in taking life and such requests are routinely approved; even more troubling is the expansion of this criterion to include patients who are competent or partly competent, as well as newborns (e.g. with spina bifida).

The difficulty of limiting the scope of euthanasia points to the inherent moral problem. It was originally explained and justified as the patient's decision, with the doctor acting merely as agent of the patient's wishes. But more and more, it has become the decision of the physician. And this is not only because of professionalization or strong motives on the physician's part. When a physician administers a lethal injection, even at a patient's express request, it is not the decision of the patient alone. It involves the autonomous intention to kill by the physician. The same moral structure is involved in abortion, where the physician cannot be seen merely to be the instrument carrying out the autonomous decision of the pregnant woman.

The laxness of the requirement of consent is paralleled by a loosened interpretation of suffering. In one case, a fifty-year-old woman who had lost two sons, one to suicide and the other to cancer, repeatedly asked her psychiatrist, a Dr. Chabot, to help her die. Dr. Chabot assisted her to commit suicide and was prosecuted but later acquitted. This woman was not terminally, indeed not even physically, ill. The suffering considered sufficient to warrant assisted suicide was emotional, resulting from what was analyzed as a depression in a narrower sense without psychotic characteristics in the context of a complicated grieving process. (This and other revealing cases are included in H. Jochemsen's *Euthanasia* [Oxford: Latimer Studies, 1995].)

Although the Dutch originally accepted euthanasia in the 1980s if there was a clear and "persistent" request by the patient, the evidence suggests that the transition to nonvoluntary euthanasia has occurred. One of the important lessons of the Dutch experience has been to show the fluidity of the criteria. Those very reasons for euthanasia, enthusiastically recommended by Bishop Spong, reasons that have become rallying cries in the debate, have not functioned in the Netherlands as safeguards against nonvoluntary euthanasia. They actually combine to widen the practice and weaken the barriers. The right of choice allows the patient to develop his or her own interpretation of the degree and quality of the suffering, at the expense of objective criteria or alternative options. When the degree of pain is interpreted by the physician for people who are incompetent or not able to make clear requests, the principle of choice and autonomy is compromised. Thus the criteria tend to merge and weaken each other (see Jochemsen, p. 24).

Theological Viewpoints

There are a number of important theological themes relevant to the discussion of euthanasia. A thorough treatment would consider the doctrines of the providence and sovereignty of God, creation, the effects of sin in the world, redemption, and eschatology. For our purposes we will consider only the topics of suffering, death, and the image of God as the fundamental points at issue here because of the role they have played in the position offered by Bishop Spong.

Suffering

There are two generalizations about suffering currently accepted in our day that shape many people's views about medical care at the end of life. The first is that suffering is an unqualified evil; the second, that suffering should be removed at all costs. Understanding why these two generalizations are in conflict with Christianity is an important factor in seeing the error of Bishop Spong's approach and in recovering an authentic Christian view (see Kilner, *Life on the Line*, p. 103 ff.).

First, there may be a good purpose, within God's providence, for the experience of suffering in our lives. That general point is in line with the experience of many people recorded in Scripture. And yet we have to be careful not to overstate the case, because it must be remembered that (1) in the light of creation, suffering is not a good in itself, (2) we should not directly associate our suffering with that of Jesus Christ; the purpose of Christ's death was unique, and (3) we must not encourage perverted views of the Christian life whereby people unwisely accept avoidable suffering (see Hauerwas, pp. 31–32).

In any event, suffering cannot be directly sought. The paradox of suffering is related to the paradox of finding one's life only by losing it; people can gain the value of suffering "only when they oppose suffering as a genuine evil" and yet experience God's goodness in the midst of it (Kilner, p. 104).

Mindful of these caveats, some benefits of suffering can be described. (1) The experience of suffering is a legitimate course in the "school of virtue." Suffering can be the means of growth in perseverance, maturity, wisdom, and obedience to God. Just as bravery cannot be developed in an armchair by thinking correctly about courage, but requires the experience of danger, so certain essential qualities of firmness of character and obedience to God come only through the school of suffering. (2) A true perspective on life and self often requires suffering. It clarifies priorities, exposes weakness and self-centeredness, and restores trust in God as the source of strength. (3) Our suffering may provide a benefit to others: this benefit may come from our providing an example of how suffering can be endured, or more directly, because our suffering creates the capacity to empathize with, help, and comfort others (cf. 2 Cor. 1:3–4: "Praise be to the God of all comfort who comforts us in all our troubles, so that we can comfort those in any trouble with the comfort we ourselves have received from God.")

This perspective on suffering is part of the response to the second modern generalization, that suffering should be removed at all costs. The modern attitude, which is reflected in Spong's position on pain, is that a fundamental dichotomy exists between suffering and the "pursuit of happiness," at least the kind of happiness associated with personal comfort, pleasure, and success.

If we set the agenda for our own lives, then it makes sense to avoid suffering. But if we are taking God's perspective, then the ultimate test of whether we are really centered on God's will for us may be how we deal with suffering.

A Christian perspective must accept that things may not actually make sense here and now. There is an eternal dimension in which all our experiences have meaning. But if we insist that our sufferings are to be seen as fair and meaningful in the light of our present experiences, then we are going to be frustrated and disappointed. Kilner goes further:

> When people find meaning only in those things that they experience as meaningful, they have made themselves God. At that point their experiences rather than God's will become authoritative, in line with the utilitarian spirit of the age (*Life on the Line*, p. 108).

The relevant Scripture here is again from Paul's letter to the Corinthians:

Therefore we do not lose heart. Though outwardly we are
wasting away, yet inwardly we are being renewed day by
day. For our light and momentary troubles are achieving
for us an eternal glory that far outweighs them all. So we
fix our eyes not on what is seen, but on what is unseen
(2 Cor. 4:16–18).

When we insist on being the arbiter of meaning for our own
lives, especially in situations of suffering, we usurp the role of
God and we severely limit the possible meanings. This is true not
only of our view of suffering; it is the crux of the matter in our
view of death.

Death

The cessation of physical life is only one aspect of death,
although it has become the most prominent or exclusive aspect
in contemporary attitude and discussion. For the Christian,
death involves the passage to eternity. Precisely because death is
not the end of existence but the passage to a new state, physical
death need not be seen as of ultimate importance. For this reason, Christians need not "hang on" to life, striving to extend life.
We can choose to forego life-prolonging treatment if it does not
offer proportionate benefits.

For the Christian, death involves a judgment on one's life.
From a biblical point of view, death brings one before the judgment seat of God; it marks the end of illusion and deceit, the
end of the possibility of hiding from oneself and from God. The
secular mind rejects this connection between death and judgment. There is no one to be accountable to and no forum where
one will be answerable.

Thus it matters little if one's final exit from life is made in a
spirit of trust or fear, of contentment or cynicism, because only
the exit itself matters.

Because a Christian sees the soul as answerable to God, our
attitude at the point of death is of great importance. Taking the
timing or method of death into one's own hands reveals a fundamental lack of trust in God and perhaps a continuing desire
to take the role of God for oneself. This point was made clearly
and strongly in the 1975 Church of England position on
euthanasia:

For the Christian, then, death signifies the ultimate help-lessness of man before God and his ultimate dependence on God. His faith bids him wait upon God in patience and hope. It is this insight, it seems, which prompts the almost universal Christian feeling that suicide is wrong (*On Dying Well*, pp. 19–20).

Bishop Spong seems completely oblivious to this aspect of Christian spirituality. Instead of respecting the long and pro-found Christian tradition of preparing oneself for dying (a tradi-tion to which Anglicans such as Jeremy Taylor and William Law have made important contributions), Bishop Spong seems to think that modern medicine has reduced the whole issue to one of the quality of life versus biological existence.

The problem ignored by Bishop Spong has been forcefully expressed by Kilner:

The desire to control death becomes more suspicious when we recall that death is a means God has used to keep in check the rebellious human attempt to become God. The original temptation to eat the special fruit was a temp-tation to "be like God" (Gen. 3:5).... Just as people ate the fruit because doing so promised desirable results (Gen. 3:6), so people today continue to try to usurp control over God's next limitation, death, by deciding when it should occur based on expected desirable results. From this per-spective, deciding when someone should die is a striking but not surprising manifestation of pride and, ultimately, rebelliousness (*Life on the Line*, p. 110).

The Image of God

Some traditional accounts of the *imago Dei* interpreted the image of God in terms of rationality, will, or imagination, that is, in terms of a property or capacity that human beings share with God that sets us apart from animals or other parts of creation. From that point of view, it makes sense for Bishop Spong to talk about the image of God "passing on" or being removed from a person whose mental capacities fall below a certain point.

But if we are sensitive to the theological, philosophical, and moral implications of this view, we will find it an unacceptable description of human personhood, because it depends on our wavering capacity for response. We have remarked earlier on the detrimental implications of this view of grace. We need to develop a description of the image of God in relational terms. People are created in the image of God because they are fundamentally relational creatures, not only in friendships, families, and marriage, but in terms of basic personal identity. Theologically, the Trinity indicates the essential connection between personality and relationality. This view has been developed by Karl Barth and many other theologians who represent the best of the Catholic, Orthodox, and Protestant traditions.

The carelessness of Bishop Spong and his reluctance to think through the implications of the positions he advocates are shown very clearly by his basing his argument for assisted suicide on the notion that we may lose the image of God and become bearers only of biological existence. The kind of separation of soul and body (Cartesian dualism) that this notion implies is shocking.

From a relational point of view, the image of God does not vary with the functioning of mental capacities; it encompasses the unique human being in the womb who will speak and think and love in the future, but is an object of love now, as well as the elderly or diseased person lapsing into dementia or unconsciousness. They are still unique individual persons, objects in relationships of love, whose personhood does not disappear as a result of weakened capacities.

Works Considered or Consulted

Bouma, Hessel, D. Diekema, E. Langerak, T. Rottman, and A. Verhey, eds. *Christian Faith and Medical Practice*. Grand Rapids: Eerdmans, 1989.

General Synod, Church of England, Board for Social Responsibility. *On Dying Well: An Anglican Contribution to the Debate on Euthanasia*. London: Church Information Office, 1975.

Hauerwas, Stanley. *Suffering Presence*. Notre Dame: Notre Dame University Press, 1986.

Jochemsen, H. *Euthanasia: A Christian Evaluation*. Latimer Studies, 49. Oxford: Latimer House, 1995.

Keown, John, ed. *Euthanasia Examined: Ethical, Clinical, and Legal Perspectives.* Cambridge: Cambridge University Press, 1995.

Kilner, John F. *Life on the Line: Ethics, Aging, Ending Patients' Lives, and Allocating Vital Resources.* Grand Rapids: Eerdmans, 1992.

Kilner, John F., Arlene B. Miller, and Edmund D. Pellegrino, eds. *Dignity and Dying: A Christian Appraisal.* Grand Rapids: Eerdmans, 1996.

May, William F. *Testing the Medical Covenant: Active Euthanasia and Health Care Reform.* Grand Rapids: Eerdmans, 1996.

Wennberg, Robert. *Terminal Choices: Euthanasia, Suicide, and the Right to Die.* Grand Rapids: Eerdmans, 1989.

Wilkinson, John. *Christian Ethics in Health Care.* Edinburgh: Handsel Press, 1988.

Contributors

C. FITZSIMONS ALLISON is the retired bishop of South Carolina. His varied career includes teaching at the University of the South (Sewanee), from which he obtained his B.A., teaching at the Virginia Theological Seminary, and being rector of Grace Church in New York. A church historian, he obtained his doctorate from Oxford University and soon thereafter published *The Rise of Moralism*. His other books include *Fear, Love and Worship; Guilt, Anger, and God*; and most recently (1994), *The Cruelty of Heresy*. Bishop Allison served on the General Board of Examining Chaplains, the Board of Regents of Sewanee, and is a member emeritus of the board of Trinity Episcopal School for Ministry.

EDITH M. HUMPHREY is a lecturer in the Faculty of Religious Studies at McGill University in Montreal. She has also lectured at the Universities of Ottawa, Toronto, Bishop's, and Carleton. Her Ph.D. is in New Testament studies from McGill. Dr. Humphrey also holds degrees from the University of Toronto (B.A.) and the Royal Conservatory of Toronto (A.R.C.T.). She is the author of *Ladies and the Cities*, a work on the Apocalypse and the Shepherd of Hermas. She is a member of the Primate's Theological Commission, Anglican Church of Canada.

PETER C. MOORE is the dean president of Trinity Episcopal School for Ministry, Ambridge, Pennsylvania. He was graduated from Yale University (B.A.), Oxford University (M.A., theology), the Episcopal Divinity School (M.Div.), and Fuller Theological Seminary (D.Min.). He is the founder of FOCUS, The Fellowship of Christians in Universities and Schools, and former rector of (Little) Trinity Anglican Church, Toronto. He is the author of several books, including *Disarming the Secular Gods; One Lord, One Faith;* and *A Church to Believe In.* He also has written chapters for several volumes, including *Modern Anglican Liturgies, Anglican Essentials,* and *The Anglican Communion and Scripture.*

EPHRAIM RADNER served as associate priest at Emmanuel (Episcopal) Church, Stamford, Connecticut, and is currently rector of the Church of the Ascension, Pueblo, Colorado. He has been a teacher and director at Matana Theological College, Burundi, Africa, and a visiting lecturer at Yale University. He is a graduate of Dartmouth College (B.A.) and Yale University (Ph.D., theology). He has co-edited several volumes, including *Reclaiming Faith* (1993) and *Inhabiting Unity* (1995), and his book, *The End of the Church: A Pneumatology of Christian Division in the West,* will be published soon.

RUSSELL R. RENO is an associate professor of theology at Creighton University and has served as an acting instructor and teaching assistant at Yale, from which he earned his Ph.D. in 1990. He holds a B.A. from Haverford College, where he majored in religion. He has published many articles in journals, such as *The Thomist, Pro Ecclesia,* and *Mission and Ministry.* He was a residential fellow at the Princeton Center for Theological Inquiry, and his book, *The Ordinary Transformed: Karl Rahner and the Christian Vision of Transcendence,* was published in 1995.

DAVID A. SCOTT is the William Meade Professor of systematic theology and a professor of ethics at the Virginia Theological Seminary in Alexandria. He has studied at the Goethe Institute and Tubingen University and holds a Ph.D. in systematic theology from Princeton University. He is a graduate of Amherst College and the Episcopal Divinity School, where he was an instructor in theology. Dr. Scott served in Liberia with the Holy Cross Mission. He has published many articles in scholarly journals, monographs, and chapters in volumes, such as *A Wholesome Example: Sexual Morality and the Episcopal Church,* and is a member of the board of the *Anglican Theological Review.*

STEPHEN M. SMITH is a professor of theology and ethics at Trinity Episcopal School for Ministry. He was graduated from Stanford University, received his M.Div. from Fuller Theological Seminary, and holds an M.A. and a Ph.D. from Claremont Graduate School, where he wrote his dissertation on the interaction of nineteenth-century Anglican theologians with German liberalism. He has written several articles for the *Evangelical Dictionary of Theology*, including those on "kenosis" and the "theology of hope," and is finishing a book on the parables. He is a member of the board of the Episcopal Committee on Religion and Freedom.

JAMES M. STANTON was consecrated the sixth bishop of Dallas in 1993 and serves as the president of the American Anglican Council. He was ordained a deacon in the Diocese of Los Angeles in 1977, and a priest in the Diocese of San Joaquin that same year. He has served in San Joaquin, Iowa, and in Los Angeles before coming to the Diocese of Dallas. He received a D.Min. degree from the Southern California School of Theology at Claremont, and a D.D. from the University of the South and Nashota House.

GEORGE R. SUMNER, JR., has served as a missionary in Tanzania and Navajoland, as a parish priest in Connecticut and Massachusetts, and is presently the rector of Trinity Church, Geneva, New York. He has a Ph.D. in systematic theology from Yale University, where he wrote a dissertation on Wolfhart Pannenberg under the direction of George Lindbeck. He is a co-editor of *Reclaiming Faith* (1993).

DANIEL A. WESTBERG is an assistant professor of ethics at the University of Virginia. He is a Dartmouth graduate (B.A.) and obtained a M.Div. from the University of Toronto. His doctorate is from Oxford University. He has served several parishes in the Diocese of Toronto and was chairman of the Sexual Abuse Task Force for the diocese. His book, *Right Practical Reason: Aristotle, Action, and Prudence in Aquinas*, was published in 1994. He has also written articles for the *Anglican Theological Review*, *The Thomist*, *Journal of Law and Religion*, and *New Blackfriars*.

WILLIAM G. WITT is a freelance theologian living in Cambridge, Massachusetts. He is a graduate of Rockmont College (B.A.) and received his Ph.D. in systematic theology from Notre Dame. He also holds an M.A. from St. Thomas Seminary in Denver. He is seeking a publisher for his two-volume dissertation on the theology of Jacob Arminius. Currently, he is an academic administrator at Harvard University.